MIRCEA A. TAMAS

THE EVERLASTING SACRED KERNEL

> *Luz, being eternal, is, in the human being, "the kernel of immortality," as the place called by the same name is "the abode of immortality"*
> (René Guénon, Le Roi du Monde)

A REVISED EDITION

ROSE-CROSS BOOKS

2012

Copyright © 2001 by Mircea A. Tamas

This revised edition is published by **Rose-Cross Books**
TORONTO
www.rose-crossbooks.com

Printed in Canada   Toronto 2012

Cover's *Peridexion* by *Nigel Jackson*
Cover design by *Imre Szekely*
Text revision by *Nigel Jackson*

National Library of Canada Cataloguing in Publication

Tamas Mircea A. (Mircea Alexandru), 1949-
  The everlasting sacred kernel / by Mircea A. Tamas.

ISBN 0-9731191-0-1

1. Spirituality in literature. I. Title.

PN56.C68T34 2002   809'.93382914   C2002-903091-9

CONTENTS

Foreword by Nigel Jackson   V

Introduction   IX

The *Introduction* presents the objective of the book, that is, to confirm the persistence of a sacred kernel in our modern civilization. It introduces the language of symbols and the traditional triad, Cosmos – Year – Man, as the main triple significance of any sacred writing or rite.

1. Ulysses   1

Homer's epics are the first to illustrate the thesis of a sacred kernel, considering that Western literature and civilization owe a lot to the Greco-Roman culture.

2. Samson   20

The *Bible* too is a primeval source of our Western world. The story of Samson and Delilah is chosen to attest the coexistence of an initiatory and cosmic significance, alongside the religious one.

3. The Bad Wolf   40

Fairy tales, old as humankind itself, constitute excellent evidence of how the sacred kernel has been transmitted over the centuries. Two tales, Grimm's *Little Red Riding Hood* and *The Three Little Pigs*, are selected to illustrate this.

4. Dante's Devils   60

An episode of Dante's *The Divine Comedy* permits one to follow the "evolution" in time of the sacred kernel, and to develop previous symbolic considerations.

5. Shakespeare at Midnight   79

A Midsummer Night's Dream reveals Shakespeare's esoteric knowledge guiding the reader to rediscover the cosmic and spiritual aspects of the sacred kernel.

6. The Four Musketeers   100

Dumas' famous novel, *The Three Musketeers*, so often misinterpreted, proves to be an initiatory tale, hiding a profound spiritual meaning, even if the author was unaware of it.

7. Dracula's Castle   122

This chapter, closer to our modern times, elucidates one of the modern fixations: Dracula and the vampires. Jules Verne's story, *Carpathian Castle*, is considered in connection with the surviving sacred kernel.

8. Black and White   142

The strange novel *The Narrative of Arthur Gordon Pym of Nantucket* by Edgar Allan Poe gives the opportunity to better understand how modern literature uses the ancient spiritual heritage. The important symbolism of black and white helps uncover other faces of the sacred kernel.

9. The Twins   166

Mark Twain's *The Prince and the Pauper*, and a more recent one, *The Scapegoat* by Daphne du Maurier, represent illustrations of an everlasting spiritual meaning misunderstood by our modern civilization.

10. The Eye of the Heart   188

The last chapter presents an extraordinary story, *The Little Prince* by Antoine de Saint-Exupéry. Considered mainly "children's literature," the story unveils a powerful spiritual kernel and introduces the traditional concept of "the eye of the heart," well known in Islamic tradition.

Ten Years Later – Avowal   208

The closing section emphasizes why is so importance to open the "eye of the heart" and choose between "the wheat and the darnel."

FOREWORD

THE MEDIEVAL image of the *Peridexion* (illustrating the cover of the present work) conveys a symbol of the axial Tree of Paradise situated at the numinous Centre: it bears upon its boughs the solar fruit of immortality for the initiate who can attain by conquest to the "Sanctuary of Peace," the "Land of the Living," and amid its branches and foliage the "birds of the air" take refuge, representing spiritual beings of the Angelic world. For those birds that wilfully stray and turn away from this blissful "Pure Land," devouring dragons lie in wait on either side, the delusive potencies of Mâyâ and Samsâra.

The Gospel tells us that this Paradisiacal tree, which symbolises the realisation of the "Kingdom of Heaven," grows from a minute seed-point and this is in fact precisely what the title of Mircea Tamas' fruitful book explicitly refers to – that imperishable kernel of transcendent and uncreated Light, which exists at the sacred Centre, within the locus of the heart that is the vital centre of the being.

From this seed-kernel, called Luz by the Kabbalists of the Middle Ages, the divine order unfolds in resurrection through the cycles, and microcosmically it is identified with a small bone at the base of the spine (the *Os Resurrectionis* as it was termed) from which man arises in renewal upon the day of the Greater Resurrection (*Qiyamat*). The letter *Yod* is a Hebraic representation of this centre-point of supernal Unity and this can also denote the brow-centre, the station of the "Divine Eye" (*Divya-chaksu*).

Thus, as the symbol of the Divine Principle, there could be no more apt theme than the seed-kernel of immortality for the title of

The Everlasting Sacred Kernel

Mircea Tamas' important book which takes as its subject the incorruptible existence, timelessness and renewal of Traditional ideas even within the cultural and artistic productions of a late and negative historical cycle such as the man of this *Kali-yuga* encounters. This is certainly an unusual work, even by the standards of so contrarians a canon of writings as those penned by such luminaries of Tradition as René Guénon (Sh. Abd al Wahid Yahya) and Ananda K. Coomaraswamy, in whose track the author plows his furrow.

Where those great authorities expounded the tenets of Traditional metaphysics with an authoritative and crystalline clarity, Tamas judiciously applies these eternal truths in a highly original species of *ta'wil*, of hermeneutics and exegesis by which a diversity of materials, from Dante Alighieri and Homeric epic to fairy tales and the 19th century novels of Edgar Allan Poe, Mark Twain and Alexandre Dumas and even works of children's literature are seen to yield startling glimpses and vistas of the eternal verities of Tradition. In this way Mircea Tamas' book presents a spiritual-cultural perspective which is both timelessly archaic and endlessly fresh and vital and therein lies the startling originality of this work.

But the author's employment of Traditional metaphysical interpretation and symbolic exegesis is never mechanical, dryly literal or simplistic but rather demonstrates a delicate and living faculty of esoteric insight grounded in the Divine Intellect and realised via the theophanic "Eye of the Heart."

Tamas' book evinces this power of understanding and awareness of the "sacred everlasting kernel" of Truth which has even been carried into modern times under an obscuring, sometimes distorting, cover of modern acculturation to survive unsuspected in places which might even seem unlikely and in open view. But following the oft-times compelling intricacy of Mircea Tamas' esoteric elucidations one is convinced that the transcendent essence of Traditional knowledge and themes have indeed been transmitted, in a concealed manner, in our modern world if one only has the "eyes to see" and the "ears to hear."

Mircea Tamas is under no illusions as to the formidable challenge such a task of spiritual discernment presents in a world-age

Foreword

infested by spiritual counterfeits, anti-spiritual subversions and infernal falsifications designed by the Counter-Initiatic agencies of the Adversary to lead man astray from the Straight Path and deeper into delusion and dissolution – occultism is anathema to this line of approach and he has deplored the degeneration whereby the schools of Hermetism have become involved with and been finally identified with little more than mere magic and deviation. Thus one can trust the author's rigour in regard to the metaphysics of the Primordial Tradition and this makes for a book which is both profoundly satisfying and beneficial.

This work is replete with initiatic and esoteric insights but one might call attention in particular, as an representative example of Mircea Tamas' methodology, to the 5th chapter "Shakespeare at Midnight" which explores the imagery, themes and significance of William Shakespeare's play "A Midsummer Night's Dream" in very profound ways relating to the function of the summer solstice as the *Janua Inferni* and unfolds a wondrous exposition of the deep esoterism which vivifies Shakespeare's play in the context of the mysterious role of carnivals and masques in the High Middle Ages: certainly the reader of this chapter subsequently finds him or herself watching the drama of Puck, Oberon, Nick Bottom, Titania and the other protagonists of this play through new eyes and beholds a very real demonstration of the genuinely primordial and initiatory content of the Shakespearian corpus.

These interconnected essay-chapters invite careful reading and demand from the reader a degree of spiritual maturity, clarity and intellectual sobriety – some of the insights conveyed in chapter 4, "Dante's Devils," would likely have at certain times and places been regarded as extremely secret and reserved for the very few in the sense that they are easily misunderstood and misinterpreted by those of defective understanding, the immature and by the type of crude misapprehension typical of occultists as well as of those mired in lower "moralism" of a dualistic nature. Mircea Tamas' words on the fall of Lucifer and the metaphysical implications thereof are extremely profound, paradoxical and illuminating but as with all true metaphysics, characterised always by orthodoxy and regularity, he advances here a doctrine for a veritable elite, those whose intellects are as it were spiritually ripe for this precious quality of penetrating insight - in a profane epoch of senescence, confusion and decline at the End of Time, characterised by what the author has elsewhere termed the "wrath of gods," the number of those capable of fully appreciating these sometimes startling insights, flashes and illuminations will always be a select one.

Nonetheless for those attuned to Tamas' uncompromising fidelity to the eternal "pattern of the heavens," as Plato called it, a perspective grounded totally in the immutable truth of Tradition, this important book with its marvellous essays provides a sure entry-point into the sacred realm of metaphysics and aligns the understanding with an authoritative exposition of Traditional knowledge illustrated in a number of highly unusual ways which will simultaneously surprise, delight and enlighten the attentive reader. "The Everlasting Sacred Kernel" is one of those rare books which the right reader is destined to discover at the right time and place and which for the right individual may well hold the possibility of indicating the authentic path to the supreme Centre.

Nigel Jackson

INTRODUCTION

SOMETIME ago, on a beautiful, fresh morning, I was riding my bicycle in a park, close to my home. I was thinking of everything and nothing. Suddenly, like a bolt, a picture came into my mind and made me freeze; I realized, at that very moment, the secret meaning of my harmless physical exercise: a modern paraphrase of the traditional symbol of the Chariot of Light.[1] The bicycle, a modern, profane vehicle, was revealing a new, deep significance, a sacred one: the front wheel became the symbol of Heaven, the rear wheel the symbol of Earth, and the crossbar was the *Axis Mundi* itself. Riding the bicycle changed into a spiritual journey, along the axis of the universe. A very challenging query was coming to life from the intelligence of my heart: is it possible to still have a sacred kernel hidden in our Western modern existence?

The main difference between our modern civilization and the traditional ones is that now we play at being gods, imposing our individual desires, ideas and originality, unaware that, in fact, we are puppets and that God, the supreme Principle, is the Master Puppeteer. The modern world has cut its ties with the Principle; on the contrary, God was close to the members of traditional civilizations, and they knew that individuality was nothing compared to the One-and-only, that they were just puppets on a string. In a traditional society, their whole life was a reflection of God. The myths were

---

[1] See René Guénon, **Symboles fondamentaux de la Science sacrée**, Gallimard, 1980, p. 267, and Ananda K. Coomaraswamy, **Traditional Art and Symbolism**, Princeton Univ. Press, 1977, p. 380.

The Everlasting Sacred Kernel

real, the beliefs were certitudes, and the rites were not superstitions, but spiritual instruments. In a traditional society, every gesture, every activity was a sacred one, imitating what the gods did *in illo tempore*, at the beginning of the world.[2] Eating, working, hunting, dancing, singing, playing, each one represented a sacred rite, an organized activity (Sanskrit *rita* = "order"), following a divine model and having a spiritual meaning. A traditional person knew that mankind, at the moment of birth, was blessed with a holy lore, the Tradition descended from Heaven. For the modern person this descent is just another legend.

Our modern society is terribly "human" and *ipso facto* profane; most of the traditional *karma* (Sanskrit *karma* = "ritual activity") becomes show business and entertainment, while the supernal kernel is forgotten.[3] Is it possible then, without error, to transmute symbolical, sacred significance ("showing through signs") to our present world, to charge a bicycle with mythical signs? The answer is definitely affirmative for a very profound reason: the sacred hidden marrow of the World is the projection of the supreme Principle, One without a second, who wants to play and creates the universal Existence as a sport in his image.[4] The spiritual, sacred sparks, proceeding from the everlasting divine Fire (Hindu Agni as *Âtmâ*, Kabbalah's *Ein-Sof* as dark flame) to support and give life into the Cosmos, will always be there. It only seems that they are missing because human mentality has changed and turned away from the traditional knowledge of the celestial principles.[5] It doesn't matter if the modern and profane people label the sacred heritage of the traditional societies as superstitions, myths or legends. The spiritual

---

[2] Mircea Eliade, **Le mythe de l'éternel retour**, Gallimard, 1979, p. 34.

[3] Physical activity, so appreciated nowadays, has also a sacred origin. See Ghazi bin Muhammed, **The Sacred Origin of Sports and Culture**, Fons Vitae, 1998.

[4] "Brahma's creative activity is not undertaken by way of any need on his part, but simply by way of sport, in the common sense of the word" (**Brahma Sûtras** II.1.32-3). See Ananda K. Coomaraswamy, **Selected Papers: Metaphysics**, Princeton Univ. Press, 1977, p. 150.

[5] We understand "tradition" and "traditional" defined as "what was transmitted" from the beginning of the World, as an unbroken golden chain anchored to the supreme Principle.

Introduction

kernel, inviolable and unchangeable, is alive. We just have to see it with the Eye of the Heart.

There is yet another question to be answered: is it possible for any kind of object (such as a bicycle) to be considered an expression of the divine archetypes or is it only the human imagination that plays tricks on us? To answer, we introduce the "metaphysics of *ekapâda*." *Ekapâda* means "one-footed" in Sanskrit and represents the *Axis Mundi* as celestial Ray (or as the "seventh Ray") of the spiritual Sun. Before manifesting itself, the supreme Principle (Hindu *Brahma nirguna*, Brahma without qualifications and attributes) is a Dragon without eyes or feet, a "black hole," a turtle retreated inside its shell, the peacock with its tail furled. Producing the universal manifestation (the whole Existence), the Principle opens its eyes and forms one foot, the axis of the universe, with this foot it jumps (like Vishnu) three steps, manifesting the "Three Worlds" (corporeal, subtle and angelic). The *Axis Mundi* – the solar Ray, the unique foot – producing the Existence, multiplies itself into "one thousand feet" (Sanskrit *sahashrapâda*),[6] i.e., a multiplicity of solar rays, reflecting the unique Ray. *Ekapâda*, like Brahma, is neutral. *Ekapâda* is father and mother, and son and daughter, and friend and fiend, and dragon and hero, and brother and sister, and husband and wife, and alive and dead, and one and multiple. For that reason the "feet," everything in the Cosmos, are explanations of *ekapâda* and symbolic assistants in the quest for the supreme Truth. A tree, a bicycle, a house or a vase, are all projections of the one and only foot and, therefore, represent operative aids during a spiritual task, allowing us to "participate" to the Most High.

As Ananda K. Coomaraswamy said, "Natural or artificial objects are not for the primitive [that is, for the traditional mentality], as they can be for us, arbitrary symbols of some other and higher reality, but actual manifestations of this reality"[7]; therefore, "that a safety pin or button is meaningless, and merely a convenience for

---

[6] Coom., **Metaphysics**, p. 391. See also Ananda K. Coomaraswamy, **La doctrine du sacrifice**, Dervy-Livres, 1978, p. 47.
[7] See Coom., **Trad. Art**, pp. 295.

us, is simply the evidence of our profane ignorance."[8] The pin or the button, Coomaraswamy explained, is a symbol of the Sun that "connects all things to himself and fastens them; he is the primordial embroiderer and tailor, by whom the tissue of the universe, to which our garments are analogous, is woven on a living thread"; and "the proof that the meaning of the safety pin had been understood [by the traditional man] can be pointed to in the fact that the heads or eyes of prehistoric fibulae are regularly decorated with a repertoire of distinctly solar symbols."[9] We have in our collection, besides the bicycle, a hair pin, two thousand years old, 14 cm long, from an ancient Dacian city called Ratiaria, conquered by the Romans, who made it the capital of the province Dacia Ripensis; the pin has a wolf head,[10] with the eyes made of carneols and holding a ring in his teeth: the ring obviously is the "Sun-Door."

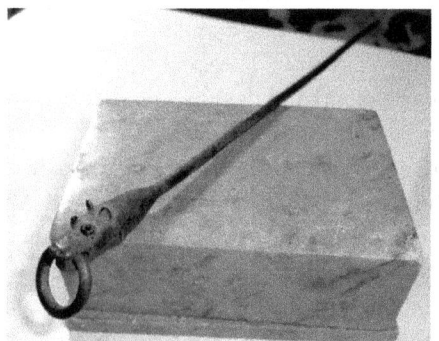 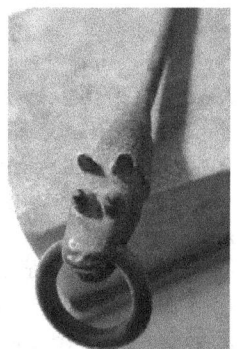

---

[8] *Ibid.*, p. 298.
[9] *Ibid.*, p. 299.
[10] The ancient Dacians' standard was a flying dragon with a wolf head. We will discuss later the symbolism of the wolf.

Introduction

Between *ekapâda* and *sahashrapâda* there is a "broker," archetype of the multiplicity, the "two-footed" (*dwapâda*), by definition the World being the domain of duality (in the Cosmos, all the couples coexist: good-bad, warm-cold, etc.). The primordial duality represents the two fundamental principles called Heaven and Earth and is symbolized by the two wheels of the bicycle, principles that are actually One without a second, and two only from a mundane point of view. But the "two feet" could express, from a spiritual point of view, the immortal and the mortal "soul," the sacred kernel and the profane skin. Consequently, in some initiatory rituals the neophyte has one foot uncovered (the axis of the universe, the naked truth) and the other one covered (the world). Titian's famous painting, "Sacred [the nude woman] and profane [the dressed woman] love," also illustrates this meaning.

We see the beauty of the science of symbols: it gives us "a thousand feet," better, it affords "a thousand eyes," a multitude of points of view, all valid, like the indefinite number of solar rays; for that reason, the Hindu doctrines are called *darsanas* – "points of view." Kabbalah, the Hebraic tradition, selects three as fundamental meanings of any symbolism: the Cosmos, the Year and the Man (**Sepher Yetsirah** III.2), and they can be traced in any orthodox doctrine of any traditional society. Moreover, any rite has as its kernel this triple significance and it is a good exercise to come back to the bicycle's symbolism. First, from a cosmological point of view, the bicycle is the entire Cosmos or universal manifestation, the two poles, Heaven and Earth, and the axis representing the principles sustaining and developing the World; as well, the wheel itself is an image of the Cosmos, the hub being the Principle, and the rim the World, created and supported by transfer from One (the center) to many (the spokes). Secondly, the rotation of the wheels simulates the movement of the Cosmos, the whirled development of the worlds starting from the immutable Principle. This rotation is also an emblem of the Year or Time, because the production of the Universe obeys the law of cosmic cycles (that is why after night comes day, and again night, the whole Existence being governed by cycles). Thirdly, the bicycle is Man's vehicle, the rider being the immortal "soul" of any human being. Riding the bicycle signifies a divine initiation, a spiritual voyage from Earth to Heaven, redemption, and liberation (Sanskrit *moksha*).[11]

Another important fact is that a symbol is universal, and so is not affected by particularities such as geographical location, nationality, religion or culture. For example, meditating in front of a Christmas tree or in front of a standing Ganesha statue makes no difference. The Christmas tree is in Christian tradition a symbol of the *Axis Mundi*. All the ornaments, which are hanging from the boughs, represent the multicolored elements of the Cosmos, comparable with the colors radiated by the secret flame of *Ein-Sof* (**Zohar** I.15a). The standing Ganesha is usually "one-footed," this foot being the axis of the universe, the unique Ray. His four arms, the trunk and the other foot (lifted) are the manifestation rays, the innumerable spokes that produce the Universe; they are the boughs of the Christmas tree. The main difficulty is not selecting the symbol, but rather our qualification to recognize it. The less profane our mentality is, the deeper our comprehension of the absolute Truth gets. Thus, by choosing a bicycle to sustain our spiritual efforts the effect is not going to be less efficient.

The Quest for the sacred kernel is, consequently, a spiritual adventure with a benefic internal change for any person capable of seeing with the heart, and our modern world still provides symbolic supports for this Quest. It is the objective of this book to prove this. The domain is incommensurably vast, as large as the Cosmos itself. The book will try then to limit itself to a small region, focusing on Western culture (identified today with the modern world), and mainly on Western literature. It is well known that Western

---

[11] We must define the meaning of the word "initiation," which was used in many ways. Initiation, etymologically speaking, is a "beginning" and an entrance into a new domain. Profane scholars have used the term for all kinds of fields. We have to stress, though, that initiation is primarily about spiritual achievement and not about social rites. For a traditional society, initiation represented a series of sacred rites leading to a spiritual realization. The neophyte, the Man, can be male or female; here Man should be understood as Sanskrit *mânava* "a mental being," image of the Hindu *Manu*, the "Lord of the World."

Introduction

culture was influenced at the beginning by two major spiritual currents: Hebraic and Greco-Roman, the first expressed in the Holy *Bible*, the second in the mythological stories and philosophy. With the rotation of the wheels and time elapsing, the sacred writings became modern literature. Similarly to the example of the bicycle, it is still possible to unveil a sacred kernel in Western literature, whether ancient, medieval or modern.

This is not an easy task, considering that the simplifications and the shortcuts the moderns are fond of cannot apply here. Descartes, the French philosopher, was one of the first scholars in the Western world who turned people's mentality away from traditional, sacred thinking, offering instead profane, rational judgments. He insisted that any idea had to be "clear and distinct," and all modern sciences are based on this axiom; hence the obsession with systems, classifications and simplifications. Unfortunately for the rational mind, the metaphysical order is beyond systems and "clear and distinct" ideas. A system means limitation but the supreme Principle is infinite. Unveiling the sacred kernel will never offer a unique, limited solution; a symbol will never translate only one concept.

Ganesha is considered in Hindu tradition the god protecting such a task as the present one, the task of reaching the sacred kernel. He is the lord of beginning, of initiation (Latin *initium*, "beginning"), and the inspiration for traditional writers. He also helps us understand the path from skin to kernel. Ganesha is not only *ekapâda*, "one-footed" (as *Nrtya Ganapati*, "dancing Ganapati"), but also *ekadanta*, "single tusked,"[12] stressing the idea of One without a second as definition for the supreme Principle. Ganesha is this One, the Center of everything. On the other hand, his name means "the lord of multitude" (Sanskrit *gana* = multitude, *isha* = lord, Grimes 41). Ganesha is One and multiple, he is the only Ray, but reigns over the one thousand rays and that is why he has 108 names and 32 forms. The spiritual doctrines and the sacred symbols present the same characteristic: they are one (*ab intra*) and multiple (*ab extra*). We can never expect to build a system or a confined method to

---

[12] John A. Grimes, **Ganapati**, State Univ. of New York Press, 1995, pp. 61, 75.

The Everlasting Sacred Kernel

explain the sacred knowledge. In the metaphysical order ("beyond the physical field") if we drop a stone from a tower, it may fall, or it may fly.[13]

For example, any traditional government, divine or human, has two sides: spiritual authority and temporal power. Ganesha is the lord of wisdom and the emblem of spiritual authority; his brother, Skanda, the lord of war, is the emblem of temporal power.[14] We find something similar in Greek tradition: Hera, the Queen of gods, has only two children, two sons: Hephaestus, the lord of divine fire, and Ares, the lord of war.[15] We could assume a tendency to limitation and schematizing but no, Hephaestus is not the lord of wisdom, even though he is related to Light. More likely, Ulysses can be compared with Ganesha from this point of view. Ulysses is considered the wisest of the Greeks and he is called *polytropos*, that is "with many forms," like Ganesha. His real name, though, is "Nobody," which is a perfect name for a divine person.[16]

The sacred kernel is such a "nobody." Though invisible, it has many forms and aspects, some opposing each other, some creating an Aristotelian perplexity. All these names and forms, escaping the ordinary rules and profane reasoning, contribute to express in words what is nameless and indefinable.

We are prepared now to begin the Quest. Since Ulysses turned up, it is not a bad idea to consider for the next step the sacred kernel of Homer's important poems, the **Iliad** and the **Odyssey**, focusing on some of Ulysses' deeds.

---

[13] "Sometimes the dragon jumps into the abyss, sometimes he doesn't," **Le Yi: King**, Adrien Maisonneuve, Paris, 1975, I, p. 31 (the traditional commentary). See also **The I Ching**, Dover Publications, 1963, p. 57.

[14] René Guénon, **Autorité spirituelle et pouvoir temporel**, Les Éditions Véga, 1976, p. 62.

[15] Hephaestus is born "one-footed" or lame and his body is, like Ganesha's body, deformed. He was raised in a cave, and so was Ganesha.

[16] **The Odyssey of Homer**, Harper & Row, 1975, tr. by Richmond Lattimore, IX.365; Greek *oydeis*, "nobody," was considered related to Ulysses' Greek name, Odysseus. "Tao, the Way, is forever nameless" (Lao tzu, **Tao Te Ching**, Penguin Books, 1967, XXXII.72); Tao is in Chinese tradition the supreme Principle.

Chapter One

ULYSSES

THE HINDU tradition tells that Ganesha, listening respectively to Vyâsa (Grimes 76) and to Vâlmîki,[1] wrote down the two extraordinary poems, *Mahâbhârata* and *Râmâyana*. Vyâsa and Vâlmîki are probably not individuals who can be traced, but "intellectual aggregates."[2] Writing the epics, Ganesha, the lord of wisdom, has given them a divine essence; it also indicates that beyond the literal meaning and beauty, a hidden sacred significance waits to be discovered. Something similar, we assume, happened in the case of Homer's poems. Homer was blind, so he couldn't write, only dictate. Of course, his blindness is a symbolic one, pointing out that he was seeing with the Eye of the Heart (Islamic *Ayn el-Qalb*), i.e., he was seeing the spiritual world. That makes him also not an individual but more probably an "intellectual aggregate" dictating to a Greek Ganesha the celestial epics.

The more strongly a spiritual influence or a divine blessing is present in a "literary" work, the more difficult it is to comment, and usually the number of commentaries and explanations are then inexhaustible.[3] Homer's poems are not exceptions. They provoked

---

[1] Ananda K. Coomaraswamy, **Pour comprendre l'art hindou**, Tradition Universelle, 1926, p. 20.
[2] René Guénon, **Introduction générale à l'étude des doctrines hindoues**, Guy Trédaniel, 1987, p. 214.
[3] Any sacred writing, containing the words of God, has "one thousand feet," countless faces and innumerable meanings. "If the sea were an inkwell for the words of

many commentaries, ordinarily focusing on the literal, social, or historical aspects, yet the spiritual meaning was also touched in the past[4] and today.[5] Our task is, fortunately, not an impossible one. We have to prove that the sacred kernel is present. We don't have to lose ourselves in endless commentaries. We don't have to cover all "one thousand feet"; it is enough if we are able to understand the "one foot" expressed by the Kabbalistic triad, Cosmos – Year – Man.

A major event started and motivated the epics: the abduction of Helen. Before going any further we must learn its meaning, from both points of view, micro- and macrocosmically. To abduct, to steal somebody else's wife, like Paris did, is an immoral act from an external, social point of view. Yet we find this act of theft everywhere in the sacred writings. In Hindu tradition, Vritra abducts the solar herds or the rivers,[6] and Indra steals the immortal beverage, *soma* (Coom., **La doctrine**, p. 24 ff.). In the *Râmâyana*, Râvana abducts Sîtâ. In Greek tradition, Prometheus steals the celestial fire, Hercules steals the golden apples from the Garden of the Hesperides, Hermes steals Apollo's herd, and Hades abducts Persephone. In the *Bible*, Eve steals the apple and David steals Uriah's wife, Bathsheba. In fairy tales, the dragon steals the golden apples, or the sun, the moon and the stars, or the emperor's three daughters.[7]

A "metaphysics of theft" is unveiling before us. We have to transcend the moral, ordinary meaning and go deep "to steal," in our

---

my Lord, the sea would be drained before my Lord's words would be spent even though we brought the same again to replenish it," **The Qur'ân** XVIII.100 (Amana Books, 1988, p. 159).

[4] Plotinus, Proclus, Porphyry and other Neoplatonists gave us beautiful exegeses. See Félix Buffière, **Les mythes d'Homère et la pensée grecque**, Les Belles Lettres, 1956.

[5] See Titus Burckhardt, **Mirror of the Intellect**, State Univ. of New York Press, 1987, where a short but valuable article about Ulysses can be found.

[6] Sri Aurobindo, **The Secret of the Veda**, Sri Aurobindo Ashram, Pondicherry, 1971, pp. 104, 118.

[7] It has to be clearly understood that when we are talking of solar herds and celestial rivers or about the spiritual sun, these have nothing to do with the corporeal world. They are symbols of the divine, informal order, purely spiritual, beyond the soul-body domain.

turn, the spiritual, esoteric meaning. In order to understand the divine kernel and to read the symbols properly we have to be "drunk" like the Apostles were (**Acts** 2), or "mad" like Hamlet was. We have to think with our heart as Intelligence not with our mind as reason, and to be "super-rational" means for ordinary people to be mad or drunk. Only from a human point of view when somebody takes away a piece of our property from us, let's say, a piece of land, do we call it stealing. From the divine point of view how can it be possible for somebody to steal something, when everything belongs to the World and the World is a manifestation of the Principle? The thief and what is stolen are just manifestations of the Principle, so we can say "the Principle steals the Principle," which is not stealing at all. It is our human arrogance that makes us think that the World belongs to us. It is our human ignorance that makes us measure the divine works with our moral standards. If the Dragon takes away from us the solar light, we call him a thief, but the Dragon is an aspect of the supreme Principle and the sun is his property (usually his head), so who is stealing from whom?

Fiat Lux creates the Cosmos by manifesting the divine light, and the super-luminous Principle is the real owner of the World. It becomes obvious then, that taking back the light or the waters symbolizes the death of our world, the end of our cycle of manifestation and, by transposition, the end of the entire Cosmos (the "Three Worlds"), which from a human point of view means the biggest abduction ever. When the Dragon steals the light or the cows or the rivers, the Cosmos dies; also, the divine kernel is stolen, the spiritual knowledge is hidden from us and the darkness of ignorance covers the dying world, as well as our heart and eyes. In the sacred writings, a symbol for absolute, divine Knowledge is the Virgin, *Madonna Intelligenza* for Dante, *Shakti* for Hindu tradition, and Helen of Troy is exactly this "virgin," symbolizing the spiritual light. Thus, the abduction of Helen illustrates the end of a cosmic cycle, the end of a world, the end of the sacred wisdom, when the Dragon steals and hides the spiritual sun, the celestial rivers, i.e., life and knowledge. In the Aztec tradition there was a ritual of extinguishing the fires at the end of a cycle, and even in our modern world, when celebrating the

The Everlasting Sacred Kernel

New Year, it is the custom to turn off the lights just before midnight.

According to the traditional doctrine of the Year (of the cosmic cycles), the death of a world (if we are talking about macrocosms) or being (if we are talking about microcosms) equals the birth of a new one. That is why the Aztecs would kindle a new fire and in the first second of the New Year, the lights are turned on. In our modern world, full of automation and electronics, even symbolizing the transfer from the old, dying cycle to the new one looks easy and simple (turning a switch off and on), but this simplicity hides all the spiritual meanings of this transfer.

The Greeks started an implacable war to bring back the light. It is not very difficult to understand the significance of this war. To begin a new cycle, to produce a new Cosmos, to resurrect the worlds and the beings, means to liberate the abducted sun, the stolen cows or rivers, to rescue the Virgin, Helen of Troy. Maybe it sounds strange to say that Helen is the Virgin, but it is strange only to our human rational mind. The symbol of Leda's twins, Castor and Pollux, is well known from Greek mythology. Pollux is immortal, the sacred kernel, his father being Zeus; Castor is mortal, the profane skin. It is less known that Leda also gave birth to a pair of twin girls, Helen and Clytemnestra, Helen being the immortal one, with Zeus as father. Regardless of her terrestrial life, she remains the everlasting, divine maid, the Virgin.

The Trojan War is not only a cosmic war to rejuvenate the Universe, to start a new Golden Age and change the cycles. In Islam, Muhammad the Prophet explained the difference between "the lesser war" and "the Greater War." The former is an external, mundane one; the latter is an internal, spiritual one. The Trojan War is this spiritual war, which, from Man's point of view, takes place within us, the stake being the Kingdom of Heaven (**Luke** 17:21). This Kingdom is "located" in the cavity of the heart and, in some traditions, is described as a fortress. This fortress is the Hindu *Brahmapura*, "the City of God,"[8] where *Âtmâ*, the Universal Spirit,

---

[8] Ananda K. Coomaraswamy, **What is Civilisation?**, Lindisfarne Press, 1989, p. 2.

dwells, but it is also Meister Eckhart's castle.⁹ We can trace this symbolism in any tradition; this Kingdom as fortress is also Troy.¹⁰

It took ten years of war to conquer Troy: nine years of undecided battles, of death and bravura, and one last year when Ulysses' shrewdness brought the victory to the Greeks. The nine plus one years of war are, like all the other spans of time in sacred writings, symbolical and usually they represent the duration of a cycle, more or less extensive.

It is easy to illustrate a cycle by drawing a circle using a compass.¹¹ The pointed arm of the compass marks the center and remains fixed; this arm is the "one foot," the naked foot, the immutable *Axis Mundi*. The center is the place where the Principle operates as pure Presence, as pure Intellect, as Divine Will; this central point is One. The other arm of the compass traces the circumference of the circle; this movable arm is the covered foot, the "integral" of the "one thousand feet" which by rotation develops the universal manifestation and the cosmic cycles, unfolding the innumerable feet as the peacock would unfold its tail. The circumference is the symbol of the World, like the rim of the wheel, and has the number nine as its sign.¹²

We already comprehend the main significance of those ten years of the Trojan War: it is a complete development of a cosmic cycle,

---

⁹ *Intravit Iesus in quoddam castellum*, **Luke** 10:38. See Maître Eckhart, **Sermons**, Éd. du Seuil, 1974, I, p. 50.

¹⁰ In the Middle Ages, Troy became the archetype of the Center as fortress to be conquered. Also the maze was called "Troy-Town" (Caer Droia), for the maze is a symbol of the Center. Traveling through the labyrinth meant conquering the Center (or the Heart) of the Cosmos (of Man). For information about the maze see Paolo Santarcangeli, **Il libro dei labirinti**, Firenze, 1967.

¹¹ We have to keep in mind that the end of a cosmic cycle is the beginning of the next one; so the cycles are not circles but spirals and only the projection on a horizontal plane is a circle.

¹² For Pythagoras, ten was the perfect number and the circle the perfect geometric figure. The *divine Tetraktys* was the fundamental Pythagorean emblem, representing the perfect ten as the sum of the first four natural numbers: $1 + 2 + 3 + 4 = 10$. The four numbers are related to the four cardinal directions and to the two perpendicular diameters that divide the circle in quarters of 90°; hence the relation between number 9 and the circumference (Guénon, **Symboles**, p. 128).

The Everlasting Sacred Kernel

including its end. "The circle, with its central point, symbol of the number ten, is at the same time the symbol of the cyclical perfection, that is, of the integral realization of the possibilities involved in a state of existence (world)," Guénon tells us.[13] Actually, the symbolism of ten, as nine plus One, is so important to Homer that he mentions it at the beginning of the *Iliad*, not once but twice. The epic commences with Apollo punishing the Greeks. Nine days in a row Apollo has sent his deadly arrows upon the Greek army; on the tenth day the Greeks ask for mercy.[14] It is no surprise to see Apollo opening the poem; this god is like Ganesha, the lord of initiation, of spiritual deeds, he is the spiritual Sun, and his arrows are the "one thousand feet." In fact, this first episode of the epic is a synthesis of the entire poem. Agamemnon, the leader of the Greeks, has abducted a virgin, the daughter of Apollo's priest, Chryses. The virgin Chryseis is, of course, an *alter ego* of Helen.[15] Apollo starts the "war" against the Greeks, and Agamemnon on the tenth day accepts the defeat and returns the girl.[16] The nine days plus one (in divine order) are the nine years plus one (in human order) of the Trojan War.

In the second chant, the theme reoccurs as a prophecy of the whole epic. The prophecy is told by none other than Ulysses. It is a key episode and we have to remember that, besides the cosmological meaning, a spiritual one is always present. From this point of view, the Trojan War is an initiation, an inner spiritual realization, full of temptations and obstacles.[17] In Christian tradition, Jesus is

---

[13] René Guénon, **Le symbolisme de la croix**, Guy Trédaniel, 1989, p. 46. In Islam, Allâh has 99 divine attributes or names, the perfection being obtained by adding the secret name, the 100th, which is, of course, "Nobody."
[14] **The Iliad** of Homer, The Univ. of Chicago Press, 1961 (tr. by Richmond Lattimore), I.50.
[15] In Greek, the names Chryses and Chryseis mean "the golden one" that is direct related to the spiritual Sun.
[16] It is worthy to note that Ulysses is the one who returns Chryseis to her father. Her home city is Thebes, near Troy. Thebes is a symbolic name for the Center of the World and we can find a Thebes in Greece and one in Egypt. Guénon relates this name to Hebraic *Thebah*, the Ark. See René Guénon, **Le Roi du Monde**, Gallimard, 1981, p. 91.
[17] Those are the "devils" within us.

Ulysses

tempted by the Devil. In Buddhism, Mâra, the Demon, tries to subvert Buddha: first, he sends an army of devils to attack him; secondly, he sends his three daughters to tempt him. The Sirens tempt Ulysses. In the second chant of the *Iliad*, the temptation is a deceiving dream and the devil is Thersites who tries to convince the Greeks to give up the siege of Troy.[18] Ulysses stands up against the temptation, revealing himself as the spiritual leader of the Greeks. "He came face to face with Agamemnon, son of Atreus, and took from him the sceptre of his fathers, immortal forever" (**Iliad** II.185)[19]; thus, Ulysses takes the power from the supreme head of the Greeks, converting the scepter from temporal to sacerdotal power. And now Ulysses, as the true leader of the spiritual Quest, describes the prophetic sign seen by the Greeks before leaving for Troy (**Iliad** II.284 ff.). A plane tree and a spring with shining waters mark the axes of the sacred coordinate system.[20] A snake ascends to "the uttermost branch tip" of the plane tree and reaches a nest with nine sparrows: the mother and the eight children. The snake swallows the nine birds and then Zeus "made him a monument, striking him stone." The snake is the dragon that at the end of the cycle "steals" the lights, "eats" the worlds, and recovers his "powers," absorbing them back into the Principle (the non-manifestation).[21] He is also the spiritual father, the vertical axis, identical with the tree itself, the fixed arm of the compass. The she-bird is the mother, the substantial principle of the universal manifestation, the movable

---

[18] Theristes was "the ugliest man" in the world, deformed, "bandy-legged and went lame of one foot." He is the emblem of the Dragon. *Ab intra*, the Dragon is the supreme Principle, so all the temptations are coming from God himself. That is why Zeus sent the deceiving dream.

[19] Hephaestus had wrought the golden sceptre for Zeus (**Iliad** II.100). It is a symbol of the lightning, the lightning being not the natural phenomenon but the "one foot," the celestial Ray. With this sceptre Ulysses will crush Thersites, the devil, expressing the activity of spiritual Light.

[20] The solar Ray (vertical axis) reflected in the waters (horizontal axis) is a traditional illustration of the Divine Presence operating upon the primordial Substance. The plane tree is identical to the celestial Ray.

[21] The end of the world implies its total solidification; that is the meaning of Zeus making the snake stone.

The Everlasting Sacred Kernel

arm of the compass, the spring of water, the horizontal axis. She and the eight children are the nine of the circumference; they are the worlds and the cycles. The snake and the birds constitute the holy family of ten, the ten years of the Trojan War.[22]

The Chinese tradition will help us understand better this Homeric story. A mythological Chinese tale speaks of a solar goddess who gave birth to ten suns.[23] The suns dwell in a tree (the *Axis Mundi*, the vertical axis), in the middle of the sea (the reservoir of the generative possibilities, the horizontal axis). Following a precise order, nine of them are always in the tree while one is crossing the sky, lighting the world, fecundating the possibilities. In Greek, the word "cosmos" means "order"; following the order, the ten suns generate the worlds and rule the good course of the cycles. One day, the ten suns decide to shine together, simultaneously, and the world is burnt and devastated. An archer hero is sent to save the world and he kills nine of the suns with his arrows, the one left giving just the right light for a new world to develop.

We are ready now to translate the esoteric meaning of the Trojan War. The first nine years describe the development of a cosmic cycle or, in particular, a terrestrial cycle, from the Golden Age to the Iron Age; the tenth year, when the conquest and demolition of Troy happens, is the "end of the world," the completion of a full cycle. Homer doesn't tell us about this *Ragnarok*; his poem stops with the burial of Hector.[24] There are other epic poems, unfortunately lost, dealing with the fall of Troy. Some data have been preserved and we know that the destruction of Troy illustrates the typical calami-

---

[22] This episode is often told in fairy tales. The dragon eats the children of a she-eagle and the solar hero beheads the snake. The head will become the sun of the new world. The eagle, solar bird, will be the hero's vehicle to perfect his spiritual realization. The swallowed birds have to be compared with the children swallowed by Cronos-Saturn. Gods or birds, they symbolize the lights of various cycles or worlds. They are the golden apples or the suns of the *Axis Mundi*.

[23] Yuan Ke, **Dragons and Dynasties**, Penguin Books, 1993, p. 74 ff.

[24] *Ragnarok*, "the twilight of the gods," in the mythology of the Norsemen is described as a total battle ended with floods, earthquakes, and eventually with a huge devouring fire.

ties of the end of time.[25] When the old cycle perishes, the seed of the new cycle is already there, hiding in the ashes. That is the symbolism of the *Phoenix*, the bird that resurrects from its own ashes. Helen is this seed, she is the hidden sun, and her liberation means the beginning of a new world, means *Fiat Lux*.

The production of the Cosmos is a joint work of art of two fundamental principles, the two poles, Heaven and Earth, yet *ab intra* they are One without a second. Thus, the birth of the World and its cosmic cycles will be perceived as a double vision, a celestial and a terrestrial one. From the celestial point of view, the Principle is absolute Light, so powerful, so burning, that the worlds cannot survive or exist. This Light is the light of the ten suns shining simultaneously. Producing the universal manifestation is in this case not *Fiat Lux*; on the contrary, it is *Fiat Umbra*, the shadowing of Light. Killing the nine suns means to cripple, to veil the power of the devastating Light. We find here a second symbolism of the Trojan War. The nine years of war take place *ab intra*, in the night of non-manifestation, between two cycles,[26] each year representing the death of a sun. In the tenth year, the Light is lame enough to show "one foot" (Helen of Troy) without burning the World and bringing it to existence.[27] From the terrestrial point of view, the Trojan War is the chaos and the liberation of Helen is *Fiat Lux*. We may note that the same light of the ten suns, which produces the World,

---

[25] See **The Aeneid** of Virgil, Bantam Books, 1981 (tr. by Allen Mandelbaum), book II. Virgil describes the flames that consumed the fortress, the earthquakes that destroyed the walls.

[26] In Hindu tradition, this gap of time between two cycles is called *sandhyâ*. In reality *sandhyâ* is timeless, yet for the human mind it can be depicted as a cycle of nine plus one.

[27] In some fairy tales, the wife undertakes a spiritual journey in the quest of her husband (the spiritual Sun). She is pregnant and she has to stay this way for nine years, until she finds the solar hero. Only then the husband will touch her with his hand and will liberate her, and the child will be born. The child is the new world and he is hiding in *sandhyâ* for nine years.

also destroys it, the Principle having two faces, a benefic and a malefic one.[28]

We mentioned the spiritual meaning of the *Iliad*. The Trojan War is the war within us, aiming for the liberation of the Self from temptations, passions and all the mundane chains. It is a spiritual quest within us to discover the immortal sun, the *Âtmâ*, the virgin Helen. It is an initiation; it is the conquest of supreme Knowledge. There are two heroes pursuing the spiritual journey in Homer's beautiful epics: Achilles and Ulysses. It was said that the *Iliad* is Achilles' story and the *Odyssey* is Ulysses' story. That is not exactly true. Ulysses is very involved in the spiritual conquest of Troy, as Achilles is. Actually, we can assume that both heroes are just two faces of the same coin. They are marked as "elected"[29] heroes to follow the esoteric path. Both of them are reluctant to join the Trojan War, which presents a two-fold explanation. On the one side, the mundane chains are so strong that the devils of passions, appetites and desires are very much in control and they try to delude the "elected" one from embarking on the spiritual path. On the other side, we can assume that Achilles and Ulysses are (minor) *avatâras*, the embodiment of the Divine Presence in the World, their initiation being a model for mankind, an archetype, as the life of Jesus Christ was, in order to bring salvation. The *avatâra*'s descent[30] from Heavens is usually considered a sacrifice, and it is accepted with reluctance: the superluminous night of the Principle is much better than the shadowy day of the World. Achilles tries to hide on the island of Skyros, disguised as a girl, and only Ulysses' ruse unmasks him. Achilles appears as a projection of the Androgynous, unveiling his spiritual

---

[28] The same double symbolism appears in the case of water. Water is the perfect milieu to nourish the seeds of life; water, on the other hand, destroys the world, flooding it.
[29] The word (from Latin *eligo*) is related to elite, "most distinguished, intelligent, gifted people." That is the meaning we are interested in; the neophyte, accepted for initiation, belongs to a spiritual elite.
[30] Sanskrit *avatarana* means "coming down."

Ulysses

mark. Ulysses, in his turn, feigns madness to escape the war, and we have seen that "madness" is a mark of divine inspiration.[31]

There are two other "corporeal" marks: Achilles' vulnerable heel and Ulysses' scar. We are not going into Achilles' sacred biography, being more interested in uncovering some of Ulysses' traits that make him the archetype of the spiritual peregrine. "That scar, which once the boar with his white tusk had inflicted on him" (**Odyssey** XIX.390), is the mark that betrays him; seeing this scar, the old nurse recognizes Ulysses when he returns home, disguised as a beggar.[32] The boar symbolizes the "Lord of the World," the supreme King of a cosmic cycle, a direct image of the only Principle (Guénon, **Le Roi**, pp. 32, 58).[33] The Hindu tradition tells us that our cycle is called "the Age of the White Boar" (Guénon, **Symboles**, p. 178). We can compare the boar's white tusk with Ganesha's single tusk and it is safe to assume that Ulysses was "wounded" by God himself with the solar Ray as weapon. The boar wounded Ulysses' foot; that means the Greek hero is also, in some respect, the "one-footed."

The last remark suggests that Ulysses is a reflection of the "Lord of the World," unifying the spiritual authority and the temporal power. He is the wisest man and he is a warrior-king, that illustrating his double function; moreover, his "guardian angel" is the goddess Pallas-Athena. It is well known that Pallas-Athena, the Virgin, was born directly from Zeus' head, and she was fully armed. She

---

[31] Ulysses' feigned madness is, somehow, identical with saying that Ulysses "lost his head." In Hindu tradition, Ganesha also loses his head, which will be replaced with an elephant head full of wisdom. Ulysses' madness is identical to Hamlet's madness.
[32] The "beggar" is one of the masks of the initiate. In Buddhism, it is the mark of holiness. In Mark Twain's story, **The Prince and the Pauper**, it indicates an initiatory-like process.
[33] Guénon brilliantly promoted Ossendowski's syntagma, "Lord of the World" (See Ferdinand Ossendowski, **Beasts, Men and Gods**, Blue Ribbon Books, 1931, p. 299 ff.). We found in Christian tradition two eminent examples of this supreme function. One is Melchizedek, "king of Salem" (temporal power) and "priest for ever" (spiritual authority), **Hebrews** 7:1-3 (Guénon, **Le Roi**, p. 47 ff). The other example is Christ himself: his mock coronation (**Mark** 15:19) and his own confirmation, in front of Pilate, that he is the king, but "mine is not a kingdom of this world" (**John** 18:36) reveals him as "Lord of the World."

The Everlasting Sacred Kernel

was born "equal to her father in strength and in wise understanding,"[34] symbolizing exactly the sacerdotal and temporal powers. Ulysses' virginal guardian should be compared with Dante's celestial protector and guide, Beatrice.[35]

The goal of the spiritual quest is the "Supreme Identity" (using an Islamic syntagma) or the total "Liberation" (*moksha*, using a Hindu expression). The "elected" person transcends the ephemeral world, escapes the individual chains, leaves the indefinite rotation of the wheel of cycles and realizes that his immortal "soul," the Self, is identical with the supreme Principle. He obtains then total, absolute Knowledge. This Knowledge is the Virgin, Beatrice or Helen of Troy or Pallas-Athena.[36] During the Trojan War, Ulysses abducts the goddess, as an illustration of his spiritual achievement. He steals from Troy the *Palladium*, Pallas-Athena's wood statue that descended from Heavens as a sign of divine presence.[37]

The *Odyssey* reiterates, in some respect, the spiritual message of the *Iliad*. Ulysses' journey back home symbolizes the same spiritual realization.[38] The Virgin is not Helen anymore but Penelope. We have to understand the return of Ulysses not as going backwards but more likely as a "countercurrent" expedition, to use Coomaras-

---

[34] Hesiod, **The Homeric Hymns and Homerica**, W. Heinemann, 1936, see **Theogony** 896.

[35] Dante had a special esteem for Ulysses' *philosophy* ("love of wisdom"). Ulysses says: "Think of your breed; for brutish ignorance/ Your mettle was not made; you were made men,/ To follow after knowledge and excellence." See Dante's **Inferno** XXVI.118-120 (Penguin Books, 1977, tr. by Dorothy L. Sayers).

[36] The traditional doctrines are teaching us that a total being is not only body and soul, but also spirit. Thus, a human being, for example, is not a duality (body and mind, as Descartes invented) but a triad. The body (*Corpus*) and the soul (*Anima*) are our psycho-physical aggregate obeying the cycle of generation-destruction. The spirit (*Spiritus*) is our divine, immortal part. The "Supreme Identity" is obtained by waking up *Spiritus*, the Self. In Western traditions, this *Spiritus* is the Virgin, symbol of the celestial Knowledge and Intellect.

[37] The *Palladium* is the spiritual kernel of Troy. It is what Hebraic Kabbalah calls the "God's presence," *Shekinah*, the virgin queen.

[38] Ulysses' journey is a "sea voyage" that was often used to symbolize an initiation. "That footman (the profane) is only 'carried by the land,'/ But he (the initiate) who is 'carried by sea' is the truly learned one" (**Teachings of Rumi**, The Octagon Press, 1994, p. 239).

Ulysses

wamy's expression. In this case, Penelope is not only the wife; she is the Virgin, the goal of the initiation. She is threatened by the dragon and has to be rescued.[39] Penelope is even closer to the symbolism of Hindu *Shakti*, the virgin who is also the wife and the active energy of the supreme Principle. Penelope is not only the patron of the spiritual realization, but also she is the cosmological activity of God. It is said that Penelope was weaving a shroud for Laertes (**Odyssey** II.95). Each night she was undoing the work she did during the day. Weaving the web symbolizes the production of the World, the *Fiat Lux*, while dissolving the web during the night means the absorption of the Cosmos back into the Principle.[40] These ceaseless alternations perfectly illustrate the mesh of cycles, the production and destruction of the Cosmos, in many traditions the World being compared with a texture. The end will come only with Hindu *Pralaya*, the total dissolution of universal manifestation, which coincides with a *hieros gamos*, a sacred wedding, when the solar hero will rescue the lunar virgin and they get married.[41]

It is not the objective of the present work to follow the hero's entire journey. Each of Ulysses' adventures is a spiritual station and has a manifold symbolism. We are going to touch on just one well-known episode: the Sirens' trial. To properly understand its esoteric significance, we have to explain what we call the "metaphysics of the chain."[42] In the *Iliad*, Homer describes a "Golden Chain" as Zeus' mighty presence.

> Come, you gods, make this endeavor, that you all may learn this. Let down out of the sky a cord of gold; lay hold of it all you who are gods and all who are goddesses, yet not even so

---

[39] The dragon is present through the young suitors who invaded Ulysses' home (the Center); the suitors symbolize the "unworthy" husband, the mortal one, which at the end of time becomes devilish.
[40] For the cosmological symbolism of weaving see Guénon, **Croix**, p. 84.
[41] A legend suggests that Achilles, even though he was "killed" before the conquest of Troy, became immortal and married Helen of Troy.
[42] We already talked about the "metaphysics of *êkapada*" and the "metaphysics of theft." It is a way to stress the "superhuman" significance of the sacred kernel.

can you drag down Zeus from the sky to the ground, not Zeus the high lord of counsel, though you try until you grow weary. Yet whenever I might strongly be minded to pull you, I could drag you up, earth and all and sea and all with you, then fetch the golden rope about the horn of Olympos and make it fast, so that all once more should dangle in mid air. (**Iliad** VIII.18-26)

Aurea catena Homeri, the "Golden Chain," represents precisely the "one foot" of the spiritual Sun, the *Axis Mundi*, the celestial Ray, the "vertebral column" of the universal manifestation.[43] The "Golden Chain" produces and perpetuates all the beings, as the spider spins its web from itself. The "Golden Chain" brings the things into existence by binding them; it gives reality to the entire Cosmos; without its ties the Universe would be just an illusion.[44]

The ignorant man thinks that Penelope's web has reality by itself. He cannot see the "Golden Chain" anymore because of the bondage of the innumerable chains. Mundane chains, ropes of passions, appetites, emotions and desires, tie him. The spiritual realization means escaping from those chains of ignorance and tying in with the "Golden Chain." The Sun Dance of the Oglala Sioux describes exactly this liberation. Thongs tied into their bodies link the dancers to the central tree (the *Axis Mundi*, the "Golden Chain"). The thongs symbolize the rays of spiritual light and when the dancers tear themselves away from the cords, "it is as if the spirit were liber-

---

[43] It is safe to assume that Hephaestus, the "one-footed" god, worked for Zeus the "Golden Chain." Hephaestus is the "god of bondage"; he tied and untied with a golden chain his mother, Hera. He also used his art to forge a web that bound Ares and Aphrodite (**Odyssey** VIII.295). The bonds of Hephaestus are the bonds of Varuna. Hephaestus' web is an emblem of the "net of Heaven" (the "Golden Chain"). "The net of Heaven is cast wide. Though the mesh is not fine, yet nothing ever slips through" (**Lao zi** LXXIII.179a).

[44] The famous question from Hindu tradition: "do you know that *Sûtra* ("thread") by which this life, the next life and all beings are held together?" is referring to the same "Golden Chain" (**Brhadâranyaka Up.** III.7.1).

ated from our dark bodies."[45] It is important to understand the ambivalence of the symbol. On the one side, the thongs are the earthly ties of the body-soul aggregate. The spiritual effort will deliver us from this bondage of ignorance. On the other side, the cords are the immortal *Spiritus* of the dancers and are just aspects of the "Golden Chain." The former symbolism illustrates the arrogance of considering the strings of the worldly mesh by themselves, apart from their real Cause. The latter illustrates our spiritual humility to consider everything belonging to the supreme Principle and tied to the *Axis Mundi*.[46]

"When all the knots of the heart are destroyed, even while a man is alive, then a mortal becomes immortal" (**Katha Up.** II.3.15): these knots are the Sirens. Their name comes from Greek *seira* meaning "rope, thong, chain," but also "a cord with a noose." The Sirens represent the bondage of passions, desires and mundane attachments, the temptations that delude the neophyte. The story is well known. Ulysses is advised to "melt down sweet wax of honey and with it stop your companions' ears, so none can listen (to the Sirens' deceiving songs)"; "if you yourself are wanting to hear them, then have them tie you hand and foot on the fast ship, standing upright against the mast with the ropes' ends lashed around it" (**Odyssey** XII.47-51). The mast, of course, is the "Golden Chain," the *Axis Mundi*. Ulysses is delivered from the Sirens' bondage by wisely accepting (or conquering) the spiritual bondage, which ties him to the supreme Principle. His crew represents all his individual functions and senses, the body-soul aggregate that now is transformed ("passed beyond form") and integrated into the Self.[47] The

---

[45] Cf. Black Elk's saying (Joseph Epes Brown, **The Sacred Pipe**, Univ. of Oklahoma Press, 1989, p. 92).
[46] "A release from the bonds of Varuna, it is also a return to Varuna, to the Brahman" (Coom., **Trad. Art**, p. 447).
[47] The "sweet wax of honey" stops the human, relative function of hearing and permits one to hear the divine songs (honey is an emblem of celestial wisdom). That is why only Ulysses can hear them. The **Vêdas**, the Hindu tradition, is called *Shruti*, "that what was heard," the divine revelation being poured into human ears. In the Celtic tradition, the god Ogmios is presented as towing a multitude of men tied by their ears to a golden chain, the end of which passes through the god's pierced

total being *Corpus-Anima-Spiritus* is now realized. Ulysses, One without a second, identical with the *Axis Mundi*, is allowed to hear the Sirens' celestial music.[48] Note the ambivalence of the Sirens' symbolism. On the one side, the Sirens' are the worldly attraction; on the other side, they are God's attraction.[49]

We need to clarify one last point: the second meaning of the Siren's name, "a cord with a noose." The noose is very closely related to the two-fold symbolism of attraction. We saw, ties and bondage illustrate the attraction, worldly or divine. To attract something though, it has to be caught first, and the noose of the cord is doing the catching. In English, *string* has the meaning of a fine cord, but it is often used to describe "a series of objects threaded or hung on a string" (like "a string of pearls"). The latter meaning is exactly what Hindu tradition calls *sûtrâtma*, "the thread-self" on which the worlds or the beings are threaded, the string passing through the central aperture of the heart ("the eye of the needle"). We are more interested now in the second description, "hung on a string," which can be related to the noose. There is an informal expression "to string up" meaning "to kill by hanging"; also, coming from the same root as *string*, exists a related word *to strangle*. The etymology of those words directs us to Greco-Roman culture. In Greek, *straggo*

---

tongue. The "Golden Chain" is the way Tradition is revealed as *Logos*, Word, *ab ore ad aurem* ("from mouth to ears"); that is how any tradition was transmitted unbroken from the beginning of the World).

[48] Plato (**Republic** V.617) speaks about the celestial harmony of the eight Sirens' music. The same symbolism appears in Shakespeare's **A Midsummer Night's Dream**; Oberon says: "once I sat upon a promontory,/ And heard a mermaid on a dolphin's back/ Uttering such dulcet and harmonious breath/ That the rude sea grew civil at her song/ And certain stars shot madly from their spheres/ To hear the sea-maid's music" (II.I.149 ff.).

[49] There is, though, a fundamental difference, which is the secret of any spiritual initiation. Dionysius the Areopagite (**The Divine Names** III.1) gives us the best illustration. He speaks about God's "chain of lights." The neophyte will try to pull the chain to bring God to his heart. But God is like a rock, immutable. If we are on a boat and a rope is tied to the rock, when we pull the rope to bring the rock to us, actually the boat will be pulled to the rock. In the same way God will pull the neophyte to Heavens. Spiritual realization is not passivity; it is a very active personal effort. If we just wait for God to manifest his attraction, we will wait in vain. The only attraction will be the worldly one.

Ulysses

means "to squeeze" and *straggale* is a "cord," or a "string"; Latin *stringo* means also "to squeeze." That is why the string was mainly the cord of the gallows. Thus, we are safe to assume that "hanging" in a noose is not only the brutal deadly punishment of criminals, but also has a sacred meaning connected to the Sirens' symbolism.[50]

The final station, where the "Supreme Identity" is realized, echoed by the Sirens' episode (and other similar episodes), takes place at home, in Ulysses' own palace, that is in his own heart as spiritual Center. There are three main events describing the hero's spiritual realization: the bow contest; the revealing of Ulysses; and the killing of the suitors. The three events should take place simultaneously, in the timeless center, but for the human mind they have to be one after another. Anyway, to understand their real meaning we have to think in "countercurrent" terms and reverse their order. Meister Eckhart explained in a sermon the spiritual meaning of "the cleansing of the Temple," when Christ drove out the sellers (**John** 2:15). Our heart has to be clean and empty of any other passions and desires; only then God will come to live in his temple (Eckhart, **Sermons**, I, pp. 46-7). The same thing happens in the *Odyssey*. The suitors represent our lowest passions and appetites. They are also the residues of the dying cycle. Killing them, Ulysses purifies his own heart and also ends the old world. Then he abandons the "dark snake skin," the beggar clothing, and reveals himself as the spiritual Sun. Eventually, Ulysses produces the new world developing the solar Ray, the arrow which he sends through the twelve axes.

The bow contest takes place during Apollo's feast. Ulysses' arrow is identical with Apollo's solar arrow and is related to the Chinese story of the ten suns. It is important to note that the arrow passes through the "orifices" of twelve axes. The symbol of the axe is well known: the axe is the warlike emblem of the *Axis Mundi*. Its curious orifice is the "eye of the needle," the solar gate, *Ianua Coeli*,

---

[50] In Romanian, *strunga*, "the strait gate of a sheepfold," is related not only to the Greek and Latin words, but also to the spiritual meaning of the Gospels (**Matthew** 19:24, John 10:1-9), where Jesus is "the strait gate of the sheepfold," i.e., "the eye of the needle" and the Sundoor giving access to Heavens. Note that English "strait" comes from Latin *strictus*, the participle of *stringo*.

the center of the Center. Sending the arrow through this gate illustrates the perfect spiritual Liberation.[51] On the other hand, the arrow becomes the "Golden Chain" and Ulysses weaves the new Cosmos with this invisible string, a string called in Hindu tradition *sûtrâtma*, "the thread-self," and in the Western tradition "the chain of union." On this chain Ulysses strings the twelve signs of the Zodiac, symbol of the cosmic frame of the new World.[52]

The orifice of the axe is also connected to the name of the Sirens, "the cord with a noose." The noose has the same symbolism, it is the solar gate, but we find here again a two-fold meaning. In the myths of the Norsemen, Odin, the lord of wisdom, hung nine days and nine nights from the sacred tree Yggdrasil, the *Axis Mundi*.[53] During this hanging Odin absorbs the knowledge and he is called "lord of the gallows." The rope with the noose is here, of course, the "Golden Chain." A legend suggests that Helen of Troy died on Rhodos Island, hanging nude ("sacred love") from a tree. She was worshipped there as *Helen Dendritis* (Pausanias, **Geography** III.19.10). The twelfth card of the Tarot represents "The Hanged Man." The hanged man is upside down, hanged by one foot, and his body symbolizes the alchemical icon of the accomplishment of *Magnus Opera*, "the Great Work"; it is the symbol of the spiritual realization. His foot is aligned with the cord, stressing the symbolism of the *êkapada*.

On the other hand, the act of hanging is an act of justice. It is not only the Liberation by passing through the noose (the solar gate), from the mortal world to the immortal Heavens; it is also the punishment, the Death, and the return to the ceaseless rotation of the cycles. It is a reflection of the "divine hanging." Ulysses' battle against the suitors contains two such punishments. First, Melanthios who brings twelve shields and twelve spears to the suitors is hanged

---

[51] "OM is the bow, Âtmâ, the Self, is the arrow. Brahma is the target" (**Mundaka Up.** II.2.4).

[52] The Zodiac is also the archetype of the traditional city (Guénon, **Symboles**, p. 389). The string with twelve knots was used in the past to illustrate the golden triangle of Pythagoras. $12 = 3 + 4 + 5$ and $3^2 + 4^2 = 5^2$.

[53] H. A. Guerber, **Myths of the Norsemen**, Dover Publications, 1992, p. 33.

Ulysses

"with a braided rope," and hoisted "upward along the high column" (**Odyssey** XXII.175-6). Then, twelve serving women, who betrayed Penelope, are also hanged with a "cable of a dark-prowed ship" (**Odyssey** XXII.465). The zodiacal number twelve is present in both cases, indicating the old cycle.

The last punishment brings out the importance of "female" symbolism in Homer's epics. Following Ulysses' journey we find that women mark many of his spiritual stations: Nausikaa, Circe, Kalypso, the Sirens, Skylla and Charybdis, Eurykleia (Ulysses' old nurse), and the two "capstones," Helen and Penelope. Even if Achilles and Ulysses, together with the whole Trojan War, illustrate preponderantly a "male" initiation, transmitting a "male" symbolism, the "female" aspect is equally strong. The spiritual kernel has no preferences in this respect and any sacred story uses both masculine and feminine symbols to teach its holy lesson. The Trojan War, a men's war, has a woman, Helen of Troy, as its spiritual essence. Ulysses' sea voyage has a chaste woman as reward. Ulysses' initiation doesn't end with the killing of the suitors and the replacement of chaos with order; his spiritual realization is accomplished only when Penelope, the holy wife, says so.

The last initiatory trial is the revelation of a "secret" that only Penelope knows. This "secret" is the so-called "initiatory secret," which is, in fact, ineffable, and the sacred stories present diverse substitutes for it. The Homeric "secret" is about Ulysses and Penelope's conjugal bed, a bed built by Ulysses from an olive tree representing the *Axis Mundi*, and ornate with gold and silver and ivory, like the Heavenly Jerusalem (**Odyssey** XXIII.190-200). The olive tree, "thick like a column," is the axis of the universe and the chamber that Ulysses built around this tree is the Cosmos. The "one-footed" bed, having the tree as a post, is the Center of the World. The bed is the spiritual center where the initiate finds the supreme reward, the Virgin as absolute spirituality. Revealing the "secret" about the bed, Ulysses proves to his divine wife that he has reached the supreme Knowledge, that he is the "worthy" husband, the immortal one. Thus, Ulysses gets his reward, Penelope. The "Supreme Identity" as *hieros gamos* is now completed.

Chapter Two

SAMSON

ULYSSES' "initiatory secret" is a beautifully concise image of the sacred kernel, providing essential wisdom better than any of the explanatory doctrines and commentaries of the world. The biblical Samson possesses a similar "enigma" and, again, a woman is the "co-owner" of this secret. The *Bible* offers many examples of feminine symbolism not always praised at its real value: Eve is famous; also well known are Rachel and Leah, Jacob's wives, or Delilah, whose name is even now an equivalent of dishonesty. Like Homer's female characters, the biblical women bear a secret meaning. Rachel and Leah, for instance, became in medieval times the symbols of contemplative and active life. Delilah, who tries to uncover Samson's "secret," remained over the centuries known as a mischievous woman, but we intend to establish that her endeavor is an initiatory one, related to Ulysses' final trial and complementary to Samson's sacred symbolism, showing indissoluble ties between the "male" and "female" symbolism.

Samson and Delilah are proverbial in Western culture. Their story, dramatic and emotional, impresses profane people and, therefore, the lyrical stage has found it attractive. John Milton wrote (even though he was almost blind) a drama, *Samson Agonistes*, and Handel used it for his oratorio. The tale of Samson was the subject for at least a dozen operas, including the Saint-Saëns' masterpiece and a libretto written by Voltaire. The story, reduced to its main

Samson

idea, became part of modern mentality: a deceiving, treacherous woman is a "Delilah"; a very strong man is "Samsonian." Yet the tale hides a spiritual meaning.

From the start, the story is saying: beware of the hidden meaning! Dante would have said: "Aguzza qui, lettor, ben gli occhi al vero"[1]! Indeed, at the very beginning, the angel of God announces the miraculous birth of a child.

Every time an old cycle is dying, a *savior* descends from Heavens to rescue the seeds of the new Cosmos and replace the old world with a new one. The sacred writings mark this event describing the miraculous nativity of a child. A trace of this spiritual wonder was perpetuated in our "childish" explanation of birth. The stork brings the newborn to the parents, lowering the baby through the chimney. The stork is an emblem of the supreme Principle. When this bird flies, it looks like a flying snake. The "Feathered Serpent" unifies the bird and the serpent, Heaven and Earth, illustrating the Principle, One without a second.[2] The chimney is a representation of the *Axis Mundi*; it is the spiritual way of the fire to ascend to Heavens. The "elected" neophyte will learn the "fire route" to accomplish the Liberation. The Divine Presence uses the same route to come down in our world as *avatâra*.[3]

---

[1] "Reader, if you seek truth, sharpen your eyes,/ for here the veil of allegory thins/ and may be pierced by any man who tries," Dante's **Purgatorio** VIII.19-21 (Mentor Classic, 1961, tr. John Ciardi).

[2] Quetzalcoatl, the lord of wisdom, a most important god of ancient Mesoamerica, is the "Feathered Serpent." The flying dragon of the Chinese tradition, *Hamsa*, the swan of Hindu tradition, and the ancient Dacians' standard – a flying dragon with a wolf head, are closely related to the same symbolism. The peacock is also the birdsnake, an image of the supreme Principle; when the peacock flies, its tail is furled, which means that the World is absorbed into the Principle. The tail is the World, the "mortal" part of the Principle. A Romanian legend specifies that only the stork was capable of passing through the "Clashing Mountains" (the Sun-door, the passage to immortality), yet the rocks cut its tail. See B. Petriceicu-Hasdeu, **Etymologicum Magnum Romaniae**, Editura Minerva, 1976, p. 214. Coomaraswamy also mentions this legend in his *Symplegades* (**Trad. Art**, p. 533). The stork losing its tail illustrates Samson losing his seven locks.

[3] In full accordance with Hindu tradition, Meister Eckhart compares our "soul" with a spark. The spark's terrestrial father (the "unworthy" husband) is the fire, the wood is the mother, and the other sparks are its brothers and sisters. Yet the spark

The Everlasting Sacred Kernel

The tale about the stork bringing the newborn gets its reality from two sacred concepts: the "spiritual paternity" and the *avatâra*. The real father of any being is the Principle, the spiritual Sun. In Greek mythology, Zeus is the "Feathered Serpent." He takes the form of a swan to visit Leda, Helen and Pollux being – as a result – their immortal children. Zeus is the divine father and husband. Tyndareus is Leda's mortal husband, the "unworthy" one. Zeus is also Hercules' father. He takes the appearance of Alcmene's husband, Amphitryon, to trick the virtuous woman. Alcmene's chastity is a substitute for virginity; actually, she is the Virgin. Zeus made the divine night of love last three times longer, which is a sign announcing a miraculous birth. Amphitryon is the "unworthy" husband and that is also the function of the suitors in Ulysses' home. The myth clearly reveals that Zeus and Amphitryon are "twins," having the same appearance. Like Pollux and Castor, they represent the immortal and the mortal "soul," *Spiritus* and the body-soul aggregate, the Self and the *ego*. The traditional doctrines consider that any being has a mortal and a divine father; without the divine one, the being is not going "to be."[4]

In the same way, any child is potentially an *avatâra*, coming down into the world along the *Axis Mundi* (the chimney). Any newborn is also a potential candidate for the spiritual journey; in fact, just a few of them are qualified: the "elected" ones. An *avatâra* is a divine child who is more than a miraculous newborn. This child is an already liberated being whose essence is one with the divine father's essence. And only an overwhelming spiritual compassion makes the divine child accept the sacrifice and come down into the world. The *avatâra* doesn't need a spiritual realization, having already escaped

---

ascends to the sky, to its real father – Heaven (the "spiritual parent" of fire), forgetting its family. Moreover, for love of its heavenly father the spark forgets itself, because going up through the cold air it will become extinguished. See Maître Eckhart, **Les Traités**, Éd. du Seuil, 1971, p. 113.

[4] Ananda K. Coomaraswamy, **The Bugbear of Literacy**, Perennial Books, 1979, p. 92 ff. In Celtic tradition, Cú Chulaind, for example, has at the same time a divine (Lug) and a mortal father (See **Early Irish Myths and Sagas**, Penguin Books, 1981, p. 133).

the mundane bondage, and hanging by the noose of the "Golden Chain." The *avatâra* will embark though, on a spiritual path just for the sake of mankind, wanting to establish a pattern to be followed, to be a guide, to give a personal example.

There are usually two ways to announce the birth of an *avatâra*. The first one presents a very old couple, with a barren wife. They can be king and queen or just a poor old man and his aged wife. The second one tells about a widow or a virgin giving birth to an "illegitimate" child of spiritual paternity. In the virgin's case, often her father tries to kill the newborn; a prophecy told him that the child will take his place. Both scenarios are revealing the change of the cosmic cycles. The old king is the dying world; he is now the dragon, the same dragon he beheaded as solar hero at the beginning of the cycle.[5] His son or grandson is the new "solar hero" and the *savior* who will rejuvenate the Cosmos.[6] The infertility is also a characteristic of the dragon; *ab intra*, in non-manifestation, the dragon is sterile, blind, without feet.[7]

The birth of Jesus Christ is very familiar to the Western world. We have here all the elements that announce the birth of an *avatâra*. The mother is the Virgin, the Hindu *Shakti*. She has two husbands, the "unworthy" one, Joseph, and the divine one, the Holy Spirit.[8] Herod, who will try to kill the infant Jesus, is an aspect of the dragon and of the old cycle. "The massacre of the Innocents"

---

[5] The dragon Vritra tells Indra, the solar hero: "You are now what I was before." **Panchavimsha Brâhmana** (XXV.15.4) specifies, "The Serpents are the Suns" (Coom., **La doctrine**, p. 38).
[6] The meaning of the "solar hero" has to be stressed. The "solar" character illustrates his spiritual qualification, not a physical phenomenon. Never does a corporeal element symbolize another corporeal element. It would be superfluous. Always the corporeal order symbolizes a higher order, as the spiritual one. That is the law of symbols.
[7] In the unity of the metaphysical order, the barren woman and the virgin are not different from the dragon.
[8] In Buddhism, the Virgin is queen Mâyâ. Buddha's divine father descends upon Mâyâ taking the appearance of a white elephant.

The Everlasting Sacred Kernel

(**Matthew** 2:13 ff.) belongs to the same spiritual pattern as the birth of Perseus[9] and of Moses.[10]

Abraham and Sarah are old and they don't have a child. God says to Abraham: "your wife Sarah shall bear you a son whom you are to name Isaac" (**Genesis** 17:19). Sarah laughs since she is old and infertile; yet Isaac is born miraculously. In the same manner, Angel Gabriel is sent by God to announce to Virgin Mary that she will conceive and bear a son and she must name him Jesus; and Mary is amazed since she is a virgin (**Luke** 1:32-35). A similar thing happens to Hannah. "The Lord had made her barren" (**1 Samuel** 1:6) and Hannah prayed before God, and her husband thought she was drunk.[11] God listened to her prayer and gave her a child, Samuel. Manoah's wife is also barren, without children.

> The angel of the Lord appeared to this woman and said to her, '… you will conceive and bear a son. No razor is to touch his head, for the boy shall be God's nazirite from his mother's womb. It is he who will begin to rescue Israel from the power of the Philistines.' … The woman gave birth to a son and called him Samson. (**Judges** 13)

We are told, almost without veil, that Samson is an *avatâra*, an image of "Lord of the World," unifying the sacerdotal and temporal powers. He is predestined to become, like Christ, through his sacrifice, a *savior* and an initiatory and cosmic "exemplar." His name seems to derive from Hebrew *Shimshôn*, "sunny." Samson is an aspect of the spiritual Sun; the seven locks of his hair are the seven

---

[9] Acrisius, Perseus' grandfather, will try to suppress the newborn; an oracle told him: "Your grandson must kill you." Perseus' divine father, Zeus, came down upon Danae, in a shower of gold. The golden rain is a typical symbol for the spiritual influences. See Robert Graves, **The Greek Myths: 1**, Penguin Books, 1973, p. 238.

[10] The Pharaoh has given the order that all the boys born to the Hebrews be killed. Moses was saved, like Perseus, by an ark. It is safe to assume that here the real Virgin mother is the Pharaoh's daughter herself. The Pharaoh, like Acrisius, is the dragon-grandfather (**Exodus** 2).

[11] It is, as we already explained, a spiritual drunkenness.

Samson

solar rays, the seven *shaktis* – Samson's "powers" that generate and sustain Existence. At the same time, his long hair is a divine mark and "initiatory secret." Samson is an "elected" person, which Hebraic tradition calls *nazirite*, i.e., "vowed to God"; no razor shall touch a *nazirite*'s head (**Numbers** 6). In her prayer before God, Hannah made a vow, saying: "O Lord of hosts! If you will take notice of the distress of your servant ... and give her a man-child, I will give him to the Lord for the whole of his life and no razor shall ever touch his head" (**1 Samuel** 1:11).[12]

The long hair is bondage, a divine and a cosmic one, always mingled together. Homer describes the Greeks in his epics as "long haired." Achilles' father vowed the hair of his son to a river god; Achilles cut his long hair only to mourn Patrocles, his *alter ego* (**Iliad** XVIII.27).[13] Theseus at the age of sixteen sacrificed a part of his hair to Apollo, in Delphi.[14] The *nazirites*' or the Greek heroes' hair ties them in with God. Cutting the hair could symbolize, as in the case of Theseus or in the case of the Sun Dance, cutting the corporeal ties in order to actually realize the divine bondage. It could stress, as in the case of Achilles, the abandonment of the world. It is an initiatory sacrifice.

Greek mythology speaks of Medusa's hair being composed of appalling serpents. Medusa's symbolism is vast; it is enough to say now that she is the Dragon as an emblem of the Pole, of the immutable yet active Principle in the Center of the Wheel. Medusa's locks

---

[12] When Moses blessed the tribes he said: "May the hair grow thick on the head of Joseph, of the nazirite one" (**Deuteronomy** 33:16). The symbolism of Joseph deserves a study by itself.

[13] "Let him have time to tear his curled hair," says Lucrece stressing the fact that a deep distress or penitence is illustrated by cutting the hair. See Shakespeare's poem, **The Rape of Lucrece**, The Complete Works of William Shakespeare, Gramercy Books, 1990, p. 1179.

[14] Plutarch, **The Lives of the Noble Grecians and Romans**, Encyclopaedia Britannica, 1952, p. 2. "(Theseus) clipped only the fore part of his head, as Homer says the Abantes did (**Iliad** II.542). And this sort of tonsure was from him named Theseus." Iamblichus says that Pythagoras was "everywhere celebrated as the long-haired Samian" (**Life of Pythagoras**, Inner Traditions International, 1986, tr. Thomas Taylor, p. 5).

are the "one thousand feet" of the spiritual Sun. In Hindu tradition, Shiva's hair is Gangâ, the celestial river, having as terrestrial projection Ganges, the stream issued from a Himalayan cave. In one respect, Gangâ is Shiva's *shakti*, that is, his "energy" or "power." We said before that beheading the dragon and liberating the sun and his rays or the seven rivers, illustrates *Fiat Lux*. The hair is here a symbol of the fertile solar rays or celestial rivers producing a new cycle, the new Cosmos. In the *Râmâyana*, we find a beautiful illustration. The sage Kapila burnt to ashes sixty thousand princes, symbolizing *Ragnarok*, the fire that ended the World. No water could be found to fulfill the rites for the dead princes. The lack of water means the "abduction" of the rivers, the absorption of the manifestation back into the Principle. Eventually, Shiva released Gangâ from his hair, and seven rivers began to flow down, producing the new Cosmos.

The locks, like Samson's seven locks, are also the Sun and Agni's seven rays (**Rig Veda** I.50.8, II.5.2) representing the six directions of the spatial development of the World, plus the central, invisible "seventh Ray" (the "one foot"). The hair is the light producing the cosmos from chaos, and also the cosmic mesh with its mundane spokes. "Just as the spider emits the thread (of the web) out of itself and again withdraws it into itself, just as the plants emerge from the earth, *just as the hair grows from a man alive*, likewise the universe emerges from the Imperishable" (**Mundaka Up.** I.1.7). Hence, producing the universal manifestation means to release the "powers," to unleash the rivers, to unplait and let down the seven luminous locks, and, in the extreme, to cut the hair.[15]

We stated from the beginning that we have to forget any schematic and limited interpretations and have to understand the variety of the symbolic viewpoints. Cutting the hair, and becoming bald,

---

[15] The English word "plait" derives from Latin *plecto*, "to fold, to braid (plait)." The words "complication" and "explication" have the same Latin root and Nicholas of Cusa uses them to define God (as complication) and the World (as explication). The same symbolism is borne in the peacock's tail. "Unplaiting the hair" is a celestial point of view, indicating the Principle as "owner" of the locks. "Cutting the hair" is a terrestrial point of view, suggesting an independent existence of the World (which is the illusion created by Hindu Mâyâ).

contains a manifold symbolism, yet again the triad, Cosmos – Year – Man, permits us to organize the significance for our rational thinking.

On the one hand, cutting the locks expresses the *Fiat Lux*, when "God divided light from darkness" (**Gen.** 1:4). The primordial "cutting" represents the separation into manifestation ("one thousand feet") and non-manifestation ("without feet"), into Earth and Heaven, into "powers" and "impotence," into fertile and infertile. It is the primordial Sacrifice illustrated by the beheaded dragon. It is not fantastic to assume that hair cutting is, in some respect, a substitute for beheading. Perseus, the solar hero, instead of cutting the serpents-hair, beheads the dragon Medusa. The dragon's head becomes the turning sun of the new Cosmos, with "one thousand" rays (Coom., **La doctrine**, pp. 26, 32). The rest of the body remains "emptied of creatures" ("beardless") and without "powers."

On the other hand, the cosmogony implies the birth of Year (Time) and the evolvement of the cosmic cycle as a gradual corruption to its end. In Siouan mythology, the sacred buffalo, which loses one hair every year, illustrates the decay of the world (Brown 9); we can expect that at the end of time the buffalo will be hairless. Cutting the hair means implicitly the death of the World. Any mundane birth contains the seed of death. Cutting the seven locks implies a progressive separation from the source that feeds the hair, and in time those "powers" will decay. Thus, baldness is the characteristic of the king changed into dragon at the end of time, when the hair, apparently lost into the World, is actually withdrawn back into the Imperishable.[16] To be bald, from a cosmic point of view, illustrates the wasteland and the darkness at the end of time, the lack of hair being identical with the lack of water, vegetation, and light (Coom., **La doctrine**, p. 143).

In fairy tales, the bald and beardless character is an aspect of the Dragon. It is interesting that in one of these fairy tales the hairless

---

[16] The kings of different civilizations used to wear impressive beards, even fake sometimes. The beard is a divine sign of "power" in contrast with beardless, which represents the "impotent" dragon.

evil character is the one who beheads the solar hero.[17] Beheading the hero means a spiritual sacrifice, the supreme step of the initiation, similar to the hair cutting. It is the "ritual death" belonging to the initiatory process, followed by a resurrection, "the second birth." Indeed, the Virgin (the emperor's daughter) will place back the head of *Harap Alb* and the hero will be resurrected; that is how Ganesha got his elephant head full of wisdom. At the same time, with the hero's revival, the hairless character is punished (killed). The bald and beardless man is not only an aspect of the cosmic dragon, he is also the dragon dwelling within us, the *ego*, whose "missing" hair represents the ties of passions and appetites and desires. Sacrificing the hair is equivalent then with killing our *ego*, making our bald and beardless individuality lose for good its mundane hair, and replacing it with the invisible golden curls of the Self.[18]

A "frame of knots" sustains the Cosmos, described as a texture. Untying the knots means the death of the World. The "vital knots" keep Man, in the same way, as an organized aggregate. The Hindu

---

[17] See **The Story of the White Arab** where the hero is called *Harap Alb*, the "White Moor" or the "White Arab" (**Folk Tales from Roumania**, Routledge and Kegan Paul, 1952).

[18] The hair represents one end of the Man; the other end, the opposite one, is the heel. The hair and the heel, indicating the two poles of Man, correspond in macrocosmic order to Heaven and Earth. The hair is Samson's "strength." The heel is Achilles' "weakness." Yet from a spiritual point of view, the hair represents the mundane ties that have to be cut, and the heel is the Sun-door, the "eye" to immortality. Achilles suffers the "ritual death" being killed by Apollo's solar arrow in the only vulnerable place, the heel. Actually he is hanged in an inverted position, like the "Hanged Man" of the Tarot, with the "Golden Chain" piercing his heel. We have to think in the context of the "counter-current." In the traditional doctrines, the Man's head corresponds to Heaven and the soles to Earth. On the other hand, Man's divine position is the reverse one, with the feet planted in Heaven. In this second case, the heel becomes the real capstone. Thetis, in order to make her child, Achilles, invulnerable, dips him into the water of Styx, holding him by the heel. We see that again Achilles is in an inverted position, the heel actually being his tie with the "spiritual paternity." Homer calls Achilles "Achilles of the swift feet." A legend says that his mark was not the heel, but the anklebone that was replaced with one taken from the giant Damysos, a very fast runner. In the Hindu tradition, the head usually is the one replaced, like in the case of Ganesha. The anklebone replacement refers to a similar symbolism.

tradition compares human death with the process of cutting those knots. The hair could be such a "vital knot." Thus, hair-cutting is both "self-sacrifice" and "cosmic-sacrifice." Beheading the dragon (or cutting the locks) ends a cycle and starts a new one. Beheading the *ego* (or cutting the hair) ends the body-soul bondage and starts the spiritual bondage (the "divine Knot").[19]

Samson, as an archetypal solar hero, an *avatâra*, has to play all the scenarios. He has to be the divine king who reigns over a cycle of existence and changes gradually into a dragon. He has to be the dragon at the end of time. He also has to be the hero embarked on the initiatory path.

Coming back to Timna, Samson fights a young lion and God helps him kill the beast without using any weapons. The fight is a ritual wrestling match, a spiritual effort.[20] After a while, visiting Timna again, Samson looked "at the carcass of the lion, and there was a swarm of bees in the lion's body, and honey. He took up some honey in his hand and ate it," (**Judges** 14:9). This event sanctions Samson as "Lord of the World."

Wrestling the lion, Samson acquires its attributes. The lion is a well-known emblem of the Sun; the zodiacal *Leo* is the house of the sun. At the highest level, the lion symbolizes the supreme Principle.

---

[19] Besides the hair, there are other parts of the human body symbolizing the "vital knots," as the anklebone or the heel or the key bone. For a building, the knots are the nails that keep the edifice together. In Latin, *clavus* means "nail," a word closely related to *clavis*, "key." From Latin *clavis*, *clavus*, the French language got its *cheville*, meaning nail, plug, but also ankle. The English language used those words to name the clavicle, the "key bone". In Greek mythology, the giant Talos, the guardian of Crete, has the same vulnerable place as Achilles, the heel. A plug stopped his heel up. This plug is actually the "key," the "nail." In French, *chevillage* means to stop up with a plug.

[20] In the Greek mythology, Hercules *strangles* the Nemean lion. Theseus at the age of seven was ready to attack the Nemean lion-skin (Pausanias I.27.8). Jacob wrestled with the angel (**Gen.** 32:26); it is interesting that the angel "seeing that he could not master him, struck him in the socket of his hip, and Jacob's hip was dislocated as he wrestled with him." Jacob appears lame, "one-footed." The "socket" of Jacob's hip is, of course, a "vital knot" that was untied by the angel in exchange for a "divine knot."

The Everlasting Sacred Kernel

It is also the spiritual father.[21] On a lower level, the lion is an emblem of the justice and of the warrior-king. Killing the lion, Samson obtains the temporal power. The golden honey is an eminent symbol of divine wisdom. It is the solar nourishment, the spiritual immortal food. Honey represents the transformation of multiplicity, of mundane existences into celestial Unity, the leap from ignorance to knowledge. The way the bees change and unify the different nectars of the multicolored flowers into one kind of honey illustrates the spiritual transformation. The honey is found inside the lion as the sacred kernel is found inside the profane skin. The spiritual wisdom is in the cavity of the heart; the temporal power is the concealment, which safeguards the wisdom. Eating this honey, Samson obtains the sacerdotal power.

Samson becomes the *Sphinx*, half sage-half lion.[22] At the same time, Samson accomplishes the "Supreme Identity," celebrating a holy wedding with a Philistine girl. After Samson's miraculous birth, the *Bible* tells us right away about this first escapade. Samson went to Timna and saw a Philistine girl and he wanted badly to marry her. The Philistines are the oppressors, the enemy, like Trojans are for the Greeks. The Philistine girl should then be compared with Helen or Andromeda to understand Samson's attraction for a girl of his foes. Samson's wedding is an impossible one from an earthly point of view and a *hieros gamos* from a celestial perspective. It is the story of Romeo and Juliet; it is the marriage between the Sun and the Moon. On the other hand, if Samson is viewed as a dragon, hiding

---

[21] In the Middle Ages, there was the belief that the lioness brought forth the young which appeared to be still-born. The lion cubs would give no sign of life, but on the third day, the lion would return and animate them with his breath. See Louis Charbonneau-Lassay, **The Bestiary of Christ**, Arkana, Penguin Books, 1992, p. 10. The lion represents the "spiritual paternity," i.e., the solar fatherhood. Its breath is, conform Hindu tradition, the *sûtrâtma*.

[22] In the case of the *Sphinx*, the head is the spiritual authority and the body the temporal power. Dante (**Purg.** XXIX.108) compares Jesus Christ with another kind of *Sphinx*, the *Griffon*, thinking about Christ's two natures, the divine and the human one. A *Griffon* has the fore parts of an eagle and the hind parts of a lion. The eagle is a solar emblem and symbolizes the spiritual wisdom.

the generative "powers" or the "initiatory secret," the Philistine girl appears as a "captive virgin," and Samson is the abductor.

While the world is getting older and falls from essence to substance, from quality to quantity, from spirituality to materiality, Samson changes slowly into a dragon whose "powers" are the procreative rivers or lights. Nonetheless, he looks forward to achieving Liberation and returning to the Principle's bosom. Samson starts to govern the new cycle, the new world; simultaneously, the erosion of the "positive" by the "negative" starts to develop. The "erosion" is the normal illustration of the evolvement of a world. In Norse myths, *Axis Mundi* is the huge ash tree Yggrasil (Guerber 12). An eagle is perched on its topmost bough, representing the solar "positive" principle, and a terrible dragon, emblem of the "negative" and tenebrous principle, continually gnaws at the roots: this is the "erosion."[23] The unifying wedding that reflects the One-and-only as principle of multiplicity and source of the cycles marks the beginning of the World. The unity has to split into duality, into Heaven and Earth, to permit the cycle to evolve, and at the end of time Heaven will be so far away from the Earth that a cosmic divorce is expected, as the *I Ching* states it. Therefore, in the end, Samson repudiates his wife (**Judges** 14:20).

The whole process is presented twice; this unveils another sure sign of esotericism. In the *Iliad*, the fighting to rescue the abducted virgin is present more than once. In the *Odyssey*, each of Ulysses' stations is similar. In fairy tales, you have the feeling that the same story is told and retold. That is the way a sacred writing describes the initiation or the process of the cosmic cycles, each step being

---

[23] In Chinese tradition, during a cosmic cycle, from the Golden Age to the Iron Age, the male principle, the "positive," will be eroded by the female principle, the "negative." The traditional commentary of Kâu hexagram says: "A negativity being born, it will increase gradually, and the positive has to decline. That who marries a young girl wants his union to last a long time; or, here, the negativity increases and develops gradually, and will wipe out the positive. It is impossible such a union to last long" (**Le Yi: King**, I, p. 200, and **I Ching**, p. 154). In the Hebraic tradition, Eve starts the same process of erosion.

analogous with the previous one. In Samson's case, there is a "minor cycle" and a "major one," both very similar.[24]

In the "minor cycle," Samson challenges thirty young Philistines (**Judges** 14:11-16) to solve a riddle, the answer being the honey inside the lion – the *Sphinx*. The answer represents the "initiatory secret" of the spiritual realization and cosmic government; it is the Arcanum of Samson's existence and function. It is not a singular episode. During his initiation, Oedipus, too, solved a riddle of the *Sphinx*, in the Center of the World, Thebes; the riddle was about the cosmic cycles.[25] In one of Grimm's fairy tales, *The Riddle*, the solution to the riddle is a carcass of a horse and a raven.[26] The Princess has challenged her suitors to propound an unsolvable riddle and the King's son is the "elected" one; his riddle is exactly Samson's riddle.

We have to deal with a combined symbolism. In the initiatory process, the neophyte has to solve the dragon's riddle or to find the location of the dragon's "powers." The riddle is an important initiatory trial, a way to unveil the sacred kernel; untying the enigma means to untie the knot of ignorance. That is the case of Oedipus and of Prince Charming in some fairy tales. Ulysses' last trial represents something similar, even if both, Ulysses and Penelope, know the solution. On the other hand, the hero himself sometimes pro-

---

[24] The two cycles could be compared to the *Lesser* and *Greater* Greek *Mysteries*.

[25] Oedipus is an "elected" one, with a "biography" similar to Moses, Perseus, Sargon, and many other "heroes." For a long time his parents were sterile. At last, the Delphic Oracle announces the birth, with the gods' help, of a boy, but this child will kill his father and take his place. Oedipus (as newborn) is condemned to death by his father, but he escapes, of course, and eventually kills his parent (the king-dragon of the old cycle), solves the *Sphinx*'s riddle (proving that he reached the "initiatory secret"), and as reward marries the queen, his own mother. Obviously, the queen is the Virgin, the absolute Knowledge, and the wedding illustrates the "Supreme Identity." The moral issue (the so-called "incest") never applies to sacred stories where the "one thousand feet" are just masks of the "one foot." "The spouse of the Emperor is not the spouse only, but sister and daughter best beloved!" Dante explains (**The Banquet**, Anma Libri, 1989, III.12.14). Just for the record we note that Oedipus' name means the "swollen-footed."

[26] Grimm's **Complete Fairy Tales**, Barnes & Nobles Books, 1993, p. 625. The raven, like the honey, is an emblem of celestial wisdom and sacerdotal power; thus, it is Odin and Apollo's bird (Guerber 17 and Ovid, **Metamorphoses**, Indiana Univ. Press, 1955, II.539 ff.).

pounds the riddle. Whoever solves it, the process itself liberates the hero. It is the case of Samson and the King's son. In the cosmic process, solving the riddle illustrates the "erosion" of the "positive" by the "negative" and the development of the cycle from one end to the other when the hero takes the dragon's place. Some fairy tales describe only the end of the cycle. The dragon is the holder of the powers and only he knows how to solve the riddle. The "captive virgin" helps the hero to defeat the dragon and start a new cycle. All are related to a sacred wedding (the "Supreme Identity").[27]

Samson is the hero and the dragon. The riddle is a "knot" which has to be untied. Untying it has two consequences: first, Samson, the owner of the riddle, acquires liberation and spiritual perfection; secondly, the world is dissolved and a new cycle begins. Samson, as dragon, loses his powers. In both cases, the process is a sacrifice and has the duration of a cycle.[28]

The "minor cycle" lasts seven days, analogue with the seven biblical days of *Genesis* and corresponding to the seven rays of the Sun. It is described as a continuous feast. The banquet represents the world that declines to its end. Samson's wife "wept on his neck for the seven days their feast lasted." On the seventh day, she convinces her husband to disclose the answer to the riddle. She will betray Samson by telling the solution to the thirty young Philistines. That will finish the feast and the old world. The riddle is untied. The cosmic mesh is untied. On the other hand, Samson as a spiritual

---

[27] Oedipus's initiation ends with the spiritual wedding, which is his "reward" for solving the riddle. This wedding is the stake in Grimm's tale. In the same way, Jason marries Medea, the virgin who helped him to obtain the Golden Fleece, and Theseus marries Ariadne, who helped him to kill the dragon. In fairy tales, this scenario is also present: the "captive virgin" helps the hero to solve the riddle and kill the dragon, or to seize the dragon's "powers" (sometimes the virgin is the king's abducted daughter and also the dragon's wife, sometimes she is the dragon's daughter).

[28] Samson is at the same time hero and dragon because "to sacrifice and to be sacrificed are essentially the same"; the victim is the sacrificer himself. Prajâpati (the "lord of creatures") gives himself up (poured or emptied out), accepting to be sacrificed (Coom., **Metaphysics**, p. 108-9). Samson also gives himself up: he voluntarily tells the answer of his riddle, and so does the King's son in Grimm's tale.

peregrine accomplishes an initiation grade and a first liberation. When the riddle is untied, Samson too cuts his mundane bondage. The Philistines "bound him with two new ropes and brought him up from the Rock" (**Judges** 15:13), and Samson, with God's help, gets loose.[29]

The "major cycle" repeats the scenario, unveiling a higher level of the spiritual journey. The story also tells us that a new cycle, a new world, is ready to be produced. The similarity, either for the macrocosm or for the microcosm, stresses the symbolism of the analogy between the spires of the universal manifestation and between the grades of the initiation. Samson, after the liberation, is very thirsty. God opens a spring for him and Samson "drank; his vigour returned and he revived" (**Judges** 15:19). The thirst illustrates the ignorance and the "lack of waters" at the end of time (the exhaustion of the "powers" spread into the World). It symbolizes also Samson's "ritual death," and the dragon's complete impotence. The divine spring is the *fons vitae* that resurrects the hero and pushes him on to a superior spiritual station. It announces also the birth of a new cycle after the dragon has regained his "powers."[30]

Delilah is Samson's new wife for the "major cycle," yet she is just another mask of the same essential female character. Delilah, a Philistine too, a "forbidden" love, has, like the previous wife, an important two-fold role. As the "negative" and the infernal pole, she makes the world or the cycle decay. That is Eve's function when she takes the apple, being the serpent's associate. Samson's wife is in this case the Dragon's exponent, trying to suppress the "positive," the supernal pole, and the celestial "male" presence, which actually happens at the end of the world. From the initiatory point of view, she is the Virgin, the spiritual bride who guides the hero to realize the Liberation. She is the Initiatress. In both cases she is the activity

---

[29] Note the importance of the binding symbolism. We should recall that "religion" comes from Latin *religo*, "to bind," meaning the bondage of the religious community and also the ties with God.

[30] The Sacrifice means death and rebirth, dispersion as multiplicity and reunification as One, beheading and restoration of the head (Coom., **Metaphysics**, p. 120-1; **La doctrine**, pp. 114-7).

of the Principle. The two meanings, spiritual and cosmological, are presented in the "major cycle" in more details. The riddle is more direct, concerning the location of Samson's "powers." The process develops in four degrees, in accordance with other traditions where the cosmic cycle is considered composed of four secondary cycles. The four Ages are the pearls of the string (Hindu *sûtrâtma*), each one similar, yet not identical, with the others. The end of each secondary cycle makes the world fall deeper toward its dissolution, and passing from one cycle to another means cutting the old knots and knotting others. On the other hand, the four degrees are the steps of a celestial ladder, each one symbolizing a partial "liberation."

Delilah asks Samson: "Please tell me where your great strength comes from, and what would be needed to bind you and tame you" (**Judges** 16:6 ff.). The binding symbolism is again very active. Samson answers, "If I were bound with seven new bowstrings," and Delilah binds him; yet Samson snaps the bowstrings and gets loose. That is the first stage. Samson cuts the corporeal bondage. Also, the world is now older and less spiritual. Delilah asks a second time and Samson gives her almost the same answer. He is again bound with new ropes, yet Samson gets loose. The soul bondage is now cut; Samson is liberated from the *ego* cage. The third time Samson answers: "If you wove the seven locks of my hair into the warp of a web and fixed the peg firmly, I should lose my strength." The cosmic meaning is obvious. The hair weaves the universal texture of the Cosmos, Penelope's texture. The seven rivers or solar rays are producing the World. Yet Samson gets loose again, dissolving the web, ending the third cycle and also liberating himself from the angelic order. The last statement could be strange but the spiritual doctrines will help us. The "elected" one has to surpass the Cosmos, the "Three Worlds" (*Tribhuvana* of the Hindu tradition), i.e., the three levels *Corpus*, *Anima*, *Spiritus*, to realize the supreme and absolute Liberation and to obtain the perfect Knowledge. Meister Eckhart speaks even of cutting the ties of God and escaping from

God in order to reach the Godhead. It is not enough to tame the *ego*; the angelic bondage is angelic, yet is still bondage.[31]

"The Fourth" (*Turīya*) is in the Hindu tradition the supreme order of Reality, the house of the Principle. The fourth time, Delilah will get the right answer. Samson's "powers" are located in his seven locks. The hair is the supreme bondage. Cutting those locks symbolizes, as we already mentioned it, the supreme Liberation of Samson[32]; it also indicates the liberation of the solar rays and celestial waters, causing the complete manifestation of the Cosmos as an independent texture, which inexorable will activate its final dissolution. Delilah's cosmogonical deed (cutting Samson's locks) is similar with Judith's heroic deed (beheading Holofernes), stressing the equivalence between cutting the hair and beheading.[33] Nonetheless, if this capital act is viewed not by itself but as the conclusion of a series of ritual acts, as it happens in Samson's story, then the whole

---

[31] Ramana Maharshi says that the Self has no bondage in any of the four states, and the delusion of bondage produced by ignorance from *illo tempore* can be removed only by knowledge, and for this purpose the term "liberation" (*mukti*) has been usually accepted. The firm conviction that there is neither bondage nor liberation is the supreme purpose of all efforts. See **The Spiritual Teaching of Ramana Maharshi**, Shambala, 1972, pp. 41-2. The supreme stage is the Daoist Void or Nothingness, which, paradoxically, is identical with the complete Plenitude. This Nothingness is Meister Eckhart's Godhead (the abyss without end, the simple origin, the silent desert, in contrast with God as Creator), and corresponds to the Hindu Dragon without eyes and feet, emptied and impotent. The initiate, emptying his heart of all creatures (mundane bonds), and of God (divine bondage as Being and Creator), obtains the Nothingness and Emptiness, which is also the "plenitude and abundance of Godhead," beyond day (manifestation) and night (non-manifestation) (Eckhart, **Sermons**, I, p. 240, II, pp. 146-8, **Traités**, pp. 111-2).

[32] The sacrificer's "death" is at the same time his salvation, and the Self is the reward. In the Hindu tradition, the sacrifice means cutting off the "vital knots" (hair, skin, blood, flesh, bones, marrow), crowned with the cutting of the "topknot" hair, which speeds up the liberation (Coom., **Metaphysics**, p. 126). In Christian tradition, St. Paul explains the difference between the unveiled head (the glory of Christ, the Self) and the veiled head (the glory of man, the *ego*) as the difference between the short hair (or cut off hair) and long hair (**1 Corinthians** 11).

[33] Holofernes is the dragon. He confiscated the waters, and the children of Israel were exposed to die of thirst. Judith beheads Holofernes and releases the waters, which means the birth of a new world. See **The Missing Books of the Bible**, Halo Press, 1996, vol. I, pp. 157 ff. and Coom., **La doctrine**, p. 105.

process is not only the cosmogony but also the decaying and ending of the Cosmos. Even the final act, the cutting of the seven locks, is a sign illustrating the evolvement of the cycle to its end. Samson becomes weaker and weaker with each lock cut (**Judges** 16:20). It is an obvious process of "erosion," and at the end the Philistines "put out his eyes." Samson becomes blind, his blindness illustrating the infernal ignorance of the dying Cosmos and the dragon "without eyes," but also Samson's spiritual transformation. The hero abandons the mundane sight for the divine vision, now seeing with the Eye of the Heart.

Eventually, a last bondage is presented. The Philistines "fettered him with a double chain of bronze, and he spent his time turning the mill in prison." Samson, blind and hairless, turning a mockery of the Wheel of the World, is a precise image of the Dragon at the end of time. Then, "he was put to stand between the pillars.... And Samson put his arms round the two middle pillars supporting the building, and threw all his weight against them ... and the building fell on the chiefs and on all the people there" (**Judges** 16:26-29). The *Ragnarok* is depicted as a total destruction. The building is the symbol of the whole Cosmos and the two pillars correspond to the "Pillars of Hercules" representing the essential duality of the World.[34] The dragon-Samson absorbs the duality and the universal manifestation, ending the Existence.

The four stages are not identical, even though all are connected with binding. The first two, dealing with the individual and formal world, with the corporeal and subtle (*psyche*) orders, are described as cords and ropes of bondage. The last two, referring to the informal world and to the supreme one, are symbolized by Samson's hair. The same distinction is present in Grimm's fairy tale, *The Riddle*. The Princess must solve the riddle; otherwise, she has to marry the King's son. Two nights she orders, first her maid, secondly her lady-

---

[34] The pillars are the two "capstones," the two extreme and fundamental stations of the sun, the solstices, related to the two Saints John and the two pillars of Solomon's Temple. The columns are also connected to the motto *non plus ultra*. It means that the whole Universe is contained between them. See Guénon, **Symboles**, p. 257.

The Everlasting Sacred Kernel

in-waiting, to steal into the Prince's bedroom and listen; maybe he will talk aloud in his dreams and betray the secret of the riddle. They fail. The third night the Princess herself comes into the bedroom, and the King's son, wide-awake, gives her the correct answer. The first two trials regard the body-soul aggregate. The third one, involving the Virgin, regards the spiritual order.

Two other Grimm's fairy tales are closely connected with Samson's story. The first one is *The Devil's Three Gold Hairs* (Grimm 190). The tale starts by presenting a miraculous birth of a boy. He was born with a caul enveloping his head, as a divine mark. The king tries to kill the newborn, being afraid the boy will replace him. He places the newborn in a box and throws the box into a river. The box is the "Ark" and the "World Egg," and the newborn is the seed of the new cycle. The child of fortune escapes and marries the king's daughter, but the king, still trying to kill him, sends the boy to bring the Devil's three gold hairs. The king is not only the evil aspect of the Dragon; he is also the Initiator, the spiritual teacher who challenges the neophyte to pass the initiatory trials. During his journey to the Devil's home, the boy will be asked three questions, all symbolic and regarding the spiritual realization. The answers are known only by the Devil. Those questions compose the riddle. In this fairy tale, Delilah is the Devil's mother; she will find out the answers and will pull out the three gold hairs. The Devil is the dragon, and the three gold hairs correspond to Samson's seven locks and symbolize the double process, cosmological and spiritual, as deciphered previously. The second fairy tale is called *The Griffin*. Here the Griffin is also betrayed by his wife and will give her the answers for the riddle.[35]

In a Romanian fairy tale, *A Peasant's Tale*, the dragon takes Samson's place; also, the dragon's wife is the "captive virgin." Prince

---

[35] *The Fairy Tales* of the Brothers Grimm were published in 1812 and 1815. In 1819, E. T. A. Hoffmann writes a pseudo-fairy tale called *Klein Zaches genannt Zinnober*, in which Cinnabar, the dwarf, similar to Grimm's Devil, has three fire-like red hairs representing his bewitched "powers." Hoffmann is one of the first famous writers who discredited fairy tales and degraded their spirituality, promoting tenebrous and "Gothic" stories.

Charming comes to rescue the girl, and in order to kill the dragon, Prince Charming asks the young woman to find out where his strength comes from. Eventually, impressed by the girl's tears, the dragon gives the answer: "My power is located in a sow living in a marsh full of sweet milk. In the sow lives a hare, in the hare a quail and in the quail there are three worms. They constitute my power."[36] We can translate. The dragon is the king of the old, dying cycle. The three worms are the three gold hairs and could symbolize the "Three Worlds"; the "power" is also the sacred kernel covered by many skins, representing the spiritual seed of the new cycle, hiding in the "World Egg." Prince Charming obtains the "power," kills the dragon, and marries the virgin. He becomes the new king of the new world and the future dragon.

Regardless of their names, masks or forms, Samson and Delilah are universally present. Fairy tales offer a striking similitude with the biblical story and we have to assume that, instead of considering them as mere "children's literature," they are in reality timeless sacred writings.

---

[36] Petre Ispirescu, **Legende sau basmele românilor**, Facla, 1984, p. 200. In Peredur's story, in the Celtic traditon, a black man tells about a mound that is called the Dolorous Mound, and in the mound there is a barrow, and in the barrow there is a Worm, and in the Worm's tail there is a stone. See **The Mabinogion**, Everyman, 1994, p. 173.

Chapter Three

THE BAD WOLF

IT IS NOT easy to understand why fairy tales are considered mainly to be children's stories. The fact that the "good" always defeats the "bad" cannot be a strong enough reason. Our "moral" society just makes us think it is. Scrutinizing the fairy tales even superficially, we find a lot of absurdities, cruelties and immoral elements. A child's mind could be shocked and misled by reading or listening to a fairy tale; yet nothing of that kind happens. Everybody knows that the tale is not "real." Nonetheless, how can it be possible to let the fairy tale mark the beginning of a child's education?

Take Grimm's tale, *The Devil's Three Gold Hairs*. It starts describing how a newborn is placed in a box and then thrown into a river. That cannot be very joyful for a young child who is in the process of understanding his world. The tale explains that the king "had a wicked heart"; even so, after that, how would a child look at the adults around him? Further, the tale shows a mother who betrays her son. Even if the son were a demon, a mother wouldn't deceive him so easily. In Grimm's *Cinderella*, the two sisters mutilate their foot; one cuts her toe, the other the heel, just to fit it into the slipper; similarly, Laius mutilates the ankles of his newborn child, Oedipus. The examples could go on and on. The best-known fairy tales are full of murders and betrayals, child and animal abuse. Would then a fairy tale be the most appropriate literature for an innocent kid?

The Bad Wolf

The sacred kernel is the answer. We have seen that a cycle of manifestation, a world, evolves from a spiritual stage, a Golden Age, to a material stage, the Iron Age, while the king changes gradually into a dragon. It doesn't mean an ordinary replacement. The king is still there, but he is covered now by a "serpent-skin," like Ulysses was by the beggar's clothes. The spirituality "heard" at the beginning of the cycle is still there too, only "undercover," concentrated in a hidden kernel and buried under many layers, as the "powers," the three worms of the Romanian fairy tale, were.

There are different ways to preserve and transmit this spiritual kernel. One very efficient way is so-called "folklore," not the fabricated, but the genuine one. Sometimes "folklore" dresses up with different clothes, matching the times, yet the spiritual kernel is still there, unaltered. Fairy tales are part of this "folklore." It is useless to try finding a historical author for "folklore" or for fairy tales. The real author is an "intellectual aggregate" which has transmitted what was "heard" from the Heavens at the beginning of Existence. "Folklore," like "mythology," is a reservoir, which preserves the vestiges of vanished traditional societies, of sacred rituals and initiatory rites.

A major method to assure the unbroken transmission and survival of the spiritual lore is the "child-like" way. Children constitute a perfect ambiance to preserve unaltered the eternal wisdom. An adult would be tempted to change something, to add, to modify, to interpret, to intervene, to play god, trying to impose his originality and individuality. However, the sacred kernel being divine, the individual intervention would only damage it, and make it lose its "powers."

Young children, on the contrary, are innocent; they don't have the adult consciousness of the world. They are "unconscious," unaware of the danger of water or fire or other natural things. They are, as the Daoism requires spiritual beings to be, natural, perfectly integrated into the natural world. The young children, yet "unconscious," belong, at least virtually, to the absolute, infinite Consciousness (Hindu *Chit*): *Chit* is the supreme "unconsciousness."

The Everlasting Sacred Kernel

In Hindu tradition, the *sannyâsi*, the seer possessing the divine Knowledge, has three attributes: *bâlya*, *pânditya* and *mauna*. The last two concern his wisdom and solitude. The first one, *bâlya*, "childlike," means that the *sannyâsi* realizes a status comparable as purity, undifferentiated simplicity, and unconsciousness, to the status of a child (*bala*). The Christian tradition shares this symbolism. Jesus says: "Let the little children alone, and do not stop them coming to me; for it is to such as these that the Kingdom of Heaven belongs" (**Matthew** 19:14). The Daoist spiritual masters emphasize too the equivalence between a sage and a child.

> If you are a ravine to the empire, then the constant virtue (*De*, rectitude, natural simplicity) will not desert you and you will again return to being a babe. (**Lao zi** XXVIII)
> One who possesses virtue in abundance is comparable to a newborn babe: poisonous insects will not sting it; ferocious animals will not pounce on it; predatory birds will not swoop down on it. (*Ibid.* LV)
> As a newborn babe, the energy is concentrated, the will is one: it is the perfect harmony; the outside world is harmless, the inside virtue is fulfilled. As an adult, the energy overflows, the desires and worries rise, the outside world assaults it, the internal virtue wears.[1]
> Lao Zi replied: I tell you that we should become babies. Moving, acting, a baby has no goal, no intentions. The body is indifferent as a dry wood; the heart is impassible as extinguished ashes. For a baby, no joyousness, no sorrows. (Wieger, *Chuang tzu* XXIII)[2]

Hence, a child is the best audience and the best guardian for the spiritual kernel, being also the most adequate "elected" hero, and

---

[1] Léon Wieger, **Les Pères du Système Taoiste**, Les Belles Lettres, 1983. See *Lie tzu*, I.
[2] See also James Legge's translation, **The Texts of Taoism**, part II, Dover Publications, 1962, p. 81.

the legend about the children's terrestrial birth, the "Feathered Serpent" (the stork) bringing them into the world as virtual *avatâras*, echoes a sacred truth. It is understandable now why the solar hero of the fairy tales (or other sacred writings) is usually very young, a child. Hercules, from his cradle, chokes the serpents sent by Hera. Hermes leaves his cradle and goes off to steal Apollo's herd. Theseus is seven years old when he attacks the Nemean lion-skin, and Apollo is a child when he slaughters the dragon Python. Celtic tradition presents Cú Chulaind accomplishing his first "heroic deed" at the age of six (**Early Irish** 140); Lancelot is a boy, a "youth," when he comes to King Arthur's court, similarly with d'Artagnan, who is "almost a boy" when he starts his adventures.

The Griffin, Grimm's previous mentioned fairy tale, presents the hero, Hans, as the "youngest" boy. The hero is not only very young; he is "the youngest." There is a special reason to present the "elected" one not only as a child, but also as "the youngest."

> And Jesus, perceiving the thought of their heart, took a child, and set him by him, and said unto them: Whosoever shall receive this child in my name receives me; and whosoever shall receive me receives Him that sent me: *for he that is least among you all, the same shall be the greatest.* (**Luke** 9:47-8)

Jesus states that he is the emblem of God, but his emblem is the child. It is not only a child, but also the least among all. In the fairy tales, the youngest brother (or sister) is "elected" to be the solar hero. The laws of symbols act without error. What is the greatest in corporeal order is the smallest in spiritual order. What is the least in corporeal order is the greatest from the divine point of view. The kernel or the seed is the smallest thing, but it is the greatest spiritual entity. The biblical David kills the dragon Goliath.[3] David is very young, the youngest child of Jesse. Like Cinderella, David is away when Samuel comes into Jesse's house to find the "elected" child.

---

[3] Goliath "had a helmet of brass upon his head, and he was armed with a coat of mail" (**1 Samuel** 17:5). His scale-armour is the dragon-skin.

The Everlasting Sacred Kernel

The eldest of Jesse's sons stands in front of Samuel, who "said: Surely the Lord's anointed is before him. But the Lord said unto Samuel: Look not on his countenance, or on the height of his stature; because I have refused him: for the Lord sees not as man sees; for man looks on the outward appearance, but the Lord looks on the heart" (**1 Samuel** 16:7). The heart is the sacred kernel, the smallest; the outward appearance is the profane skin, the biggest. David, the youngest, is actually the Lord's anointed.[4]

We understand better now why fairy tales became mainly children's stories. Fairy tales are meant to be ritual tales transmitting spiritual scenarios and initiatory rites. For example, the foot-mutilation episode in *Cinderella* has nothing to do with our modern attraction for violence, blood and horror, and so much the less, with "child abuse." The elder step-sisters represent the psycho-physical aggregate, which has to be tamed and even killed, in order to be redeemed and integrated under the Self's command. The toe- and heel-cutting (Grimm 82-3), like Achilles' heel-death, constitutes an initiatory sacrifice, suggesting the beheading of the *ego*. Likewise, Oedipus' mutilation (Laius bored a hole through his ankles and tied his son's legs together with a strap) symbolizes the mundane bondage, but especially the dragon "without feet." Oedipus is an *avatâra*, and has to embark on a spiritual path, traveling from dragon state to kingship, an initiation liberating him from the bonds of his ankles, which is equivalent to saying that he gets feet, i.e., solar rays. A related scenario appears in a Romanian fairy tale (Ispirescu 240): the she-dragon abducts the "powers" (the legs' tendons) of the newborn *avatâra*, who becomes crippled, and the child has to complete an initiatory journey to get them back.[5]

The beneficiary of the fairy tale is, therefore, not any person, but the neophyte, having the purity and the simplicity of a child, and

---

[4] In Celtic tradition, Peredur is a child, the youngest of seven brothers (**Mabinogion** 152).

[5] Oedipus' transformation from dragon to king is the reverse of the mundane transformation from king to dragon. In the same way, the dragon abducting the hero's "powers" is the reverse picture of the hero abducting the dragon's "powers." The knee's tendon represents a "vital knot."

The Bad Wolf

often being indeed very young. The neophyte's model is the tale's hero, a child. During the hiding process of the spiritual lore, the fairy tales remained almost unaltered, guarded by children's innocence, by their subtle "unconsciousness." Two well-known fairy tales will illustrate plainly our point of view. This so called "children's literature," considered usually "fantastic" and "unreal," will be displayed in front of us, unveiling a higher "reality," the essential Reality.

The first one is Grimm's tale, *Little Red Riding Hood* (Grimm 140). It introduces us to another child hero, a "little maiden," a very young girl. She is the "elected" one; the "red riding hood" is her spiritual mark and also her initiatory nickname.[6] We have previously stressed the importance of the female symbolism. Helen of Troy, Delilah and many others, play a fundamental role in either the spiritual or the cosmic process. We now see in *Little Red Riding Hood* the solar hero presented as a young girl. In the spiritual order, there is no place for discrimination between male and female. Substituting the old king with the old grandmother enhances the feminine aspect of Grimm's fairy tale. We have already explained how the old king tries to kill his grandson, afraid that the young boy will take his place. The same pattern operates in the tale, even if it is presented in a softer manner.

The grandmother is the dying cycle; she is the agonizing world. The fairy tale begins by telling us that the grandmother is weak and ill, which illustrates the end of time. Also we find out that she has sent to her granddaughter the "red riding hood" as a gift. The little girl "liked it so much that she would never wear anything else, and so she got the name of Red Riding Hood." In this case, the "red

---

[6] In a traditional society, the name had a major role. It was not an arbitrary choice, depending on somebody's fantasy or taste. The name matched the nature of the owner. In the Hindu tradition, *nâma*, the name, is the spiritual principle of the individual being, while the form, *rûpa*, is its substantial principle. In the Christian tradition, anybody becoming a monk or a nun would be rebaptized with a new name. In fairy tales, many names are symbolic, indicating the initiatory process: Cinderella, Snow-White, Pinocchio, etc.

riding hood" represents the "powers" and receiving it from her grandmother the little girl is invested as the regent of the new cycle.

One day, the mother asked Red Riding Hood to take a cake and a bottle of wine to her ill grandmother, at her house in the woods; and she counseled the little girl to be careful and keep the straight path and a constant pace, not too fast, not too slow ("don't loiter by the way, or run"). It is hard to believe that a sick old person would need just wine to get better; or that a little girl would be allowed to go by herself into a forest populated with wild animals; or that a mother would not go with her daughter to see her own ill mother. Obviously, we have to read between the lines. First of all, the cake and the wine are the two elements of the Eucharist and this symbolism can be traced in many traditions. In the Christian tradition, the cake (bread) and the wine are present at the Last Supper symbolizing Jesus' sacrifice to rejuvenate the World and humanity. The cake and the wine are also the immortal nourishment, the Hindu *amrita*, and the Greek *ambrosia*.[7]

The symbolism of wine, as an immortal beverage, is well known. Omar Khayyâm and the Sufis worshipped it. It was compared with Hindu *soma* (Guénon, **Le Roi**, p. 47). It bears the same metaphysical significance as honey, milk or bread does. It illustrates the transformation of multiplicity into Unity, the spiritual process of melting the dispersed pieces into One – the Self, and the restoration of the "head of the Sacrifice." The multiplicity of flowers is melted in one sweet honey. The multiplicity of cows is melted in one white milk.[8] The multiplicity of wheat grains is melted in one white flour. The multiplicity of grapes is melted in one red wine.

The mother is, understandably, very concerned about the wine: "And don't loiter by the way, or run, or you will fall down and break the bottle, and there will be no wine for grandmother." The wine is actually not "for grandmother"; it is rather "for granddaughter." It

---

[7] Joseph's story, a very spiritual one, contains a related episode. Joseph is in prison together with Pharaoh's two high officials, the chief cup-bearer and the chief baker. The two officials symbolize the bread and the wine as components of the spiritual sacrifice (**Gen.** 40).

[8] Regardless of the color of a cow's skin, the milk will always be white.

The Bad Wolf

is the ingredient of the cosmic and spiritual sacrifice, which will "change" the World (or at least a world) and the girl's soul. The little girl's way into the woods, suggested by the mother, is her spiritual path, a very difficult journey. The neophyte has to obey the divine rules of initiation; otherwise "you will fall down." It has to be carried through at a constant pace, resisting temptations, as Ulysses did.

Grandmother's house is, we assume, located exactly in the "middle of the woods," like in many other tales. It marks the "center" of the circle, of the wheel; it marks the intersection of the *Axis Mundi* with a reference plane, which is a world. Only there, in the "center," it is possible to accomplish the spiritual transformation; only there it is possible to communicate with the angels (and exhaust the devils).

The forest is not an unusual symbol. It often appears in fairy tales and other sacred writings. In Grimm's tales, like *Hansel and Gretel* or *Snow-White*, the heroes are lost into the wild woods. In the *Râmâyana*, Râma and Sîtâ are banished to Dandaka, the same wild woods. That is how Dante's masterpiece, *The Divine Comedy*, also starts: Dante is lost into the wild forest, the *selva selvaggia* (**Inf.** I.5). Dante stresses that *la dirrita via era smaritta*, "the straight way was lost" (**Inf.** I.3). The wild forest represents the profane world or what Guénon calls *ténèbres extérieures*, "the outside darkness" (Guénon, **Symboles**, p. 217); the expression comes from the *Gospel*, Jesus prophesying that the sinners and the unfaithful will be thrown "out into the dark" (**Matthew** 8:12, 22:13, 25:30). The "outside darkness" can be compared to one aspect of the labyrinth. The maze carved upon the Cumaean gates, mentioned by Virgil in the *Aeneid* (VI.38), signifies in this case outside ignorance, mundane wandering, the ephemeral life of desires and temptations, and chaos. It is identical with Dante's *selva selvaggia*, with Little Red Riding Hood's wild woods. The profane one has lost its way and is wandering into the woods or into the labyrinth, never reaching the Center. The "elected" one is guided to the Center, fulfilling a spiritual journey.

The little girl has, as guidance, her mother's advice. And yet, she wanders, tempted by the beautiful flowers. "So she left the path and

The Everlasting Sacred Kernel

wandered off among the trees to pick the flowers. Each time she picked one, she always saw another prettier one farther on. So she went deeper and deeper into the forest". We rediscover the double symbolism, spiritual and cosmic.

From the initiatory point of view, the neophyte has problems staying on the right path. The mundane temptations are very strong and deceiving. Nowadays, we are used to blaming "human nature" for this. People are never content; when they get something, they want more or something else. That is called the "engine of progress." In a traditional society, that was "the engine of ignorance." Each flower, prettier than the one before, is an ephemeral and insubstantial temptation. It is a Siren trying to make the girl lose her way and go deeper into the woods. That is a road without end, a maze; it is a maze built of our desires, appetites, greediness and conceit.[9]

From the cosmic point of view, the varicolored flowers represent the innumerable dispersed elements of the universal manifestation, of the Cosmos. The uncolored light is a symbol of the only Principle. The myriad of colors, reflection of the unique light, is an illustration of the multiplicity.[10] Picking the flowers means absorbing the worlds back into non-manifestation. The end of time is very close. The grandmother is dying and the flowers are picked up, leaving behind a deserted field, a wasteland. And we almost have the impulse to ask: But where is the dragon?

The dragon is there all right, how could it not be? "When she got to the wood she met a wolf, but Red Riding Hood did not know what a wicked animal he was; so she was not a bit afraid of him." The dragon is there from the beginning of the journey. The little

---

[9] The countless colors and flowers correspond to the countless hairs of the Undines and water sirens. Undines' long golden hair tempts the ignorant and the profane to their death, as in the Norse myth of Lorelei (Guerber 359), the hair symbolizing here, like the flowers, the endless-like mundane bondage. See **Encyclopédie des Symboles,** Le Livre de Poche, 2000, p. 479.

[10] In Saint-Exupéry's *The Little Prince,* the flowers play the same role. The multitude of roses represents the profane world, the circumference and the skin. The unique Rose symbolizes the One-and-only, the sacred kernel and the center.

The Bad Wolf

girl, an innocent child, is "unconscious," unaware of the danger. Only the "elected" ones, with pure and childish hearts would be capable of initiating such a journey; the others wouldn't dare, being too conscious of the peril of impossible trials.

The wolf plays the devil and tempts the little girl to leave the path and pick the pretty flowers. The girl doesn't "fall down" irrevocably, even if for a while she falls into oblivion and wanders into the forest. Eventually, Little Red Riding Hood finds the way to the Center: "she remembered her grandmother again." The remembrance is a platonic one; the neophyte escapes from Lethe's bondage and wakes up like in the Greek *Mysteries*. We may compare the heroine's transformation with Dante's entrance into the Earthly Paradise. Dante finds two streams: "On this side, it removes as it flows down/ all memory of sin; on that, it strengthens/ the memory of every good deed done./ It is called Lethe here: Eunoë there" (**Purg**. XXVIII.127-130). But Dante dressed the "recollection" doctrine with theological clothes. Little Red Riding Hood, wandering into the wild woods and following the wolf's suggestion to enjoy the flowers, forgets her grandmother and her mother's counsel. She is now lost into the "outside darkness," the profane maze and the infernal chaos, due to her amnesia. The recollection of her grandmother symbolizes the recollection of the divine order and the awakening, the commencement of illumination.

In the Hindu tradition, the "deep and dreamless sleep" is an emblem of the spiritual world. When people wake up, they don't remember anything from their profound sleep; and gradually the memories of the "waking state" come back to them. From the spiritual point of view it means to fall into oblivion. The "deep sleep" state is, on the contrary, the state of divine recollection. In this state, it is no particular consciousness, the person doesn't know anything about the world, desires, and sorrows. "As a baby, or an emperor, or a noble Brâhmana lives, having attained the acme of bliss, so does it remain" (**Brhadâranyaka Up.** II.1.19).[11] Dante specifies his

---

[11] Note the reverse analogy of the celestial and terrestrial orders. The least on earth is the greatest in heaven. What is non-remembrance for the profane order (the

wandering into the wild forest: "How I got into it I cannot say,/ Because I was so heavy and full of sleep/ When first I stumbled from the narrow way" (**Inf.** I.10-12). Dante's sleep is usually interpreted as the sleep of his consciousness or of his reason and judgment. The deepest meaning is that Dante had fallen into oblivion; his sleep is, using the reverse analogy, the "waking state," the "tenebrous" state of ignorance, opposite to the blissful "dreamless sleep state" of the Hindu tradition. His sleep is the "Self's sleep" when the Eye of the Heart is closed.

There is another parallel between Grimm's fairy tale and Dante's poem. Just entered into the wild woods, Dante meets three ferocious beasts, a leopard, a lion and a she-wolf, representing the three fundamental vices (lust, pride and avarice) (**Inf.** I.31-54). The she-wolf is the worst and Dante presents it as endless greediness (**Purg.** XX.12).[12] Everybody knows that the wolf is the "bad wolf," the enemy. That is true only considering a very relative point of view, the terrestrial one. Usually, any symbol has two sides, a benefic and a malefic one, illustrating the two faces of the Principle into manifestation. For example, the death of Achilles, from a human point of view is a malefic event, yet from a divine point of view it represents his spiritual liberation, Achilles becoming immortal. Saturn was in the Greco-Roman mythology the king of the Golden Age; yet, afterwards, he became Death devouring his children. His divine marks became infernal marks.[13] The same thing happened with the wolf's symbolism.

Roman tradition considers that Saturn had shared the reign of the Golden Age with Janus. Janus, as Macrobius tells us (**Saturnalia** I.13), was considered two-headed, the janitor of the celestial and infernal gates.[14] Janus is the perfect emblem of the two-sided Prin-

---

dreamless sleep) is absolute recollection for the spiritual one, and the reverse. When Little Red Riding Hood remembers her grandmother she forgets the flowers.

[12] Red Riding Hood, forgetting her grandmother, starts to pick the flowers, wanting more and more of them. She ends her endless greediness only when she remembers the spiritual order.

[13] Saturn is described as lame ("one-footed") and armed with the scythe.

[14] The English word *janitor* is related to Janus' name.

ciple (as producing the universal manifestation). The noose of the "Golden Chain" is an illustration of this double gate. The "hanged man" could be the sage or the ignorant. For the first one, the noose is the "celestial" gate, the Gate of Liberation, and the *Ianua Coeli*; for the second one, the noose is the "infernal" gate, the Jaws of Death, and the *Ianua Inferni*. The Dragon's jaws are another symbol of the double gate. The Dragon is, as we have seen, the supreme Principle. Heaven and Earth, the primordial couple, are the Dragon's jaws: the upper jaw, fixed, is Heaven, the lower jaw, mobile, is Earth.[15]

When the "elected" one accomplishes the spiritual journey and finds Liberation, the mouth represents *Ianua Coeli*, the "supernal" gate, opened towards Heaven. The liberated being passes through the solar gate (the Sun-door) into non-manifestation, the domain of immortality and absolute bliss. The "Supreme Identity" is achieved and the Self is unified with the Principle. The same mouth is *Ianua Inferni*, the "infernal" gate for the ignorant, for the profane being. It represents the mouth of Death, opened towards Earth. The ignorant will return into manifestation, caught by the mundane noose, by the "bonds of Varuna." Hence, the Dragon is frightful and terrible only for the profane, ignorant people. For them, the Dragon is Death; for them, the Dragon is an infernal beast and a malefic creature. For the sage peregrine, the Dragon is the salvation; it is the spiritual Sun. Being swallowed by the Dragon means Liberation, and in the sacred writings the neophyte, after being devoured by the dragon, is vomited out again, which symbolizes its resurrection into the eternal and immortal order.[16]

---

[15] Yi, the 27th hexagram of the *Yi Jing*, symbolizes the jaws. A striking illustration of two-faced Janus is the Celtic *Axis Mundi*, presented as "a tall tree on the river bank, and the one half of it was burning from its roots to its tip, and the other half with green leaves on it" (**Mabinogion** 175).

[16] The Sforzesco Castle in Milan preserves the Visconti family's coat of arms representing the dragon half-swallowing a young person. For the modern visitor this picture depicts, without a doubt, the vicious beast, the devil, devouring the poor human being. It is hard to believe that a coat of arms would illustrate evil. That is the error when deciphering the heraldic symbolism. The dragon is here, on the contrary, the sign of the divine Principle, the spiritual Sun liberating the neophyte.

The Everlasting Sacred Kernel

The "Bad Wolf" is the Dragon, having all its attributes. The wolf is, like the dragon, the mask of the Principle. It is a "bad wolf" only for the ignorant, to whom it represents Death, the ferocious beast. Simultaneously with the loss of the sacred kernel, the wolf lost its benefic attributes and remained just a malefic symbol. We have already mentioned the Hindu significance of the boar. The white boar is the emblem of the "Lord of the World," the *Manu* who rules the present cosmic cycle, called *Shwêta-varâha-Kalpa* or the "cycle of the white boar." In various traditions, we can trace the importance of the boar's symbolism. Ulysses was wounded by a boar and marked as an "elected" one. Sometimes, the bear contests the boar's supremacy, as an illustration of the revolt of temporal power against the spiritual authority (Guénon, **Symboles**, p. 177). The two English words, "boar" and "bear" are obviously etymologically related, as Guénon pointed out; they derive from an Indo-European root, *var* or *vri*. The question is how does the wolf fit into this pattern?

We should note first that "wolf" comes from the Sanskrit *vrka*, a word derived from the same root as boar and bear.[17] Hence, we can assume that the boar, the wolf and the bear are connected not only linguistically but also symbolically, composing a sacred triad, corresponding to the Christian meaning of the three Magi. If the boar is an emblem of a supreme ruler, the "Lord of the World," and the bear is, without any doubt, an emblem of temporal power and of the warriors, there is only one position left for the wolf: the spiritual authority. Sometimes, the boar takes on the spiritual authority function, yet if we want to have the whole picture we must admit the triadic representation.

The wolf changes its significance dramatically. Far from being "pure evil," the wolf is first of all an emblem of wisdom and of spiritual initiation; the wolf is the Initiator (*Guru*), the divine guide, and the sacerdotal power. We still can trace in mythology this celestial symbolism. In the myths of the Norsemen, Odin, the lord of

---

[17] Sanskrit *varâha*, "boar," is evidently related to *vrka*, "wolf," and also to *(v)riksha*, "bear." Derived from *vrka* we find Lithuanian *vilka*, Slavic *vluku*, Gothic *Vulf*, Greek *(v)lykos* and Latin *(v)lupus*.

The Bad Wolf

wisdom and initiation, has as emblem, besides the raven, the wolf. In the Greek tradition, Apollo, the god of spiritual initiation, representing the spiritual Sun, is called Apollo Lykos, that is, "Apollo the Wolf," his twin sister being "Artemis the she-Bear." They are the two branches of the supreme power, the sacerdotal and temporal authorities. The related Greek word *lyke* means "light," Apollo Lykos being also the "lord of the divine light." Thus, the wolf symbolizes first the spiritual light and wisdom, and only when the sacred kernel became hidden, did he change into a "creature of darkness."[18]

The Dacians' standard represented a dragon with a wolf's head.[19] The standard is always the essential emblem of a nation, its pride. As in the case of Visconti's coat of arms, it is impossible to consider the dragon and the wolf of Dacians' standard as infernal beasts. A she-wolf was the mother of the Roman twins, Romulus and Remus; the whole Roman Empire descended from a wolf and again, it is hard to believe a malefic significance here.

The "Bad Wolf" is, consequently, "bad" only for the lost people wandering into the wild forest. For a sacred society, the Wolf is the "spiritual father" and the face of the supreme Principle; for the neophyte, the Wolf is the Initiator, the Dragon that will devour the body-soul aggregate, liberating the Self, *Spiritus*. The wolf also plays the role of the old king, the dragon of the dying cycle, the "wicked" grandfather. In Grimm's tale, swallowing Little Red Riding Hood's grandmother and taking her place, the wolf actually identifies himself with her, unveiling his role; in a way, the grandmother is the Wolf's *Shakti*, its mundane "cover." The wolf, dressed as a woman (like Achilles), reveals the androgynous status of the Principle as Being.

The wolf, substituting the grandmother, swallows Little Red Riding Hood. From a cosmic point of view, it represents the end of the

---

[18] The wolf is not the only animal bearing a name connected with the spiritual light. The Sanskrit *go* means "cow" and "light" at the same time, stressing why the herds symbolize the solar rays.
[19] Mircea Eliade, **Zalmoxis the Vanishing God**, The Univ. of Chicago Press, 1972, p. 10.

The Everlasting Sacred Kernel

world, the abduction of Helen of Troy and of the fertile light. The dragon swallows the multiplicity, the myriad of flowers, simultaneously with the little girl. Each old cycle contains the seeds of the new cycle, the elements that are saved from the final cataclysm; inside the wolf, the little girl represents that sacred seed, which will produce and will reign over the new cycle. We previously mentioned the "evil" grandfather placing the newborn in a box. The wolf itself is this ark here. From a spiritual point of view, it means the end of the *ego*. The wolf swallows *Corpus* and *Anima*, it is a "ritual death," the neophyte's self-sacrifice.

A hunter will liberate the little girl and the grandmother, marking the birth of a new world and the spiritual resurrection of the neophyte. They will eat the cake and drink the wine, accomplishing the indispensable sacrifice, the Eucharist. In fact, they eat and drink the wolf's meat and blood. Many traditions emphasize the primordial sacrifice necessary to produce Existence. The beheading of the dragon operates *Fiat Lux*, the dragon's head becoming the new sun; also, the dragon's body is cut into pieces, a sacrifice representing the transfer from Unity to multiplicity, from uncolored light to a myriad of colored flowers, from one foot to one thousand feet, meaning the birth of the Cosmos.[20]

The primordial sacrifice, richly developed in the Hindu tradition, is also present in the second well-known fairy tale we want to talk about: *The Three Little Pigs*.[21] The tale is so familiar that it would be tedious to look at its plot; yet, some commentaries are required.

The three little pigs are similar to the three royal brothers or sisters from other fairy tales. The story tells us that a "bad wolf" swallows the two elder pigs, but could not devour the youngest. The three brothers symbolize the triad *Corpus-Anima-Spiritus*; they are in fact one, and only for initiatory purposes are presented divided. The reverse analogy operates without error. The youngest little pig sym-

---

[20] "A thousand heads has Purusha, a thousand eyes, a thousand feet." The gods will cut Purusha, the supreme Principle, to produce the manifestation. "When they (the gods) divided Purusha how many portions did they make?" (**Rig Veda** X.90.1.11).
[21] The version we present is part of **English Fairy Tales**, Wordsworth Classics, 1994, pp. 126 ff.

bolizes *Spiritus*, the eldest *Corpus*. We find the same pattern in Grimm's *Cinderella* and Shakespeare's *King Lear*. Cinderella's elder step-sisters are the body-soul composite, the mortal individuality, and so are Goneril and Regan, Cordelia's elder sisters.[22]

The wolf eats the body-soul aggregate, first the eldest little pig (*Corpus*), then the second-born brother (*Anima*), but he cannot reach the youngest (*Spiritus*). That means that the dragon swallows the hero and vomits him out, activating the spiritual awakening. The wolf devours the duality (the elder brothers) and proclaims the unity (the youngest little pig). In *The Three Little Pigs*, the wolf uses his breath to blow the pigs' houses in. In fact, the wolf exercises his "paternal" spiritual powers. As the lion animates the cubs in the third day with its breath, so the wolf uses its breath three times, eventually the youngest pig being spiritually "born."

The fairy tale, as we expected, presents also a cosmological symbolism regarding the renewal of the Cosmos and the change of the cycles. Between the "existential parameters" that define (and condition) our world, two are frequently used to symbolize the development of a cycle: space and time. The space-time frame of coordinates is amply employed by the modern sciences, but the traditional writings were the first to consider it in describing the cosmogony. At the same time, the two main types of symbolism, spatial and temporal, are in direct connection with the two main types of populations, sedentary and nomadic. The former are founders of cities, fixing the space with their stable buildings; the latter dissolve the space with their wanderings and provisory dwellings, free as the wind.[23] In a way, it is tempting to regard the elder little pigs, with their impermanent houses destroyed by the Wind, as representing the nomads, and the youngest little pig, with his solid home made of bricks, as the sedentary type. The wolf, eating the elder brothers,

---

[22] The difference between the mortal *ego* and the immortal Self is stressed by the fact that Cinderella's sisters are step-sisters. Shakespeare's Cordelia, the *Spiritus*, has a suitable name; it comes from Latin *cord*, "heart," and *cordatus*, "wise" (in the traditional doctrines, the Intellect is located in the cavity of the heart).

[23] For a discussion of the two types see René Guénon, **Le règne de la quantité et les signes des temps**, Gallimard, 1970, pp. 197 ff.

devours time, and concentrates space into its center (the youngest little pig). In fact, there is a wider symbolism, spatially and temporarily, and the Hindu tradition gives us a valuable clue.

> In a Year's time a Man, this Prajâpati, was produced ... and Prajâpati was born in a Year. He broke open this golden egg [the "World Egg"]. There was then, indeed, no resting-place: only this golden egg, bearing him, floated about for as long as the space of a Year. At the end of a Year he tried to speak. 'Bhûr!' he exclaimed; and there was the Earth. 'Bhuvar!' he exclaimed; and there was the Atmosphere. 'Svar!' he exclaimed; and there was the Sky. (**Satapatha Brâhmana** XI.1.6.2-3)

The Hindu cosmogony combines the birth of the "Three Worlds" (*Tribhuvana*) with the birth of Time (*Kâla*, the Year). The "Three Worlds," called also *Tripura*, the "Three Towns," come into existence not only as syllables, but also as the three immense steps of Vishnu who produces the tripartite manifestation by measuring space. The wolf destroying the houses and eating the two elder pigs represents then the Dragon contracting back the unfolded space and reducing the "Three Towns" to its center (the youngest pig's house). Yet the end of the Cosmos is called the "end of time" and not the "end of space" because when the cycle dies time changes into space (Guénon, **Le règne**, pp. 215-7). Time disappears, the succession changes into simultaneity, and space is compressed into its primordial and eternal center; only into the paradisiacal center "the time can change into space" (*Ibid.*, pp. 218-220). The Dragon (identical with Time) devours time and that is the significance of the youngest little pig's next three trials. The wolf, furious that he couldn't eat the youngest pig, tries three times to lure him outside, each time fixing an earlier meeting time: at six o'clock in the morning, then at five o'clock, and finally at three o'clock; it is a time reversal: time is flowing in countercurrent to its origin and to its own destruction.[24]

These three trials illustrate, besides the absorption of time, the reassembling of multiplicity into Unity, and the double movement, one centripetal, from circumference to center, the other vertical, from "down here" to "up there," both movements *à rebours*, in "countercurrent."[25] The first morning, the youngest little pig collects turnips from a whole field, similar to Little Red Riding Hood who picked the flowers. The second day, this time earlier, the little pig climbs an apple tree and gets a basket half-full of apples. We see the centripetal movement from a "field of turnips" (the circumference with the innumerable points) to half the way between the circumference and the center (a "basket *half* full of apples"), and the ascension from field (the lowest level, the Earth) to tree (the intermediary level, the Atmosphere). In the last trial, the youngest little pig finds himself, very early in the morning, on top of a hill with a butter-churn he bought. Now the centripetal movement reaches the target (*one* butter-churn) and so does the ascension from tree to hill (the highest level, the Sky). The top of the hill symbolizes the Earthly Paradise on the Mount of Purgatory; the butter-churn plays the role of the "World Egg" in which the little pig (the spiritual germ) will hide. That is again a "countercurrent" operation, a return to origin, and if we compare with the Hindu text from *Satapatha Brâhmana* we see a perfect match, only upside down. The fairy tale presents the reverse of the cosmogony, i.e., the *Pralaya* – the dissolution of the Cosmos, when time is annihilated and space is reduced to the paradisiacal center.

---

[24] "Common sense" forces the tale to specify that the third meeting takes place at three o'clock in the afternoon. In fact, this "three o'clock" is earlier than the "five o'clock" of the previous meeting, and the tale stresses that the little pig "started early in the morning and went to the fair."

[25] The reassembling of multiplicity back into unity is a well-known Masonic adage; "the soul is purified into the body," says Meister Eckhart, "in order to reassemble what is spread outside" (**Sermons**, I, p. 95). Regarding the two movements, note the coincidence between "the highest" and the "innermost," that is, between the "transcendence" and "immanence." "When I say 'the innermost,' I want to say 'the highest,'" explains Meister Eckhart (**Sermons**, I, p. 244).

The Everlasting Sacred Kernel

It is true that after the end of a cycle, a new cycle has to start. In the Hindu tradition, the production of the universal manifestation is sometimes illustrated by the "Churning of the Milky Ocean." The angels (*dêvas*) and the titans (*asuras*), using mount *Meru* as a shaft and the dragon as the pulling rope, are doing the churning. We discover the same symbolism in *The Three Little Pigs*. The youngest pig (the *avatâra*, the solar hero), arrives on top of the hill, and hides in the butter-churn: "he crept into it, and was just pulling down the cover when the churn started to roll down the hill." The butter-churn, rolling down the hill with the *Spiritus* hidden inside it, is a beautiful image of the birth and evolvement of the new cycle. It represents the biblical fall, the development of a cosmic cycle from the Golden Age to the Iron Age, the rotation of the churn being, of course, a substitute for the rotation of the cosmic Wheel. It shows also the spiritual kernel hidden in the Center of the Wheel.[26]

For a complete presentation of the cosmology, Purusha's sacrifice and the Eucharist must be present too. The self-sacrifice will be officiated by the wolf. We have said before that the stork brings down the newborn *avatâra* through the chimney. The wolf will descend as a "divine presence" in the world using the same route; the story asserts that "the wolf was coming down the chimney" into the

---

[26] The butter-churn rolling down the hill is also an illustration of the birth of Time. The end of a cycle, like its beginning, is timeless (Guénon, **Le règne**, p. 218), and the little pig inside the churn, on top of the hill, symbolizes this "non-temporality" as reflection of supreme Eternity. "This Principle, at rest within the One, is Eternity," states Plotinus (III.7.6); on top of the hill, where "the wheel ceased to turn" (Guénon, **Le règne**, p. 215), the little pig inside the churn represents Plotinus' Soul united with the One, the Seed at rest in the Center of the Wheel. When the churn starts to roll down the hill, the Seed (Soul) awakens from rest and starts a Movement that produces the Cosmos and Time: "To bring this Cosmos into being, the Soul first laid aside its eternity and clothed itself with Time.... For the Cosmos moves only in Soul ... and therefore its Movement has always been in the Time which inheres in Soul" (Plotinus III.7.11). See Plotinus, **The Six Enneads**, The Univ. of Chicago, 1952, tr. Stephen MacKenna and B. S. Page. "That which is prior to the sun is the Timeless (*akâla*), without parts. But that which begins with the sun is Time, which has parts. Verily, the form of that which has parts is the year. From the year, in truth, are these creatures produced.... In the year they disappear." (**Maitri Up.** VI.15).

The Bad Wolf

house of the youngest little pig. It is self-sacrifice, leaving the bliss of the Heavens for the mundane sorrows; it is also a cosmological sacrifice. The wolf comes down along the *Axis Mundi*, the only possible way, reaching the fireplace where a big pot full of boiling water is waiting for him. The fireplace is a typical symbol for the Center. In the Center of the World, all the contraries are reconciled; water and fire illustrate a paradigmatic couple of opposites, the boiling water representing the wedding of water and fire, as a perfect emblem of the *coincidentia oppositorum* that describes the Center. Therefore, it is not a surprise to have the primordial sacrifice depicted as a deadly baptism in the boiling water. The little pig, the solar hero, accomplishes the sacrifice, boiling the wolf to death.[27] And then, the little pig "ate him for supper." It is the Last Supper; it is the Eucharist; it is the immolation that produces and vivifies the new cycle, and consecrates the youngest pig as the new king enthroned in the Center of the World.

The fireplace and the big pot full of boiling water, we saw, symbolize the Center. But what does the house itself signify? And what about the two other houses of the elder little pigs? Could the fact that the wolf blew those two houses in have a special meaning? We think that all these legitimate questions deserve an answer.

---

[27] Minos of Crete was killed in the same way (Diodorus Siculus, **Bibliotheca historica** IV.79). Minos, whose name is identical with the Hindu *Manu*, is a projection of the "Lord of the World" for a minor cycle. (Guénon, **Le Roi**, p. 13).

Chapter Four

DANTE'S DEVILS

THERE ARE many symbols describing the cosmogony, the Year (cosmic cycles), and the Cosmos itself. Penelope, weaving and unweaving Laertes' shroud, has already illustrated the doctrine of the cosmic cycles and of the two phases (expiration-inspiration, birth-death) of Existence. In the same way, the construction and destruction of an edifice (or its walls) symbolize the evolvement of the existential helix, the generation and corruption of the worlds. The city, the palace, the house, and the temple, were all used to represent the Center, defining the World as "complication," or the World, defining the Center as "explanation."[1] In a traditional society, all those buildings were sacred and masonry was a divine métier. Nonetheless, only the temple remained in the modern world an obvious sacred place; and only the temple preserved this meaning in its very name.

The word "temple" comes from Greek *temno*, "to cut"; hence, Greek *temenos* "a piece of land cut off" and "a piece of land sacred to a god"; hence, Latin *templum*, "a sacred place." Cutting off a piece of land means actually to separate somehow this portion from the outside land. The outside land becomes in this case the "outside

---

[1] "Complication" and "explication" ("folding" and "unfolding," from Latin *plecto* "to fold") constitute Nicholas of Cusa's terminology and express the non-manifestation and the manifestation. The peacock's tail describes perfectly the two phases.

darkness," the wild woods, a profane and tenebrous place. The land inside the cut becomes the sacred kernel, the self-illuminated place, the "temple," the grandmother's house, Ulysses' palace, and the city of Troy.

In Latin, we find an Indo-European word *seco*, "to cut"; its root provided the words *sacer*, "saint, sacred," *sica*, "dagger" and the English *scythe*. The Latin *sacer* has the same spiritual meaning as the Greek *temenos*. The related Latin word *sacrificium*, "sacrifice, immolation," means "to render sacred" and from there, "to perform a sacred rite." It implies that a *sacrificium* requires a "cutting": cutting a piece of land, that one becomes sacred; cutting the bread or an animal, that means performing a sacrifice.

Cutting the head of the Dragon symbolizes the primordial sacrifice. The same sacrifice is illustrated in the *Bible* by the scission of Heaven and Earth (**Gen.** 1:6).[2] In the Sumerian mythology, the god Enlil separates Heaven (An) and Earth (Ki) by cutting Anki (the supreme, androgynous Being) in two halves. Enlil uses a bronze dagger and it is safe to assume that it is a curved dagger, a *sica* or a scythe. Saturn (Cronos) uses a scythe to emasculate his father. When the sacred kernel became hidden and lost for the profane world, the scythe remained the emblem of Death. The curvature of the scythe suggests the circularity of the cycles and the wheel as a symbol of the Cosmos.[3]

Another kind of cutting is the circular furrow dug by Romulus at the foundation of Rome (Plutarch, **The Lives**, p. 19). We know that in ancient and medieval times a surrounding ditch protected any fortress or city. The ditch is more than a defensive structure; it is the "cutting" that makes the place sacred; it is a symbolic furrow cut by a curved plough. The historians are still confused and cannot give a satisfactory explanation about the so-called "furrows" which cut the European continent from place to place.

In the case of a simple house, the walls themselves replace the ditch. For a fortress or a castle, the surrounding ditch and the walls

---

[2] The word "scission" comes from Latin *seco*, "to cut."
[3] Hermes' sword is curved. The Dacians' sword was called *sica*, the "curved dagger."

belong to the same sacred function and coexist. The house lost the ditch, but the walls symbolize the same ritual "cutting," which make the house sacred and separates it from the "outside darkness" and chaos. Many legends speak about human immolation being indispensable to make the walls last (Eliade, **Zalmoxis**, pp. 179 ff.). The word "wall" derives from Latin *vallum*, "rampart"; thus, the primitive function of the wall was to protect and defend.[4] It is primarily not a physical protection, but a spiritual one, similar with the cherubs' role to protect the Garden of Eden (**Gen.** 3:24).[5]

The most enigmatic and famous example of a protected city is Atlantis. Beyond the historical debate about the existence and location of Atlantis, Plato's description matches perfectly the symbolical picture of the Center of the World. The mountain and the island are the favorite symbols of a spiritual center. Atlantis is built on a mountain located in the center of an island. The mountain is the *Axis Mundi*, the Hindu *Meru*. Plato tells us that Poseidon, god of the Sea, to protect Atlantis, enclosed the city with two circular ramparts and three circular fosses, alternating land and water.[6] Atlantis became inaccessible; no man could get to the spiritual center (Plato, **Critias** 113). Poseidon built the enclosures, playing the role of the Grand Architect of the Universe: the sacred "cutting" is so important that the gods themselves are involved as masons, and build the divine enclosure. Greek Thebes, another holy city representing a

---

[4] The root *var* or *vri*, which has produced Sanskrit *varâha* and *vrika*, means also "to cover, to protect, enclosure, walls" (Guénon, **Symboles**, p. 179). In the Iranian tradition, Ahura Mazda asks Yima to build a *Vara*, i.e., an "enclosure" to preserve the germs of all the animals and plants, *Vara* being similar to Noah's Ark. Sanskrit and Iranian *vara* is close to Latin *vallum* (to be compared with Sanskrit *sûrya* and Latin *sol* designating the sun). The Celtic *var* means "fortified city"; from this word the Hungarian *varos* and Romanian *oras* derive, with the same meaning.

[5] The garden is also a "sacred place," a symbol for the spiritual center. The word "garden" is related to the Slavic *gorod*, *grad*, "city," Romanian *gard*, "enclosure," and English "gird." Virgil says that Ascanius "girded Alba Longa with walls" (**Aeneid** I.379).

[6] The word "fosse" comes from Latin *fossa*, "ditch, canal." *Fossa* is mainly a defense structure, reinforcing the *vallum*, the bank of earth (rampart). Romanian *sat*, "town," comes from Latin *fossa*, emphasizing the sacred function of the enclosure. Similarly, the Chinese *chéng* means, at the same time, "wall" and "city."

spiritual center, is too built miraculously: Amphion, the son of Zeus, erected the walls by using the sounds of his divine lyre to move the stones.[7] The Christian tradition generalizes the symbolism of construction, considering the production of the whole Cosmos: "Every house is built by someone, of course; but God built everything that exists" (**Hebr.** 3:4).

Poseidon also erects the walls of the city of Troy, and Apollo, the god of spiritual wisdom, helps him. The construction of the Trojan enclosure presents a symbolism that anticipates the Trojan War and emphasizes the spiritual significance of Troy. Laomedon, the king of Troy, didn't pay the gods for their work. Poseidon, in revenge, flooded the land and forced the king to offer his own daughter, Hesione, as a victim, to a sea-dragon. Hercules rescues the virgin, who is chained to a rock, but Laomedon doesn't keep his promise to reward the hero; eventually, Hercules conquers Troy, destroying the walls and capturing the virgin Hesione (Ovid, **Metamorphoses**, XI.194 ff.). It goes without saying that the Trojan walls were rebuilt, and destroyed again by the Greeks in the Trojan War.[8] The construction and destruction of the walls illustrate the evolvement of the cycles, the birth and death of the worlds.

The Hindu tradition preceded the modern "Big Bang" theory by thousands of years. In the Hindu tradition, a cosmological doctrine states that the Cosmos was produced due to *Parasabda*, the "primordial sound." Amphion, using the sounds of the lyre to build the walls of Thebes, is just an illustration of the cosmogonical operation of the "supreme sound," *Parasabda*.[9] The same sound, as an aspect

---

[7] Amphion has a twin brother, Zethus. Amphion represents the immortal Self and Zethus the mortal *ego*.

[8] Troy was rebuilt, says a legend, by two architects from Crete, Belin and Lev, imitating the labyrinth of Knossos. See Santarcangeli, chap. I.

[9] We said before that the primordial Tradition was "heard" (*Shruti*). As the external ear has a labyrinthine shape, so the spiritual center should be meandrous to capture the divine revelation. In the Chinese tradition, the ear is the sign of wisdom and Lao Zi was called "Long Ears." On the other hand, the internal ear with its semicircular canals (called the labyrinth) controls the orientation in space; that makes the ear also an emblem of the "seven rays" as spokes of the Cosmos. We may note that connected to sound is light, having the same symbolism, spiritual and cosmogonical

of the supreme Principle, has the power to end the Cosmos. The destruction of the walls of Jericho is a very good example:

> The Lord said to Joshua: Now I am delivering Jericho and its king into your hands. All you fighters will march round the town and make the circuit once, and for six days you will do the same thing. But seven priests will carry seven trumpets in front of the ark. On the seventh day you will go seven times round the town and the priests will blow their trumpets. When the ram's horn rings out, the whole people must utter a mighty war cry and the town wall will collapse then and there. (**Joshua** 6:2-5)

The end of the Cosmos takes "seven days," a symbolical period of time mirroring the duration of the biblical creation. God is involved in the destruction of the walls as He is in their building. An interesting detail is the circumambulation that Joshua, the priests, and the warriors have to perform. Hector and Achilles performed also three rotations and a half along the circular walls of Troy.

There are many symbolical aspects of the circumambulation. It could illustrate the "complication" (the absorption of the Cosmos) and the "explication" (the production of the Cosmos), when marching in circles is actually marching along a spiral path toward or from the center. It could be also a representation of the labyrinth, which, in many cases, is composed of seven circular meanders.[10] In a medieval manuscript, the labyrinth is even called the "town of Jericho"

(*Fiat Lux*). Therefore, Egyptian Thebes was built having the shape of God's eye (See Jackson Knight, **Vergil, Epic and Anthropology**, Barnes & Noble Inc., 1967, p. 220). The Easter bunny synthesizes the two symbols: it has very long ears, and, according to legend, it sleeps with its eyes open.

[10] When Ascanius girded Alba Longa with walls he also taught the Latins the game called "Troy." They had to ride their horses tracing a labyrinthine path, which was an image of the maze of Crete (**Aeneid** V.770-789). Similarly, Theseus and his companions executed in Delos a dance called "the Crane," consisting of a series of serpentine figures and representing the Cretan labyrinth. This dance accompanied Theseus' sacrifice to Apollo (Plutarch, **The Lives**, p. 7). Note that the crane is an image of the "Feathered Serpent."

Dante's Devils

(Santarcangeli, chap. X). A French manuscript recorded the visit of the Seigneur de Caumont to Crete in 1418, and his statement about the meandering house built by Daedalus, a house termed a labyrinth and now called by many the "city of Troy" (Santarcangeli, chap. V). Sometimes, the maze is carved on the walls or at the entrance, as in the case of the Cumaean gates, and in Greece, in some cases, the meanders drawn on the walls are surrounding the house. The labyrinth reinforces the symbolism of the walls and occasionally the walls of the edifice themselves are composing the maze. Nonetheless, the maze is subtler than the walls. The walls seem to be more corporeal, protecting against physical elements, while the maze is more sophisticated; therefore, it is easy to consider it as a defense against evil and impure psychical influences (Knight, **Vergil**, part two, chs.V-VI).[11]

In fact, to understand the relation between the labyrinth and the wall of a sacred city we have to go back to the symbolism of "cutting." The "cutting" or the wall, as a result of a divine activity, has two sides: one side, directed inwards, is bright and full of child-like simplicity and clarity; the other side, directed outwards, is tenebrous and intricate. The labyrinth appears as a projection of this exterior side. When the "cutting," *fossa* or *vallum*, is performed to make a place saintly, implicitly the labyrinth is born. The sacrifice with its "cutting" automatically establishes a distinction between the *templum*, or the "sacred place," and the rest of the world, which becomes the labyrinth as "outside darkness," the maze of profanity and ignorance. The neophyte has to find the way, as Little Red Riding Hood did in the wild woods, and reach the center of the labyrinth, which is the sacred city, Troy or Thebes. The "outside dark-

---

[11] In the Christian Orthodox tradition, there is a striking example of the circumambulation's protective role. When the Russians attacked Constantinople in 860, and the city was almost conquered, the Virgin's robe was carried around the walls and ramparts, and the Russians gave up the siege. See Philip Sherrard, **Byzantium**, Time-Life Books, 1966, p. 34. In a fifth-century ivory plaque, Constantinople is represented as an empress wearing a crown symbolizing the walls of the city (Sherrard 15), which invites a deeper view on the symbolism of the crown.

The Everlasting Sacred Kernel

ness" plays the protective role very well: it will never permit the ignorant to escape the maze.

On the other hand, the "cutting" makes the "holy place" (city, fortress, garden, etc.) inaccessible and inviolable, as Atlantis and the Garden of Eden became. The labyrinth is in this case the very characteristic of the "cutting" itself, and the game "Troy," associated with the construction of the walls, comes to emphasize this symbolism; as a sacred ritual, it has the power to "activate" the protective, labyrinthine role of the wall. But again, the defensive role has to be understood in its highest significance. Like the "outside darkness," the labyrinthine wall forbids the access of the profane, ignorant people, while the "elected" ones will find their way toward the Center.

The labyrinthine wall has not only a guarding function, prohibiting the hostile and non-qualified elements from getting inside, but also a conserving one, preventing the inside elements from dissolution and dispersion. Herodotus and other ancient authors mentioned in their works a magnificent Egyptian labyrinth composed of 12 roofed yards, and Diodorus Siculus and Pliny were convinced that the Egyptian maze was the model that inspired Daedalus to build the Cretan labyrinth. Some modern scholars suggested that the Egyptian maze was a representation of the Zodiac (Santarcangeli, chap. IV), and they were right. The labyrinthine wall enframes and orders the elements of the city as the Zodiac enframes and orders the Cosmos. The Zodiac is the celestial archetype of the terrestrial town (Guénon, **Symboles**, p. 121), and it encloses the Universe as the "cutting" encloses the "sacred place." The "chain of union," which surrounds the Masonic Lodge, usually has twelve knots, being a reflection of the Zodiac (Guénon, **Symboles**, p. 388). The "chain of union" encloses and keeps together the elements of the Lodge, symbolizing the Zodiac framing the Cosmos; untying the knots means the dissolution of the walls and the destruction of the city, i.e., the end of the world.

In the Christian tradition, the *Book of Revelation* presents the end of the world and the birth of a new one in the same manner. "I saw a new heaven and a new earth; the first heaven and the first earth

Dante's Devils

had disappeared now, and there was no longer any sea. I saw the holy city, and the New Jerusalem, coming down from God out of heaven, as beautiful as a bride" (**Revel.** 21:1-3). The Heavenly Jerusalem is described as having twelve gates, obviously a symbol of the Zodiac.[12] If the production of a new Cosmos is symbolized by the foundation of a "sacred place," of a spiritual center, of a holy city, the destruction of the old world has as its emblem the ruin of the cities and especially of the Great City, Babylon that became a symbol of evil, illustrating the decadence of the Cosmos: "The Great City was split into three parts and the cities of the world collapsed" (**Revel.** 16:19); "Babylon the Great has fallen, and has become the haunt of devils and a lodging for every foul spirit and dirty, loathsome bird" (**Revel.** 18:2).[13]

The last quotation seems to be confusing; how can a "sacred place" become an "evil place" full of devils? In point of fact, to symbolize the decaying of the cosmic cycle, the "holy city" of the Golden Age is described as an "evil city" of the Iron Age. Saturn, the regent of the Golden Age becomes Satan, *princeps hujus mundi*.

However, from a macrocosmic point of view, the "chain of union," the labyrinthine frame, or the Zodiac, keeps together and orders all the elements of the Cosmos, from the most luminous to the most tenebrous. The countless elements or knots are reflections of the Center of the World, of the supreme City, *Brahmapura*, and so they can be represented in their turn as enclosures or cities. More than that, the Hindu tradition replaces the innumerable knots (or cities) by three fundamental ones, describing the Cosmos as *Tribhuvana*, "The Three Worlds" (the Earth, the Atmosphere and the Sky). Those "Three Worlds" are called also "The Three Towns," *Tri-*

---

[12] In the Hindu tradition, the Paradise of Vaikuntha, the celestial abode of Vishnu, has also a zodiacal design. See Burckhardt, **Mirror**, pp. 102 ff.

[13] Note that Babylon means "the Gate of God" and, at the beginning of the old cycle, was the exact replica of the New Jerusalem. In the *Bible*, the decay of the world is also suggested by the change of Babylon into Babel, the Tower, the name Babel being identical with Babylon.

pura,[14] and we can visualize instead of one city as Center, three cities concentrating the three main tendencies (*gunas*) of *Prakriti*: *tamas* (ignorance, error, and darkness), *rajas* (greed, unrest and desire), and *sattva* (wisdom, bliss, and light) (**Bhagavad-Gîtâ** XIV.5-18). *Tribhuvana* is present in Dante's *Divine Comedy* as *Inferno*, *Purgatorio*, and *Paradiso*, and Hell (*Inferno*) contains the "city of Devil (Dis)," mirroring the "city of God" situated in Paradise.[15]

From a microcosmic point of view, the labyrinth or the "chain of union" keeps together the elements of Man (being). The dissolution of the walls is identical with untying the vital knots and it means the death of the being. If we consider the total being as composed of *Corpus*, *Anima* and *Spiritus*, the labyrinth symbolizes the *sûtrâtma*, which strings all Man's states of existence, or in the case of an individual being, all its modalities (Guénon, **Symboles**, p. 392). The Center (the supreme City, *Brahmapura*, the Temple) is the heart of Man where the "Kingdom of Heaven" has to be found. The spiritual realization is an inner journey, a labyrinthine one, from city to city until all those cities are purified and absorbed into the supreme City. When Jesus Christ said, "I have power to destroy the Temple of God and in three days build it up" (**Matthew** 26:61), describing His resurrection, Christ was also describing the spiritual realization.[16]

There is a perfect analogy between Macrocosm and Microcosm: *Tribhuvana* or *Tripura*, "The Three Towns," correspond to *Corpus*, *Anima* and *Spiritus*. Now we understand why the Bad Wolf blew the

---

[14] Heinrich Zimmer, **Myths and Symbols in Indian Art and Civilization**, Harper & Row, 1962, p. 185.

[15] *Ab intra* "The Three Towns" are one and only one City. In the Hindu tradition, Shakti is called "The Fairest Maid of the Three Towns" (Zimmer 190). Shakti is one, but she appears different in each city. That is why in the Greek mythology the maid of *Tripura* is described as "the triple Hecate" (Selene reigns in the Sky, Artemis on Earth and Persephone in Hell). Helen of Troy is also a representation of this Shakti.

[16] Dante, during his infernal journey inside the city of Dis, at one time, loosed himself by taking off the rope girdle that he was wearing. The gesture is similar to the dissolution of the wall, the untying of the inferior knots, marking a partial liberation and a spiritual achievement (**Inf.** XVI.106-114).

two houses in. The three little pigs' houses are the cities of *Corpus*, *Anima* and *Spiritus*; they are the spatial equivalents of Christ's three days, which bear a temporal symbolism. Destroying the first two houses means the destruction of the *ego*'s walls and the absorption of the mortal elements into the immortal Self, which dwells inside the holy city and the third house.[17] The three houses are the *chakras* of the Tantric doctrine; *Kundalinî*, the "Serpent Power," will pass from *chakra* to *chakra*, until the final Liberation. In the same way, the Bad Wolf passes from house to house facilitating the spiritual realization. The three houses and the labyrinth are inside us, and so are the devils and the temptations. From the microcosmic point of view, the biblical fall happened within us, and gradually the "holy city," the heart, was invaded by devils; therefore Babylon has become the haunt of devils. Liberation, teaches Meister Eckhart, is obtained when we chase all these evil forces from the heart, purifying our soul and emptying it for God, in the same way Jesus Christ chased the merchants from the Temple.[18]

There is a difference, though, between the Devil and the devils. We remember Grimm's fairy tale, *The Devil's Three Gold Hairs*. The Devil plays the dragon's function and appears as an aspect of the Principle itself. Even if it is hard to believe, the Devil, like the Bad Wolf or Saturn, had a benefic side, which was mainly lost in Christian times, and the Devil became pure evil.[19] Nonetheless, the Christian tradition preserved the symbol of the *amphisben*, the two-

---

[17] "If what has been built on the foundation survives, the builder will receive a reward. If the work is burned up, the builder will suffer loss" (**1 Corinthians** 3:14-15).

[18] In the Christian tradition, the three houses represent the satanic temptations as mundane ties. In this case, God's House is "The Fourth" one, the heart. The "tempter" is, interestingly enough, Peter. He tries to stop Christ from going to Jerusalem, and Jesus "turned and said to Peter, 'Get behind me, Satan! You are an obstacle in my path, because the way you think is not God's way but man's'" (**Matthew** 16:23). Also Peter, during the Transfiguration episode, says: "'Master, let us make three tents, one for you, one for Moses and one for Elijah.' – He did not know what he was saying" (**Luke** 9:33).

[19] Saturn, who was the regent of the Golden Age, became a devilish character in the Middle Ages, the astrologers presenting him lame, armed with the deadly scythe and devouring his children. Even his name was related to that of Satan.

headed serpent, representing united Christ and Satan (Guénon, **Le Roi**, p. 30). Also, we have already explained the two-folded function of the Dragon, a benefic one for the spiritual peregrine and a malefic, deadly one, for the ignorant; the Devil is just another name for Dragon.[20]

Brahma nirguna, the supreme Principle, one without the second, produces the worlds "by simply way of sport," as pastime (**Brahma Samhitâ** XVII). Playful, the Principle unveils one of its many faces and manifests the Cosmos; playful, the Principle unveils another face and "falls" as Dragon, together with the World; and, revealing another face, the Principle comes down as solar Hero to save the decaying Cosmos and behead the Dragon. At the same time, the Principle remains immutable, infinite, without parts, unchanged in itself. Brahma is, therefore, the Creator, the Savior and the Devil alltogether, the same as his Shakti is the one-and-only, yet has many faces. The Principle is the supernal Sun, super-luminous, absolute and unmovable; yet it "comes down" as *Oriens* (*Sol Invictus*, the Savior) and also "falls" as a lamed, "mortal" sun to produce and maintain the Existence. This last one, evolving with the decaying cycle, appears as Dragon, the Devil, the solar essence being eventually forgotten. The Savior doesn't belong to the world: "You are from below," says Jesus; "I am from above. You are of this world; I am not of this world" (**John** 8:23); instead, the Devil is *princeps hujus mundi*, belonging to this world, and the world belongs to him. The Hero (the Savior) and the Dragon (the Devil) are the two faces of the same Principle as supreme Artist.

The marvelous Hindu epic *Mahâbhârata* offers an excellent exemplification. The virgin Kuntî, tells the poem, uses Shiva's spell and asks the Sun to come down and be her husband. And the Sun obeys and comes down to her. His complexion was "honey-yellow," the color of wisdom. "By his wizardry he had split himself

---

[20] In Romanian, the devil is called *dracul*, a word derived from Latin *draco*, "dragon." Dracula's name means "devil" regarded as "dragon."

Dante's Devils

in two, and thus came there and went on shining in the sky."[21] That is a very important statement. The Sun, emblem of the supreme Principle, sacrifices himself and operates the "cutting": it is the scission of Heaven and Earth; the two halves of the Sun are the twins, the immortal and the mortal one (**Rig Veda** I.164.38). But the truth is that the Principle is without parts and will never split. The supernal Sun will be forever, infinite, immutable, and unchangeable. Only for the benefit of the world it seems that the Sun splits in two. The "mortal" sun comes down and will be the father of a solar hero, Karna. Note that Kuntî will remain a virgin and she, afraid of her family, will set the child in a basket and throw him into the river (**Mahâbhârata** I.104, III.292).

The "mortal" solar half, which comes down, has two faces: its first aspect is the *avatâra*, the second one is the fallen angel, the dragon. The miraculous birth of Karna (similar to Christ's birth) illustrates the first aspect; Karna is the "incorporation" of the "coming down" sun, and only seems to be "mortal"; essentially, he belongs to the "immortal" solar half that "went on shining in the sky." At the same time, the fact that, like in other tales we discussed, the child is left in an ark floating on the waters suggests the existence of a dragon; that represents the opposite face of the solar half, the "fallen" sun, which is the real "mortal" one.[22]

Aditi, the solar, infinite mother, gives birth to eight suns; she throws away the eighth sun, Mârttânda, the mortal one, which falls into "this world" (**Rig Veda** X.72.8). Similarly, Hera drops Hephaestus, abandoning her child, because he is lame and deformed (**Iliad** XVIII.394). In time, Hephaestus, working in his smithy inside the mountain, was considered a satanic character: his lameness became the devil's lameness; his fire became the fire of Hell, its celestial origin being forgotten. Therefore, Mârttânda and Hephaestus, both connected to celestial light and presented as fallen

---

[21] **The Mahâbhârata**, Univ. of Chicago Press, 1981, tr. and ed. by J. A. B. van Buitenen, III.290.
[22] At the end, Karna himself becomes the dragon. Arjuna's arrow will behead Karna and his head will become the new sun.

gods, could symbolize the Devil as Lucifer, the fallen angel, whose name means "light giver." Kuntî also abandoned Karna; Karna could symbolize accordingly both the *avatâra* and the fallen angel.[23]

We encounter a very complicated symbolism.[24] The solar god asked by Kuntî to come down is the *avatâra*, yet an *avatâra* is also her son, Karna. Karna, the abandoned child, could play the role of the fallen angel, the same as his father, the mortal solar half, can.[25] In this last case, the fallen sun is the king-dragon of the old cycle trying to suppress the newborn. We already know the sacred scenario: the "fall" of the cycle brings the change of the solar king into a dragon; the new solar king will behead the dragon. In fact, the solar heroes and the dragons are just the effects of the Principle's pastime. The Vedic statement *sarpyâ vâ âdityâh*, "the serpents are the suns," illustrates their common origin and essence.[26]

Manifesting the Existence implies not only a static cosmogony but also a dynamic movement of the cycles that makes the Cosmos operational. The *Bible* describes it as a "fall"; it is a "fall" from the "city of God" to the "city of Devil," it is the natural evolvement of

---

[23] Eventually, the solar brothers brought Mârttânda back into Heaven and the gods also accepted Hephaestus into Olympus, events illustrating the alchemical "rectification." The alchemical *vitriol* illustrates, by using its letters as initials, the operative sentence, *Visita Interiora Terrae, Rectificando Invenies Occultum Lapidem*, "Visit the Interior of the Earth, in Order that You May Find the Hidden Stone by Rectification" (M. Caron and S. Hutin, **The Alchemists**, Grove Press, 1961, p. 137). The "rectification" is a spiritual recovery, following the "fall," and is similar to *Kundalinî*'s awakening and ascension from *chakra* to *chakra* (Guénon, **Symboles**, p. 229). The emblem of the alchemical *vitriol* is the "green lion"; note that green, which is the color of the stone the Holy Grail was made of, is the color of regeneration ("rectification") and indicates the absolute Truth (Latin *viridis*, "green," and *veritas*, "truth," are very close phonetically).

[24] The same intricate symbolism appears in Jesus' statement, "It was the stone rejected by the builders that became the keystone" (**Luke** 20:17).

[25] "The Father is in me and I am in the Father" (**John** 10:38).

[26] "There were two classes of Prajâpati's sons, the Dêvas and the Asuras" (**Brhadâranyaka Up.** I.3.1). As Ananda K. Coomaraswamy has explained more than once, the Angels (*Dêvas*) and the Titans (*Asuras*), representing the powers of Light and Darkness in *Rig Veda*, have, despite their antithetic actions, the same essence. We have to remember all the time that the *Asuras* were the *Dêvas* of the past worlds and cycles.

Dante's Devils

the cycles, from a "golden age" to an "iron age." It is the fall of Lucifer, the decayed angel, yet Lucifer, identified with Satan, is not less than the solar light: his name betrays it.[27] This "fall" becomes a "coming down" when the Divine Presence "incorporates" in the world as an *avatâra*, as a *savior*, having the mission to rectify the falling cycle. "Jesus said to them: I watched Satan fall like lightning from heaven" (**Luke** 10:18), or the lightning is a symbol of the Divine Presence (*avatâra*), stated clearly in the *Yi Jing*, which suggests a halving of Lucifer: there is a damned Lucifer who falls and a blessed Lucifer who comes down[28]; and we can assume that the second Lucifer will save the first one and the decayed angel will be raised back to Heavens, in the same way Mârttânda and Hephaestus were.[29]

We have to be careful. Because of the two-fold symbolism, the infernal forces can easily be mistaken for the celestial ones. *Ab intra*, the two Lucifers are one; *ab extra*, from a mundane point of view, the Devil is very real and distinct from the Savior: it is the Enemy.[30] It takes a high spiritual realization to dissolve the devilish side, to untie the labyrinthine path and reach the Center where the oppositions are appeased, where the two Lucifers are indeed One, where the Dragon's mouth is the solar gate of Liberation.

---

[27] The lion, a solar symbol, is the sign of both the Messiah and the Antichrist, says St. Hippolyte (Guénon, **Le Roi**, p. 30).

[28] The Savior is the benefic "image" of the Principle; the Devil is its malefic "image." The Divine Presence, *Metatron* of the Hebraic *Kabbalah*, has two faces, a bright, angelic one, Mikael, and a tenebrous, demonic one, Samael (Guénon, **Le Roi**, p. 29). They are "brothers," having the same essence; better, the Devil is the "anti-brother" of the Savior, and in Dante's *Inferno* it becomes a "reverse image," a monkey-like imitation.

[29] "At the beginning the sun was down here; the gods raised it to the upper world" (**Maitrâneya Samhitâ**). Jesus said: "Now sentence is being passed on this world; now the prince of this world [Satan] is to be overthrown. And when I am lifted up from the earth, I shall draw all men to myself" (**John** 12:31-32). The destruction of the Beast coincides with the ascension of the Savior. The two Lucifers are actually one. Note that "I shall draw all the men to myself" illustrates the function of the "Golden Chain."

[30] "The prince of this world comes, and has nothing in Me" (**John** 14:30).

The Everlasting Sacred Kernel

A Romanian legend calls the God "brother" and the Devil "non-brother"; they work together to create the Cosmos. The God creates an even land (illustrating the Oneness) and the Devil molds it, producing mountains and the valleys, that is, the multiplicity (Eliade, **Zalmoxis**, pp. 77-85).[31] Multiplicity, the "outside darkness," and the ephemeral world, is the Devil's domain. The Devil is divided into many devils, the same way the Dragon, as productive Principle, is cut into pieces during the cosmogonic sacrifice. Since the Devil governs the "fall" and the cyclic decadence, as change from sacred unity to profane multiplicity, the devils will be the signs of this "fall." The devils represent the profane, the chaos, the impermanence, the continuous change, the ignorance, and the turmoil of the world. They become more and more persistent and insolent while the cycle turns to its end. From the microcosmic point of view, the devils and Hell are inside us, as the Kingdom of Heaven is. All our desires and appetites, our greed and egotism, our fears and mental turbulence, express the devils. The devils are not so much the physical appetites, but the psychical ones. All the spiritual methods stress the importance of pacifying the soul and the mind. The mental waves, the elusive, turbulent thoughts, imagination and the emotions are the biggest enemies of spiritual realization. These are the temptations, the sirens' songs, and the devils. Ultimately, the *ego* is the city inhabited by the devils, i.e., the individuality, the ephemeral, relative body-soul composite, which has to be purified and reabsorbed into the Self.[32]

---

[31] The God's emblem is a bee and the Devil's emblem is the hedgehog. It is easy to note that both the bee and the hedgehog have a spine as a common element; the difference is that the bee has *one*, while the hedgehog has a *multiplicity* of spines.

[32] Ananda K. Coomaraswamy wisely proves that *anima* (the soul, mentality and sentiment, the "tempter") represents Hell and the devils. This soul has to be "lost" in order to be saved; this soul has to be "killed" and "tamed" in the Holy War (*jihâd*). As Rûmî says, "this soul is hell" and "the soul and Shaitân are both one being." The killing of this soul is his redemption, when the fallen angels, Lucifer, Phosphorus or Scintilla, become again what they were before, the light of the supernal Sun. Coomaraswamy also notes that the Devil, whom we call the "enemy," "adversary," "tempter," "dragon," doesn't actually have a personal name. Also, Hebrew *Sâtân*, "opponent" (and English "devil," from Greek *diabolos*, "slanderer"),

Dante's Devils

The "legion" of devils is also a description of multiplicity. The traditional doctrines, all of them, define the supreme Principle as One, or furthermore, as Non-dual (Hindu *advaita*). Contrary to the One, multiplicity describes the impermanent, relative, changeable Existence. The multiplicity is symbolized by the innumerable points of the circumference, points that become One in the center of the wheel. At the beginning of the cycle of manifestation, the multiplicity is less evident, closer to the center, and more qualitative. As the world decays, the points move centrifugally away and, with the increases of the circumference, the multiplicity increases. It is what Guénon defines as the fall from quality to quantity (Guénon, **Le règne**, p. 18). He also explains this evolvement of the world from the "city of God" to the "city of Devil" using an Islamic concept about *les fissures de la Grande Muraille*, "the fissures of the Great Wall" (Guénon, **Le règne**, pp. 230 ff.). This Wall is in the Islamic tradition the "rampart" that protects against Gog and Magog (**Qor'ân** XVIII.92-99) and many *hadîth* tell about the crack in the wall, which will bring the end of the world.[33] The Great Wall is the "cutting" which protects and separates the whole Cosmos from the "outside darkness," and so any wall is, from a traditional point of view, a specification of the Great Wall, having the same functions. As the Cosmos degenerates, the protective Wall cracks and fissures start to appear.[34] Through these fissures the satanic, tenebrous forces (Gog

---

is not a personal name. Abu Sâ'îd says that the evil called himself "nobody," refusing like Buddha, to accept a name and be identified with a "personality." For all these see Coom., **Metaphysics**, pp. 23 ff., *Satan and Hell*. We remember that Ulysses too called himself "Nobody." As we explained, the solar heroes and the dragons are just puppets of Brahma's play, "images" and "masks" of the one and only Person, the Principle. "Nobody" means not only that those puppets don't deserve a personal name (which would make them independent), being illusory in comparison with the Principle, but also that the real Person is beyond *nâma-rûpa*, "names and forms." "The nameless was the beginning of heaven and earth" (**Lao zi** I.2); the Principle "can not be named" and is "for ever nameless" (**Lao zi** XIV, XXV, XXXII). "We can give it no name" (Plotinus V.3.13).

[33] Émile Dermenghem, **Muhammad**, Harper & Bros. 1958, pp. 20-1.
[34] In Dante's *Purgatorio* (XXXII.130-135) a dragon's tail produces the fissures in the cosmic wall.

and Magog) begin to break in[35]; at the same time, the Divine Presence inside the walls retreats and hides. At the end of the cycle, the whole city (Cosmos, world) will fall into the devils' power.[36]

Dante's "Dis" is such a city.[37] As *The Divine Comedy* describes a spiritual journey, we recognize both meanings of the "satanic town": on the one hand, it symbolizes the decadence of Man, who is lost in the wild woods, overwhelmed by ignorance and inferior appetites; on the other hand, the initiation is a journey from city to city, in which case Dis is only a station of this spiritual path.

Dante mentions more than one city in his divine poem. From the beginning he states the goal of his journey: the holy city, Christ's city (*sua città*), located in Paradise (**Inf.** I.128). Of course, this city is the opposite of the city of Dis and, to reach it, a purification of the "satanic town" and the taming of the devils are mandatory. In fact, the whole *Inferno* is a city, "the city of desolation" (*città dollente*), having the famous inscription *lasciate ogni speranza, voi ch'entrate* carved on its gate (**Inf.** III.1-11).[38] Dante starts his spiritual voyage passing through this gate, suggesting that the spiritual process takes place inside him, where all the cities are to be found, eventually the Kingdom of Heaven being reached. The first major station inside the *città dollente* is Limbo, where the pagan philosophers and heroes are. They dwell in a noble castle "girt with seven high walls around and

---

[35] The satanic forces are, as Guénon specifies, psychic or subtle forces. Sometimes, they are symbolized in tales by dwarfs or giants, and connected with the subterranean fire of the smiths. That is why Hephaestus had a satanic image (Guénon, **Le règne**, p. 232). The fissure admits, as any other symbol, a two-fold meaning. From a beneficial point of view it represents the "eye of the needle," the gate of communication between the neophyte and the Principle. In Shakespeare's *A Midsummer Night's Dream*, the Wall, a personage of the play-within-the-play, says, "I, one Snout by name, present a wall:/ And such a wall as I would have you think/ That had in it a crannied hole or chink,/ Through which the lovers, Pyramus and Thisby,/ Did whisper often very secretly" (V.I.155-159).

[36] That is the meaning of Shakespeare's poem *The Rape of Lucrece*. For him, the conquest of Troy is the satanic invasion of the city. Lucrece is the virgin, the chaste maid, whose rape echoes the rape of Troy.

[37] Dis is the name of Pluto, the god of Hell, and so it became the name of Satan. See Cicero, **The Nature of the Gods**, Penguin Books, 1972, II.66-68.

[38] The inscription plays the role of the Cumaean labyrinth.

moated with a goodly rivulet" (**Inf.** IV.106-8), and we recognize again the importance of the "cutting."

The city of Dis is also described as a guarded sacred fortress: "We now were come to the deep moats, which turn/ To gird that city all disconsolate,/ Whose walls appeared as they were made of iron" (**Inf.** VIII.76-8). The walls "made of iron" remind us of the rampart built against the devils Gog and Magog: "I'll place a rampart between you and them. Bring me blocks of iron" (**Qor'ân** XVIII.92-4), and the well-known supposition that Dante used Islamic sources. The city of Dis represents an important station of Dante's initiation. The most significant fact is that Dante and his guide, Virgil, have no access inside the fortress; the devils "slammed the gate" in Virgil's face. The city of Dis appears inviolable and inaccessible, as a "sacred place" is. We encounter here Satan's monkey-like imitation. The vices and appetites, the inferior desires and emotions, all these devils dwelling inside the city, are violently reacting against sacred purification during the initiatory process. The *guru* ("spiritual master") teaches his student that the first sign of a spiritual achievement is the brutal reaction of the *ego* that will try to preserve the *status quo*. That is why a genuine initiation is not an individual, autodidactic operation. The result would be illusory. A real initiation requires a regular attachment to a sacred organization, and a spiritual *guru*, both capable of transmitting a divine influence or blessing.

Dante knows it very well, and he tells us that a celestial messenger (*da cielo messo*) comes down and chases the devils and opens the gate (**Inf.** IX.85-90). That is a crucial episode, which unveils the truth about initiation. Anybody who thinks that a spiritual realization is an individual (human) operation commits a huge mistake. The initiatory process consists of a series of personal efforts, that is true, but without the intervention of a celestial grace, of a divine influence, those efforts would be worthless, a pure illusion. That is why just before the descent of the celestial messenger, and after the violent reaction of the Erinnyes, Dante puts us on guard: "O voi, ch'avete gl'intelletti sani,/ Mirate la dottrina, che s'asconde/ Sotto il velame de li versi strani."[39] The celestial messenger will overcome the hateful reaction of the infernal appetites and subhuman emotions, and will purify the city.[40]

From the Year's perspective, the city of Dis, a mockery of the city of God, marks the end of a cosmic cycle. Dante enters Dis soon after midnight (**Inf.** VII.98). Midnight is the balance and the crucial point between the old and the new cycle. It is the time when, according to the reverse analogy, everything is upside-down, just before the spiritual rectification.[41] Therefore, the city of Dis, full of devils, appears as a parody of a holy place, inviolable and inaccessible; therefore, Dis (Lucifer) itself is described standing upside-down and having a monkey's fur (**Inf.** XXXIV.73-90).

The Romans celebrated this particular time at the winter solstice as *Saturnalia*, when everything was upside-down, and all the normal rules were disregarded. The summer solstice has the same significance, even more accentuated, since it corresponds to *Ianua Inferni*. That makes Shakespeare's play, *A Midsummer Night's Dream*, a very attractive one, provided that a sacred kernel is hidden there.

However, knowing Shakespeare's esoteric reputation the play deserves our full attention and that will be our next trial.

---

[39] "O you whose intellects keep their sanity,/ Do you mark well the doctrine shrouded o'er/ By the strange verses with their mystery" (**Inf.** IX.61-63).
[40] That is the meaning of "the cleansing of the Temple," when Christ drove out the sellers or when Ulysses killed the suitors.
[41] According to a well-known hermetic adage, the celestial things are as the terrestrial ones, only reversed. Related to this, the midnight symbolism offers two sides: it is the darkness of the infernal pole but also the divine "black light" of the supernal pole ("God enters the Garden of Eden at midnight," **Zohar** I.92b).

Chapter Five

SHAKESPEARE AT MIDNIGHT

IN HINDU tradition, the Great Wall has two legitimate gates: *dêva-yâna* ("the gate of gods") and *pitri-yâna* ("the gate of ancestors"), corresponding to the winter (north) and summer (south) solstices. The first one is the gate through which descend divine messengers and celestial influences, through which comes down the *avatâra*, or ascend the "liberated" ones, the "elected" beings that have achieved a complete spiritual realization. The second one is the gate through which the beings come back into Existence, chained by their ignorance to the worldly rotations of the cycles. This gate communicates also with the domain of the ancestors, with the realm of the past cycles, with Death, that is why it is called *Ianua Inferni*. In our Western tradition, their janitor is, as we already mentioned, Janus *Bifrons* ("two-faced").[1] The divine Homer gives us a hint about the meaning of the two gates in the *Odyssey*; no doubt, Homer's gates, "the gate of gods" and "the gate of men," are identical to the Hindu solar gates, only, as René Guénon explained, they are regarded from a

---

[1] From an absolute point of view the Principle is the only Gate, which appears from our mundane perspective divine and human, with two faces. "I am the Gate," states Jesus (**John** 10:9). "The gates were opened by Deity and Humanity, and the lover (neophyte) went in to see his Beloved (God)," Ramon Llull, **Book of the Lover and the Beloved** 43 (See **Doctor Illuminatus, A Ramon Llull Reader**, Princeton Univ. Press, 1993, p. 195).

The Everlasting Sacred Kernel

celestial point of view, not a terrestrial one, which is why the north and south appear reversed (Guénon, **Symboles**, p. 244).[2]

The gate has a vast symbolism and there are many examples in various traditions about its sacred meaning. The gates of the temple, palace or city, are all praised in a special way.[3] We know that Babylon means "the gate of God," *Ianua Coeli*. In the Bible, Jacob describes the spiritual center as "a house of God; this is the gate of heaven!" (**Gen.** 28:17); also, the Psalmist says: "Take pity of me, Lord, look on my suffering, you who lift me up from the gates of death, that in the gates of the daughter of Zion I may recite your praises, rejoicing that you have saved me" (**Psalms** 9:13-14).[4] In Daoism, "The gateway of the mysterious female is called the root of heaven [*Ianua Coeli*] and earth [*Ianua Inferni*]" (**Lao zi** VI).[5]

The sacred enclosure is not a "closed system." It is surrounded by a continuous, protective and inviolable barrier, yet there are ritually designated openings – the gates. The Romans followed sacred rules, as in the *Mysteries*, to found Rome. They dug a round trench, called *Mundus* ("the sky" and also "the world"), and Romulus used a plough to drive a deep and continuous furrow round the bounds; where they designed to make a gate (*portae*), there they took out the

---

[2] "At the head of the harbour, there is an olive tree with spreading leaves, and nearby is a cave that is shaded, and pleasant, and sacred to the nymphs who are called the Nymphs of the Wellsprings, Naiads. There are mixing bowls and handled jars inside it, all of stone, and there the bees deposit their honey.... It has two entrances, one of them facing the North Wind, where people can enter, but the one toward the South Wind has more divinity. That is the way of the immortals, and no men enter by that way" (**Odyssey** XIII.102-112). Porphyry wrote a famous commentary about this cave. The honey inside the cave corresponds to Samson's honey inside the lion. The Nemean lion's cave has also two entrances. All are related to a solar symbolism.

[3] For an illustration of the gate's importance in different traditions see Titus Burckhardt, **Principes et méthodes de l'art sacré**, Dervy-Livres, 1976, pp. 107 ff.

[4] The gates of Zion represent "the gate of gods." "The Lord loves the gates of Zion more than all the dwelling of Jacob. Glorious things are spoken of you, city of God" (**Psalms** 87:2-3).

[5] The "mysterious female," called also the "dark, obscure female," should be compared to Shakespeare's "heavenly Rosaline" who is a dark woman, because "No face is fair that is not full so black" (**Love's Labour's Lost**, Act IV, scene III). Here the darkness is the super-luminous, supernal Night.

share, and left a space (Plutarch, **The Lives**, pp. 19-20).[6] If the sacred enclosure represents the entire Cosmos or the "Three Worlds," gates are required to permit communication with the "two nights." A "divine" gate allows communication with the supernal Night, the "super-luminous darkness," the night of non-manifestation, domain of silence, void, non-action, and the realm of the supreme Principle, *Brahma nirguna* (the "midnight Sun"). The "human" gate facilitates communication with the infernal chaos, the "outside darkness," the night of ignorance and profane. If the enclosure symbolizes just a level of existence, then it requires gates to communicate with the upper and lower levels of existence (*chakras*).

Samson's tale contains a strange episode, which parts the story in two. Just before meeting Delilah, and after ending the relationship with his first Philistine wife, Samson is trapped in Gaza. "Samson however stayed in bed till midnight, and rising at midnight, he seized the doors of the town gate and the two posts as well; he tore them up, bar and all, hoisted them on to his shoulders and carried them to the top of the hill facing Hebron and there he left them" (**Judges** 16:3). The hill is comparable to Dante's Mountain of Purgatory, and Samson's ascension to the top of the hill suggests his liberation through the heavenly gate; actually, Samson identifies himself with the gate during the entire ascent. We find something similar at the end of Samson's tale, when he destroys the building full of his enemies by breaking its two middle pillars (**Judges** 16:29-30). In this case, the ruin of the house (of the walls) symbolizes the end of the Cosmos, as we have already explained. Nonetheless, the two pillars, like the two posts, invite us to a further investigation.

The most famous pillars during ancient times were *Herculis Columnae*, the "Pillars of Hercules," considered as marking the extreme, the limit of the civilized world. The adage *Non plus ultra*, connected to these columns, emphasizes the separation ("cutting") between order and chaos. The *Herculis Columnae* constitute the Gate of the

---

[6] The trench is the image of a celestial archetype, the gates corresponding (as in the case of the Heavenly Jerusalem) to the zodiacal signs.

Great Wall, of the zodiacal frame of the Cosmos.[7] This Gate is though not any gate, but symbolizes the solar gates, the gates of Janus – the solstices. The "Pillars of Hercules" mark, from a celestial point of view, the limits of the sun's path, limits that couldn't be trespassed without changing order into chaos (Guénon, **Symboles**, pp. 256-7).[8]

As we said before, the "cutting," *vallum* or *fossa*, represents not only a protection against the evil forces or an obstacle against ignorance, but also a frame to sustain and order the elements of the enclosure. Any alteration of the sacred frame would shatter the harmony, the balance, and the peace, leading to chaos and demonic invasion. When the ten suns of the Chinese tradition disobey the celestial order and decide to shine together, the Cosmos falls into chaos, the world becomes a burnt, uninhabitable desert. The sun's path, the zodiacal frame, is broken. Restoring the order, that is, "recreating" the Cosmos, imposes punishment (sacrifice) on the "trespassers," the nine suns being killed by the hero's arrows. When Phaeton, Helios's son, drives his father's chariot, the solar vehicle, he cannot follow the zodiacal path, and his "trespassing" destroys the order, burning the world. Zeus punishes him, using his arrow – the lightning.[9] Remus, Romulus' twin brother, is punished and

---

[7] The sacred place inside the "cutting," or inside the wall, represents, in the largest acceptance of its meaning, order, i.e., the Cosmos. The "outside darkness" is the chaos. When the devils take possession of the sacred enclosure, order falls back into chaos. See Mircea Eliade, **Images and Symbols**, Princeton Univ. Press, 1991, p. 38 and **Le mythe**, p. 20. The ancient interdiction of passing beyond the "Pillars of Hercules" (*Non plus ultra*) was actually a warning about the chaos prevailing outside. Dante explains Ulysses' death as a consequence of his last voyage beyond *Herculis Columnae*. Ulysses drowning in the ocean means that chaos swallowed the hero, making him an inhabitant of Hell. See Dante's *Inferno*, XXVI.106-142.

[8] The two pillars indicate the two solstices. Hercules' twelve labours correspond to the twelve zodiacal signs, stressing the celestial symbolism of *Herculis Columnae*. Porphyry specifies that the solstitial gates are the limits of the solar journey.

[9] One of the Erinnyes' functions, says Heracleitus the Obscure, is to make sure that the sun follows the zodiacal frame without trespassing its limits (Buffiere, IV, chap. V, note 25). The Erinnyes are the infernal goddesses of punishment, and Dante shows them guarding the city of Dis (**Inf.** IX.37-57). In other words, anybody perturbing order (cosmic, social, religious or pure spiritual) should be punished and

killed because he jumps over the sacred "cutting" of Rome (Plutarch, **The Lives**, p. 19). After that, a Roman rule stipulated the death penalty for the soldier who crossed the wall of the camp instead of using the gate (Knight, **Vergil**, p. 219).[10]

Crossing and violating the sacred "cutting" represents a "fall" from order to chaos. It endangers not only the sinner but also the enclosure itself, creating a "fissure" in the wall through which the evil forces could penetrate into the city. The "cutting" is a continuous line, as Christ's robe was one piece without any seam.[11] Any interruption of this continuity means a profanation, a sacrilege, erosion of the inviolability, a loss of divine unity, and a "reversal of the poles."[12]

The safe place for crossing is the gate.[13] Even so, not everybody is allowed to enter or exit the gate. Ulysses is punished because he passes beyond *Herculis Columnae*, the solar gate, without a divine guide, and Guénon considers it an illegitimate initiation. This kind of trespassing is equivalent to "looking back," to falling back into profanity and ignorance.[14] The gate is the legitimate way to com-

---

thrown into chaos by the Erinnyes; hence the sacred symbolism of various capital punishment methods.

[10] As Plutarch says, the trespasser is called a "profane." The walls are sacred and nobody is allowed to touch or damage them, the offender being put to death. See Fustel de Coulanges, **The Ancient City**, Lee & Shepard, 1901, book III, chap. IV, notes 11 and 13.

[11] In the *Yi Jing* the continuous line symbolizes the supernal, active Principle, *Qian*. Also, Nicholas of Cusa describes God as an infinite, continuous line.

[12] In the *Yi Jing* the discontinuous line is *Kun*, the infernal, passive Principle. Breaking the line means a reversal from supernal to infernal pole, from sacred to profane: hence the "superstition" about the black cat crossing somebody's path.

[13] The *avatâra* comes down "crossing" the "gate of gods." The word *avatâra* derives from *tarana*, "crossing," hence *avatarana*, "crossing back (down)" (Coom., **Metaphysics**, p. 325).

[14] From the same microcosmic point of view, Icarus, the son of Daedalus, failed his liberation, disobeying the ordered path. Note the similitude with Phaeton's macrocosmic symbolism. The initiatory ritual forbids the neophyte to look back during his journey. Lot's wife was punished because she looked back (**Gen.** 19:26). "Looking back" represents the temptations of the profane world, the nostalgia due to mundane desires and emotions. Cupid asked his wife, Psyche, not to answer or even look up to her sisters. Psyche broke her promise and she fell from sacred to pro-

municate with the upper or lower levels of the "Three Worlds" (*Tribhuvana*); to pass through the gate safely, a divine guidance is needed; if not, the neophyte, as any ignorant, will be punished for trespassing. Dante, to accomplish his journey in Hell, needs a celestial messenger to open the gate of Dis.[15] Ulysses is guided by Circe's advice to pass Skylla and Charybdis (**Odyssey** XII.70-110). Usually, the gate is very well guarded: cherubs, lions, dragons, monsters or sphinxes are the *dvârapâlas*, "the guardians of the door," punishing the intruders and testing the "elected" ones. The "Clashing Rocks" have the same function.[16]

In order to fully understand the symbolism of the gate we must return to Janus *Bifrons*. First, the crossing itself has to be perceived as a two-way crossing, towards and from the enclosure, in both cases a similar meaning being unveiled. "I am the Gate," says Jesus. "Anyone who enters through me will be safe: he will go freely in and out" (**John** 10:9). Samson's exit through Gaza's gates symbolizes his salvation and spiritual liberation. On the other hand, Yvain's entrance through the palace-gate means the same salvation.[17] As a

---

fane, failing the initiation. See Lucius Apuleius, **The Golden Ass**, Penguin Books, 1985, p. 103.

[15] With God's help even crossing the wall is not a "trespassing": "with my God I leap the rampart" (**Psalms** 18:29). Virgil, Dante's first guide, is incapable of opening the gate, a much higher influence being required. Note how Dante has to use the gate to communicate with the infernal circles, starting with the main gate of Hell and continuing with the seven gates of the castle in Limbo.

[16] Skylla and Charybdis constitute such a gate, called the "Clashing Rocks" (or "Clashing Mountains"), a motive widely spread in different traditions. Skylla and Charybdis should be compared with Calpe and Abyla, the two rocks of the Straits of Gibraltar, which represent *Herculis Columnae*. In the Hindu tradition, the *yakshas* are the guardian angels of the gates of cities, palaces or shrines. When a city is endangered a *yaksha* in the form of an ass brays and the city is lifted into the air. See Ananda K. Coomaraswamy, **Yaksas**, Oxford Univ. Press, 1993, p. 56. The symbolism of the ass deserves a special study.

[17] Chrétien de Troyes, **Arthurian Romances**, Dent & Sons, 1982, p. 192. We learned that usually the spiritual realization is symbolized by reaching the center and entering into the holy city. But if the city is the city of Dis (Devil), sheltering the *ego*, if it is a prison and an entrapment for the Self, the liberation is obtained by escaping. Therefore, when Joshua's spies "crossed" the wall of Jericho, escaping, that was not profanation, but liberation. Note that they used a rope, which is a reflection of the

profanation, the evil forces trespassing from outside into the city, through the fissures of the wall, or the crossing of the wall towards "outside darkness," present the same malefic meaning.

The gate not only permits a two-way crossing, it also reveals a double path, actually a "double" door. *Ianua Coeli* is the solar gate, the gate of liberation, the Vedic "barricade of the sky," which, as Coomaraswamy tells us, divides the mortal realm under the Sun from the immortal realm beyond him (Coom., **Trad. Art**, pp. 524, 535).[18] In Grimm's fairy tale, *The Sleeping Beauty*, the entire wall represents the "barricade of the sky." A hedge of thorns surrounds the castle and any prince trying to cross it is put to death. Only when the "elected" one, i.e. the Prince, comes to save the Virgin, does the hedge of thorns change into a hedge of flowers. It parts to let him pass and then closes behind him as a thick hedge. In fact, there is a gate, a hidden, dangerous gate that uncovers itself as *Ianua Coeli* for the Prince and as *Ianua Inferni* for the profane and ignorant princes. *Ianua Inferni* is the second "face" of the Gate.

Ianua Coeli, as a divine gate, reflects the heavenly One-and-only, the spiritual unity, the child-like simplicity; this gate has to be conquered by spiritual knowledge.[19] *Ianua Inferni*, as worldly gate, reflects the multiplicity and accepts numerous meanings; it is wide

---

"Golden Chain," having a "redemption" role (**Joshua** 2:15). The same meaning has St. Paul's escape from Damascus (**Acts** 9:25). For the city as prison, see Shakespeare's *A Midsummer Night's Dream*, Act I, scene II, 30.

[18] When Yvain, or Gawain, passes through the palace-gate, which operates as "Clashing Rocks," the moving gate cuts off a part of his mule's tail (Troyes 192). The same thing happens to the Romanian stork, as we saw previously. The tail (remember the peacock's tail symbolism) represents the root of manifestation and mortality. The dragon's tail from Dante's *Purgatorio* (XXXII.131) is also related to this symbolism.

[19] Daoism, Plotinus and Meister Eckhart insist upon the simplicity of the Principle. Nicholas of Cusa also describes *Ianua Coeli* as *coincidentia oppositorum*, as the way towards unity: "I have learnt that the place wherein Thou art found unveiled is girt round with the coincidence of contradictories, and this is the wall of Paradise wherein Thou does abide. The door whereof is guarded by the most proud spirit of Reason, and, unless he be vanquished, the way in will not lie open" (**The Vision of God**, The Book Tree, 1999, p. 44). "That indeed is the door to the world of Brahma, an entrance for the knower and a shutting out for the ignorant" (**Chândogya Up.** VIII.6.5).

open for all kind of influences and thus, very dangerous. Both gates, as we specified at the beginning of this chapter, are directly connected to the symbolism of the "two nights." We already encountered those "nights." Samson got his liberation from Gaza at midnight: that is the supernal night[20]; Dante entered the city of Dis at midnight: that is the infernal night.[21]

The night of the summer solstice is "infernal" rather in the etymological sense of the word,[22] and we should call it more adequately a "cosmological" night. Thus, it is easier to understand why such a night can be connected at the same time with entities of Hell, with the subtle domain of *psyche* and the world of dreams, and with the spiritual realization of the *Lesser Mysteries*, all belonging to the cosmological order.

Shakespeare's *Midsummer night* is this "cosmological" night, a night that has an important role in Shakespearean plays.[23] *A Midsummer Night's Dream*, besides having night as the major background, ends with Theseus' statement: "The iron tongue of midnight hath told twelve" (V.I.349). The "balcony scene" from *Romeo and Juliet*, a very spiritual scene, takes place also around midnight and the nature of this night is unveiled by Romeo when he says: "It is the east, and Juliet is the sun!" Indeed, if night represents the ignorance of the

---

[20] Jesus was born as *avatâra* at winter solstice and at midnight (Guénon, **Symboles**, p. 240).
[21] About the symbolism of the "two nights" see René Guénon's excellent article *Les deux nuits* in **Initiation et réalisation spirituelle**, Éd. Traditionnelles, 1980; as Guénon explains, the "two nights" are, in an absolute sense, the two faces of the same unique Principle, as the two gates, *déva-yâna* and *pitri-yâna*, are. The supernal night corresponds to the metaphysical order, while the infernal night corresponds to the cosmological order (Guénon, **Initiation**, p. 241).
[22] The word "infernal" comes from Latin *inferus*, "below."
[23] As in Homer's case, it is not clear who was/were the individual/s bearing the name of Shakespeare. But as Juliet says: "What's in a name? that which we call a rose,/ By any other name would smell as sweet;/ So Romeo would, were he not Romeo call'd,/ Retain that dear perfection which he owes/ Without that title: - Romeo, doff thy name;/ And for that name, which is not part of thee,/ Take all myself" (**Romeo and Juliet**, Act II, scene II). We already explained the metaphysical meaning of "Nobody." See also how Dante hid the name of mysterious *bella donna* Matilda in *Purgatorio*, from XXVIII.43 to XXXIII.118.

Shakespeare at Midnight

"outside darkness," the rising sun (*Oriens*, Jesus Christ) is the spiritual dawn of illumination and Juliet is, as Helen or Beatrice, the *Madonna Intelligenza*, the Virgin.[24] *Hamlet, Prince of Denmark* starts exactly at midnight when the cosmic gate opens to give access to the ghost.[25] Night has a central role in *King Lear*[26]; in *Love's Labour's Lost*, a curious allusion about "the school of night" is made.[27] Also *Twelfth Night* has a significant name related to Christmas (winter solstice) festivities, though Olivia uses the popular expression "midsummer madness" (summer solstice) (Act III, scene IV).[28]

The examples could go on, but we don't have to continue. To prove that there is a sacred kernel in Shakespeare's work connected to our subject, it is enough to focus upon *A Midsummer Night's Dream*. The play is a marvelous, symbolic festival.

The carnivals and festivals were at the beginning not profane celebrations, but sacred. They had a precise, technical motivation and were related to the solstitial and equinoctial gates. Like the Roman *Saturnalia*, celebrated during the winter solstice, those carnivals usually mark the passage from the old to a new cycle. It is a period of unrestrained revelry and licence, when the most inferior possibilities of the old cycle are released, in an obvious attempt to exhaust them. During those days of the ending cycle, a controlled, ritual chaos replaces the existing social order, the normal hierarchy turning upside-down. Villains play royal roles; inferior priests occupy bishop's functions (Guénon, **Symboles**, pp. 162 ff.). The laws, rules

---

[24] Romeo says: "Call me but love, and I'll be new baptiz'd;/ Henceforth I never will be Romeo." It is obvious that Romeo is the neophyte (with a new name) following, like Dante, the *bhakti-marga*, the Love-initiatory path. Note that Romeo crossed the wall to get inside Juliet's garden (Act II, scene I).
[25] The gate is *pitri-yâna* of the summer solstice, communicating with the realm of ancestors.
[26] Night is connected with the wild tempest, the heath and with Edgar faking possession by devils.
[27] Frances Yates, **The Occult Philosophy in the Elizabethan Age**, Ark Paperbacks, 1983, p. 150 ff. Dame Yates presents a very convincing hypothesis about Shakespeare's involvement with Elizabethan occultism.
[28] Note the Fool, whose name is Feste (medieval French for "feast," "festival"). The spiritual symbolism of the Fool in Shakespeare's plays requires a separate study.

The Everlasting Sacred Kernel

and morality are temporary abolished; the inferior passions are set free. It is a monkey-like imitation of the rites and spirituality of a "golden age."[29] The *coincidentia oppositorum* of Paradise is imitated as a total confusion and mixture. The Cosmos is imitated as "anticosmos." *Diabolus simia Dei*, says Tertullian, i.e., "Satan is God's ape," and the witches' festivals, "the Sabbats," are held about the time of Christians' festivals in evil mockery, a very important one being held at summer solstice (Eve of St. John the Baptist).[30] The ass, a medieval emblem of the malefic forces, is worshipped in the church.[31] Finally, we should mention the important role played by the mask during carnivals, the masks (including the ass head) representing here mainly psychical, inferior influences and evil entities, exposed in order to be purified.[32] It is something very much like real chaos itself, expected in the city of Dis or as a result of many fissures that have developed in the wall; to simulate such a situation, the solstice gate is opened deliberately. The midsummer night, illustrating this gate, gathers all the cosmological meanings.[33]

---

[29] Guénon stresses that such a festival doesn't mean at all a return to a "golden age." On the contrary, it represents the "upside-down world," illustrating the satanic aspect of Saturn.

[30] Montague Summers, **The History of Witchcraft & Demonology**, Castle Books, 1992, p. 112. The Sabbats started usually at midnight.

[31] "I," says the Lord, "will instruct you and teach you the way to go; I will watch over you and be your adviser. Do not be like the ignorant horse or mule..." (**Psalms** 32:8-9). The Egyptian "red ass" was an emblem of satanic forces. Jesus enters Jerusalem riding a donkey (**Luke** 19:35), meaning that the Redeemer subjugated evil (Guénon, **Symboles**, p. 162). The medieval "feast of ass" and "feast of fools" were parodies, almost sacrileges, accepted to end the old world.

[32] In Shakespeare's plays, the travesty replaces the mask. The sacred symbolism of the mask is well known. See Burckhardt, **Mirror**, p. 149. The mask plays a special role in Dumas' *Le Comte de Monte-Cristo*. The return of Edmond Dantès as count of Monte-Cristo is marked by a carnival in Rome, connected with dreaming and travesties (see chaps. XXXI-XXXVIII).

[33] In the Hindu tradition, as we explained, the profound, dreamless sleep is an emblem of the spiritual world. The "waking state" is the emblem of the corporeal world. Between those two, the dream represents the subtle, psychical world, the most important domain of the cosmological gate. That is why Shakespeare's play is a festive "dream" describing the operations during the midsummer night. It is worthwhile to quote Homer's description of this solstitial gate. After Odysseus kills the suitors, "Hermes of Kyllene summoned the souls of the suitors to come forth,

Shakespeare at Midnight

The midsummer night represents therefore the opening to the infernal world and, at the same time, marks the end of the cycle when its most inferior possibilities are manifested, stirred by some demonic influences that are not under control anymore. The midsummer night, as "the gate of men," illustrates also the changeable, relative, perishable and ephemeral Existence, the madness of cyclical rotation, and the "country of dreams." Eventually, as a crucial point, as a balance between old and new, the birth of a new Cosmos, of a new order is announced, the victory of spirituality, marked by a spiritual wedding and the consecration of the regent of the new cycle. These we can find all in Shakespeare's play, *A Midsummer Night's Dream*.

The Shakespearean night, without any doubt, symbolizes primarily ignorance, the chaos of the dying world.[34] Nonetheless, we can distinguish three levels in the play, corresponding to a triple Hecate: infernal, mundane (psychical) and spiritual.

The plot takes place at "mid-time," the temporal "turning point."[35] This crucial point is marked not only by the solar aspect (summer solstice), but also by the lunar one, the moon being a striking emblem of the play. From the beginning, Shakespeare specifies that the "old moon wanes" and "another moon," "the next new moon," is coming (I.I.3-4, 83), the "new moon" announcing a new cycle, a new Cosmos. In the Zodiac, the moon corresponds to the summer solstice; also, Janus is *Lunus*, having a lunar face. The world

---

and in his hands he was holding the beautiful golden staff, with which he mazes the eyes of those mortals whose eyes he would maze, or wakes again the sleepers. Herding them on with this, he led them along, and they followed, gibbering.... They went along, and passed the Ocean stream, and the White Rock, and passed the gates of Helios the Sun, and the country of dreams" (**Odyssey** XXIV.1-15).

[34] Helena prays (III.II.431): "O weary night, O long and tedious night,/ Abate thy hours! Shine, comforts, from the east,/ That I may back to Athens by daylight," where "the east" means *Oriens*, the rising spiritual Sun. Also Pyramus laments (V.I.168-172): "O grim-look'd night! O night with hue so black!/ O night, which ever art when day is not!/ O night, O night, alack, alack, alack" and, curiously enough, continues praising the wall: "And thou, O wall,/ O sweet, O lovely wall."

[35] Note that Dante's spiritual initiation starts also at "midway," the middle point of terrestrial life (**Inf.** I.1).

The Everlasting Sacred Kernel

of ancestors, as well as the country of dreams, is symbolized by the lunar realm,[36] yet the Moon, as Hecate, governs the infernal entities, the witches and the elves.[37]

The elves that populate the midsummer night and Shakespeare's play represent psychical forces, subtle influences, usually of an inferior order, called "wandering influences" in Daoism and "ghosts wandering here and there" by Shakespeare (III.II.381), favoring the end of time. They are Hecate's companions, Hecate being here the "infernal Moon," goddess of witches. "Now it is the time of night/ That the graves, all gaping wide,/ Every one lets forth his sprite/ In the church-way paths to glide./ And we fairies, that do run/ By the triple Hecate's team/ From the presence of the sun,/ Following darkness like a dream,/ Now are frolic" (V.I.365-372). Only the spiritual dawn of the new cycle (world) is powerful enough to annihilate them:

> And yonder shines Aurora's harbinger,/ At whose approach, ghosts wandering here and there/ Troop home to churchyards. Damned spirits all,/ That in cross-ways and floods have burial,/ Already to their wormy beds are gone,/ For fear lest day should look their shames upon:/ They willfully themselves exil'd from the light,/ And must for aye consort with blackbrow'd night. (III.II.380-387)

The infernal portrait is also stressed by the play-within-the-play, its central element being the nocturnal meeting of the two lovers at Ninus' tomb, followed by the double suicide, the moonlight, the

---

[36] "Fire, light, day-time, the bright fortnight (of the waxing moon), the six months of the northern (winter) solstice, - then departing, men, who know Brahman reach Brahman. Smoke, night-time, and the dark fortnight (of the waning moon), the six months of the southern (summer) solstice, - attaining by these to the lunar light (the sphere of the Moon), the yogins return" (**Bhagavad-Gîtâ** VIII.24-25). Note the perfect accordance with Shakespeare.

[37] We have to keep in mind, it is a "cold, fruitless moon" (I.I.73), those attributes being typical for the dragon and the night of non-manifestation. On the other hand, the moon is an emblem of the Virgin as *Madonna Intelligenza*.

tomb and the suicide contributing to enhance the hellish atmosphere (V.I.136 ff.). At the end of time, beside demonic and erratic entities, lunatics invade the world; the moon has disturbed the human mind.[38] The dying cycle is the realm of lunatics, ignorance and insane judgment. Shakespeare's play repeatedly speaks about blindness (of course intellectual blindness) and lack of reason.

The ending world is upside-down, as illustrated by the carnival itself. Titania describes to Oberon a perfect vision of the end of time, in total accordance with the traditional data, and abounding in symbolical meaning.

> Therefore the winds, piping to us in vain,/ As in revenge have suck'd up from the sea/ Contagious fogs; which, falling in the land,/ Hath every pelting river made so proud/ That they have overborne their continents./ The ox hath therefore stretch'd his yoke in vain,/ The ploughman lost his sweat, and the green corn/ Hath rotted ere his youth attain'd a beard;/ The fold stands empty in the drowned field,/ And crows are fatted with the murrion flock; ... The human mortals want their winter cheer:/ No night is now with hymn or carol blest./ Therefore the moon, the governess of floods,/ Pale in her anger, washes all the air,/ That rheumatic diseases do abound./ And thorough this distemperature we see/ The seasons alter: hoary-headed frosts/ Fall in the fresh lap of the crimson rose; ... the spring, the summer,/ The childing autumn, angry winter, change Their wonted liveries; and the mazed world,/ By their increase, now knows not which is which./ And this same

---

[38] Latin *mensis*, "moon," and *mens*, "mind," are related words; the mind, as the moon, reflects the spiritual (solar) light of the Intellect (Sun). A personage of the play-within-the-play is "the Man i'th' Moon" who actually is outside the moon (i.e., on earth), as Theseus observes (V.I.235-239). Starveling, who plays the Moonshine, says: "I the Man i'th' Moon; this thorn-bush my thorn-bush; and this dog my dog" (V.I.248-9). "Starveling" is a well-known nickname in various fairy tales, usually coupled with "Thirstyling," representing the fundamental elements, earth and water. Regarding the dog, in Hindu tradition, the moon is the celestial Dog, and a lunatic is a person bitten by the Dog (Coom., **What is Civil.**, p. 103).

The Everlasting Sacred Kernel

progeny of evils comes/ From our debate, from our dissension;/ We are their parents and original. (II.I.88-117)

What Shakespeare describes here is very manifest. If at the beginning of the Cosmos the primordial dyad, *Purusha* and *Prakriti* for Hindu tradition, are united into a divine, sacred wedding, governed by peace and *coincidentia oppositorum*, at the end of time they are in terrible disagreement, separated in a cosmic divorce. That is what some traditions describe as the increasing separation between Heaven and Earth. Oberon and Titania are the masculine and feminine principles, the primordial couple of the Cosmos regarded as the psycho-corporeal world. They are reflections of *Purusha* and *Prakriti*. Their divorce, illustrating the contradictions and oppositions reaching the climax, produces the hurricane and the flood of the end of time. There is chaos; the seasons are mixed up, a parody of the "golden age" when an everlasting summer was reigning, the season of Titania's paradisiacal world (III.I.147-8). The senses are mixed up too, a caricature of the primordial unity: "The eye of man hath not heard, the ear of man hath not seen, man's hand is not able to taste, his tongue to conceive," Bottom says (IV.I.209-211), and then, again: "I see a voice; now will I to the chink,/ To spy and I can hear my Thisbe's face" (V.I.190-1), and later: "Sweet Moon, I thank thee for thy sunny beams" (V.I.261). The sun has changed into the moon, it is the end; the world is upside-down, the bottom replaces the top, the back substitutes for the front. That is why the key personage, having an important role, both in the main play and in the play-within-the-play, is called Bottom.[39]

---

[39] We may note the kinship with Rabelais' *Gargantua and Pantagruel* (Penguin Books, 1969). Rabelais' work is very close connected to the symbolism of carnival, a sacred kernel, a "substantial marrow" as Rabelais himself admits, being hidden under the gross and vulgar story. It is worth mentioning that Rabelais glorifies the "bottom"; for example, the garments of the head (mask, hood, neckerchief, etc.) are attributed to the bottom (I.13) illustrating an upside-down world. Another vulgar farce, aiming at the "bottom," is Panurge's statement about his journey to the Hole of Gibraltar and the Pillars of Hercules (II.30). A popular verbal style called in French *coq-à-l'âne*, "from cock to ass," is frequently used, representing verbal nonsense (I.11 or IV.9), as Shakespeare utilizes this mainly in the play-within-the-play. About Rabelais see

Shakespeare at Midnight

Helena confirms explicitly that the world is upside-down: "the story shall be chang'd:/ Apollo flies, and Daphne holds the chase;/ The dove pursues the griffin, the mild hind/ Makes speed to catch the tiger" (II.I.230-233). The "very tragical mirth" of Pyramus and Thisbe (V.I.57), enhances the confusion and disorder.[40] The play-within-the-play itself is upside-down, "for in all the play/ There is not one word apt, one player fitted" (V.I.65); the actors are "Hard-handed men that work in Athens here,/ Which never labour'd in their minds till now" (V.I.72-3).[41]

The six craftsmen are themselves a product of the chaos, of the "anti-cosmos." Their names, crafts, and roles, which are all reflections of cosmic and spiritual rites, appear in a terrible confusion. They should be the essential bricks, the "elementary principles" of the Cosmos; instead, they are materialistic substitutes.[42] The "head" of this bunch of blockheads is the "bottom," of course, Bottom being the "shallowest thick-skin of that barren sort" (III.II.13). Bottom, as his name tells us, is the emblem of the dying cycle; he is the most inferior one, the most ignorant. Full of arrogance and self-conceit, characteristics of the end of time, he pretends to be wise

---

Mikhail Bakhtin, **Rabelais and His World**, Indiana Univ. Press, 1984, pp. 368 ff. and pp. 422-6. Bakhtin's in-passing remark, "The analysis we have applied to Rabelais would also help us to discover the essential carnival element in the organization of Shakespeare's drama" (p. 275), became a challenge for Knowles and others; see Ronald Knowles (Edited by), **Shakespeare and Carnival**, St. Martin's Press, 1998.

[40] We find again a mockery of *coincidentia oppositorum*: the play is "Merry and tragical? Tedious and brief?/ That is hot ice" (V.I.58-9).

[41] The play-within-the-play is a "feast of fools." Note that Ninus, the legendary "Lord of the World," whose name comes from Sumerian *Nanna*, "the Lord of Heaven," is called Ninny, "fool" (III.I.92-3).

[42] A few words about the Lion's role: The lion is a royal symbol, but also can be the emblem of the "Lord of the World," containing both powers, sacerdotal and temporal. At midsummer night those become just parodies. "This lion is a very fox for his valour ... and a goose for his discretion" (V.I.224-5). The temporal power has changed into a fox's slyness and weakness, and the sacerdotal power into a goose's stupidity. We can assume that the fox will eat the goose, as the temporal swallows the spiritual at the end of time. Note also the Wall's role as "cutting," parting the two lovers and providing a "fissure" ("a crannied hole," V.I.157). In Dumas' *Le Comte de Monte-Cristo* there is a chapter called "Pyrame and Thisbe" (chap. LII) in which the wall plays the same function.

and all-knowledgeable, he volunteers to play all the roles (I.II.47, 65) and even to enact Hercules.[43]

The end of time is also announced by Oberon: "And that same dew (the dew is a well-known symbol for divine influence), which sometime on the buds/ Was wont to swell like round and orient pearls,/ Stood now within the pretty flowerets' eyes/ Like tears, that did their own disgrace bewail" (IV.I.52-55). And something else; the two girls, Helena and Hermia, entangled in the amorous plot, should represent *coincidentia oppositorum*, "seeming parted,/ But yet an union in partition,/ Two lovely berries moulded on one stem;/ So, with two seeming bodies, but one heart;/ Two of the first, like coats in heraldry,/ Due but to one, and crowned with one crest" (III.II.209-214). The girls should symbolize the duality of the universal manifestation united in the One-and-only supreme Principle ("the one crest"), but at the end of time they are in conflict and completely opposite: Hermia is dark, short, strong and nasty, Helena is white, tall and weak.

To crown the carnival of the solstice night, Shakespeare introduces the "feast of the ass." Bottom – who else? – is invested with an ass-head (III.I.98); more than that, he becomes the "unworthy" husband, he takes Oberon's place. The world is totally upside-down. Bottom (the "infernal" vertex) replaces Oberon (the "supernal" vertex).[44] Titania, blinded by ignorance and hellish darkness, forgets the spiritual Principle, her consort, and worships the coarse, satanic pole: "O how I love thee! How I dote on thee!" (IV.I.44) and "Thou art as wise as thou art beautiful" (III.I.142).[45]

---

[43] Bottom's burlesque declamation as Hercules is fully significant, depicting the "Clashing Rocks," the end of time, the unlocking of solstitial gates, and the Sun's spiritual paternity: "The raging rocks,/ And shivering shocks,/ Shall break the locks/ Of prison-gates;/ And Phibbus' car/ Shall shine from far/ And make and mar/ The foolish fates" (I.II.27- 34).

[44] Oberon's name should be related to the German *ober*, "top," and to the English over, upper.

[45] In Rabelais' work we find a related episode regarding Epistemon's resurrection (II.30); it is a parody, of course, but we meet again the beheading motif. Epistemon was beheaded and Panurge healed him, putting back his head. The revived Epistemon will tell his journey to Hell, where everything looked upside-down, as at sol-

Shakespeare at Midnight

Bottom's ass-head marks a parodied sacrifice, the mockery of the sacred ritual of beheading. In the Hindu tradition, Ganesha, the lord of wisdom, received an elephant-head. The seer Dadhyanc transmitted spiritual knowledge having a horse's head. Indra used a bone of this horse-head to defeat the infernal forces, *Asuras*. Similarly, Samson used a jawbone of a donkey to kill the Philistines and to accomplish his spiritual revival (**Judges** 15:15, 19).[46] Bottom's ass-head is, on the contrary, the mark of ignorance and evil, the climax of the infernal level.

The next level, the mundane order, is, as expected, interfacing with the previous one, yet it is mainly the "country of dreams." The terrestrial existence is a dream, an illusion, or more accurately, a relative reality, dependent on a higher principle. The world has not in itself a reason to be, it is an ephemeral, changeable, mortal reality, a joke, a game, the Principle's sport. The supreme Principle is the Puppeteer and we, humans, are just puppets on strings, strings tied to the "Golden Chain" (III.II.14, 240, 288-9).[47] The puppets-protagonists running in circles describe the mad vortex of the mundane cycles: Helena runs after Demetrius, Demetrius runs after Hermia, Hermia after Lysander, and this one, bewitched, runs after Helena. At the same time, they are suffering amazing changes, living an agitated dream, the sleep as a trance being often present.[48] Also the play-within-the-play insistently is presented as an illusion, it being stressed that the lion is not a real lion and so on. Everything is a dream.

---

stice festivals: the devils were good fellows, the poor men became great lords, an anti-pope writer became pope, the kings and popes were servants. Famous heroes were hard-handed workers, very similar to Bottom and his companions. Rabelais' *Gargantua and Pantagruel* deserves special attention.

[46] In this case, the ass reveals a beneficial face, being connected to the spiritual symbolism of the Hindu horse-head (Coom., **La Doctrine**, p. 119). Related to this, we note Mimir (Odin's *guru*) and Orpheus' oracular heads (Eliade, **Zalmoxis**, p. 34).

[47] We already suggested it at the beginning of our work. About the "Puppet Complex" see Coom., **The Bugbear**, pp. 92 ff. Related to this, let us mention Pinocchio's symbolic story and the episode when he is transformed into an ass.

[48] See, for example, III.II.415-445, and IV.I.39, 81.

The Everlasting Sacred Kernel

About the world as a dream, Shakespeare has a famous predecessor, Philo of Alexandria. Philo emphasizes in his work the mutability of worldly things; he compares life with a dream-state, where all the things related to the body are dreams. The mortal world is not real in itself, it is a dream full of confusion, upside-downs, and nothing is stable and secure. Powerful kingdoms disappeared, powerful men became slaves. The human beings wander about as if in a deep sleep, without being able to arrive at anything, for all things are like shadows or phantoms. The men awake are not different from those asleep. They walk in a sort of giddiness, and create dizziness and confusion. Heavenly things are dressed with brilliant light; earthly things are covered by dense darkness. Heaven is everlasting day, free from all participation in night or any kind of shade. And so is the spiritual man, he is spiritually illuminated and really awake, compared with the profane ones who are asleep and living the illusion of dreams.[49]

It is not difficult to remark Shakespeare's concordance with Philo; the dream and the night, the changes and the confusion, all are there, in the play. The question is where is the light, the illumination? And this question takes us to the third level, the highest.

Here, the spiritual meaning is combined with the cosmological one, focusing on the birth of a new Cosmos. In different traditions, this birth follows a spiritual wedding, when the One, the unity of the supreme Principle is stressed, the new cycle and the new Existence being the fruit of this union. In Shakespeare's play, the symbolic wedding is that of Theseus and Hippolyta, marked by a new moon and backed up by two other weddings, those of Lysander with Hermia and of Demetrius with Helena. The spiritual wedding produces the "reversal of poles," the abrupt, sudden, timeless transformation of profane to sacred, of "iron age" to "golden age," of confusion to *coincidentia oppositorum*, reabsorbing multiplicity into Unity. The ignorance and blindness, the phantoms and dreams are clarified and replaced by wisdom, order, intellectual (heart) vision and spiritual awaking. Oberon, "the highest," has the power to op-

---

[49] **The Works of Philo**, Hendrickson Publishers, 1997, pp. 445-447.

Shakespeare at Midnight

erate this transformation, using the magic herb "Whose liquor hath this virtuous property,/ To take from thence all error with his might,/ And make his eyeballs roll with wonted sight" (III.II.367-9). Oberon says: "I with the Morning's love have oft made sport" (III.II.389), unveiling his relation with spiritual dawn. Oberon operates the divine illumination due to the rising Sun, the *Oriens*, coming through the "eastern gate, all fired-red" and then changed to "yellow gold" (III.II.391-3).

And it is something else. Shakespeare's play talks about a strange character, who actually is invisible, without name, having no active role in the *Dream*. He is "Nobody," the celestial Orphan, the *avatâra*, the divine child coming from the East (India; II.I.22).[50] This "lovely boy" of "an Indian king" is meant to be the regent of the new Cosmos, of the new cycle.[51] He is the spiritual seed and the golden germ of the new world, that is why his mother, the Virgin, is compared by Shakespeare with a ship, an Ark, the "World Egg" floating on the primordial Waters (II.I.123-134). Thus, Shakespeare's play unveils to us a sacred kernel that, beyond demons and dreams, is there, bright and more vivid than ever.

We should end here the commentary upon *A Midsummer Night's Dream*. Our goal was reached. Nonetheless, a last obscure point remains unclear. Shakespeare has obvious links with Western esotericism and traditional sources. But we still don't know which esoterical branch fed his play.

We have though some hints. The first one is Oberon's miraculous herb that is a "milk-white" flower changed by Cupid into a "purple" one (II.I.166-8). This herb is very similar to *moly*, a divine

---

[50] The spiritual doctrines stress that the "elected" one has to be without terrestrial family. The *avatâra* is an "orphan," without family. Melchizedek, "Lord of Peace" and "Lord of the World," was an orphan: "he has no father, mother or ancestry ... he is the Son of God" (**Hebrews** 7:3).

[51] Note that the "Indian king" is the legendary "Priest John," another name for the "Lord of the World." The spiritual kingdom of "Priest John" (who possesses both, sacerdotal and temporal power) was located not only in India, but also in Tibet, Ethiopia or Mongolia. See Robert Silverberg, **The Realm of Prester John**, Doubleday & Co., 1972.

plant with black roots and a milky flower, given by Hermes to Ulysses (**Odyssey** X.275-306). The change of color from white to dark red suggests an alchemical process, white and red being not only connected to the theological virtues, described by Dante, but they are also Hermetic colors symbolizing the *Lesser* and *Greater Mysteries* of Alchemy, *the white stage of the Work* and *the red stage of the Work*; the first stage eventually is transformed into the second one. It is tempting to link Shakespeare to Hermetic tradition. Another hint comes to corroborate this hypothesis: the fact that a character is named Hermia. The plot of the play starts with Hermia's love problem, but that is not enough to draw a conclusion.[52] Nonetheless, it is more than interesting that Hermia is called "Ethiope" (III.II.258), that is, a "dark lady" like Rosaline from *Love's Labour's Lost*. In this case, we think, the "dark lady" comes to enhance Hermia's name. Ethiopia is a country neighboring of Egypt, the homeland of Hermes Trismegistus. The name Ethiopians means literally "burnt faces" (*Aithíôps*), i.e., "black faces." On the other hand, the ancient Egyptians called their country *Kêmi*, "black land," and the Arabic word "Alchemy" is related to it, black being the alchemical *materia prima* (Guénon, **Symboles**, p. 134).[53]

These last speculations suggest again a Hermetic hidden kernel in Shakespeare's play, yet they are only speculations. Fortunately, we have a third hint, a very strong and subtle one. The play presents a triple wedding with three brides, corresponding to the "Three Worlds" or the three levels of the entire Cosmos. But there is a fourth bride, as the Hindu tradition teaches us that beyond the "Three Worlds" there is "A Fourth," the world of non-manifestation, the world of the supreme Principle. The fourth bride is, of course, Titania herself, whose name has the meaning of "huge, very great size." The names of the four brides compose the following acrostic: Helena-Hermia-Hippolyta-Titania. If we separate the initials of these names we obtain H-H-H-T, that is, three times H

---

[52] Hermia's "problem" is, in fact, her revolt against the normal order, announcing the chaos to come.
[53] See also Titus Burckhardt, **Alchemy**, Penguin Books, 1971, p. 16.

and a T, the last one being the sign of something titanic or very great. It is a safe assumption to decipher the acrostic as being a key for Hermes Trismegistus, the "Thrice-great Hermes."

Now the decoding of the *Dream* is complete.

Chapter Six

THE FOUR MUSKETEERS

HERMES TRISMEGISTUS, the master of Hermetic tradition, is a universal god. He combines the traits of the Greek Hermes and Egyptian Thoth. Thoth is the lord of wisdom and sacred writing, the "heart of Re," and the seer. Hermes is the messenger of the gods, the angel,[1] the prophet, wise guide of initiation, whose mark is the planet Mercury. The planet's name comes from the Roman god Mercury, homologous with Hermes, and so comes the French *mercredi*, Latin *Mercurii dies*, for Wednesday. The English Wednesday, on the other hand, derives from Wotan's name, Wotan or Odin being in Norse mythology, as we have already seen, the god of initiation and wisdom, the inventor of sacred writing – the runes. Odin is obviously the equivalent of Hermes-Mercury. Strangely enough, the Hindu god of the planet Mercury is called Budha, meaning "wisdom," the word *budha* being very close to *wotan* or *woden*.[2] In the Assyrian and Babylonian pantheon, the deity of the planet Mercury is Nabu, the god of spiritual learning, wisdom and writing, his tem-

---

[1] Greek *aggelos* means "messenger."
[2] René Guénon, **Formes traditionnelles et cycles cosmiques**, Gallimard, 1980, p. 132. Note that Budha is different from Buddha (Shâkya-Muni), yet the latter took some attributes of the former. Buddha's mother, called Mâyâ, should be compared to Hermes' mother, called Maia.

The Four Musketeers

ple being "The House of Knowledge."[3] It is not hard to see the unanimity of various traditions regarding Hermes.[4]

The Assyrians used to represent Nabu as part of a *tetramorph*, the four deities being associated to the four cardinal points. The *tetramorph* was illustrated using divine emblems: the bull for Marduk, god of Jupiter, the lion for Nergal, god of Mars, the eagle for Ninurta, god of Saturn, and the man for Nabu.[5] The last emblem is not any man, but a winged man, actually an angel, that is, "the messenger of Heaven."

The association with the four cardinal points is interesting. It suggests that besides the two solstitial gates, north and south, we should consider also the equinoctial gates, east and west. The equinoctial gates in some civilizations replaced the solstitial crucial points, having the same symbolism as passage from an old cycle to a new one. In the Christian tradition, the two representations coexisted: as "polar" (solstitial) symbolism, Christmas is celebrated; as "solar" (equinoctial) symbolism, Easter is praised. The four gates or the four cardinal points, considered together, have the same meaning in any tradition: they represent the limits of our world. Therefore, taking possession of the four cardinal directions is a sacred ritual symbolizing what the Islamic esotericism calls the realization of "ampleness" or of integral extension of the being into a specific state of existence (Guénon, **Croix**, p. 25). If the four directions are considered to be the limits of the entire Existence or Cosmos, then the ritual leads to a full spiritual realization.[6]

---

[3] In the Islamic tradition *nabî* (related to Nabu) is an *avatâra*, a savior (Guénon, **Initiation**, p. 261). The ancient Greeks had actually identified Nabu (or Nebo) with Hermes.

[4] There is also a similarity between Hermes Trismegistus and Zalmoxis, god of the Dacians. The ancient authors indicated Zalmoxis' Egyptian background and his close relationship with Pythagoras; it was even suggested that Hermes has a Dacian origin (Geticus, **La Dacia iperborea**, Edizioni all'insegna del Veltro, Parma, 1984, p. 52).

[5] C. W. Ceram, **Gods, Graves, & Scholars**, Alfred A. Knopf, 1968, p. 256 and Rudolf Thiel, **And There Was Light**, Alfred A. Knopf, 1967, p. 24.

[6] For the importance of the cardinal points see, for example, Black Elk's sacred teaching (John G. Neihardt, **Black Elk Speaks**, Univ. of Nebraska Press, 1993, pp.

The Everlasting Sacred Kernel

At the same time, the four crucial points are related to the Zodiac, which is, as we pointed out, the celestial archetype of any sacred edifice. The traditional capital-cities of the ancient kingdoms of India were built oriented with their four sides towards the cardinal directions. Each side had a grandiose gate, marking the solstices and equinoxes.[7] Angkor, the capital of the Khmer Empire, famous during the Buddhist domination, was a square with four gates, corresponding to the four cardinal points.[8] The "Four Signs" of Buddha's biography are also related to the four gates.[9] The Heavenly Jerusalem is described in the *Book of Revelation* as a perfect square, each side having three gates, in total twelve, corresponding to the twelve signs of the Zodiac. We see already a special relationship between 4 and 3, which deserves our attention.

The twelve tribes of Israel were parted into four, three tribes for each cardinal point (**Numbers** 2). In the Hindu society, the castes were located in a ritual order, following the solar journey (*pradakshinâ*), imitating the Zodiac. The four castes were in correspondence with the four cardinal points and the four "ages" of the cycle. The highest caste, the spiritual authority (*Brahmanas*), was situated in the north.[10] Note that there are four castes, but only three were "twice born." The Romans used an Etruscan ritual to found a city. The *orientatio* ("orientation," word derived from *oriens*, "east"), an important step of the sacred ritual, consisted of marking two perpendicular lines, *cardo* (north-south) and *decumanus* (west-east); their extremi-

---

162 ff. and Brown). Note that besides "amplitude" there is also "exaltation," that is why Black Elk considers six "powers," the four cardinal points plus zenith and nadir; only then does the sacred ritual operate upon the entire universal manifestation. The six "powers" constitute the three-dimensional cross of Guénon.

[7] Jeannine Auboyer, **La vie quotidienne dans l'Inde ancienne**, Hachette, 1961, II, chap. I.

[8] Bernard-Philippe Groslier, **Angkor, hommes et pierres**, Arthaud, 1968, ch. VII.

[9] Buddha, says the legend, met an old man at the east gate, then a sick one at the south gate, a corpse at the west gate and, eventually, a hermit at the north gate that symbolizes the "gate of gods."

[10] A. M. Hocart, **Les Castes**, Paul Geuthner, 1938, p. 55.

ties represented the locations of the gates[11]; on the other hand, this partition into quarters coexisted with a division into tribes, that is, etymologically speaking, a "three-way partition."

This apparent hesitation between 4 and 3 is another way to express the supreme One as duality into the World. The third card of the Tarot represents the Empress; the fourth card is the Emperor. Emperor and Empress, they are the two poles of the universal manifestation, their sacred wedding symbolizing the One, the only Principle.[12] The unification of 4 and 3 is a mystery, reflected in Py-

---

[11] Jean-Claude Redouble, **Dictionnaire de la civilization romaine**, Larousse, 1970; see "urbanism."

[12] Regarding the "sacred wedding" we should keep in mind that the same symbol could be applied to the *Lesser Mysteries* and to the *Greater Mysteries*. Therefore, René Guénon expresses the Androgyne as the union of Heaven (*Purusha*) and Earth (*Prakriti*), which concerns the Universal Man as comprising the universal manifestation and not only the formal manifestation (and the Earthly Paradise) (**Croix**, pp. 27, 43-4, 146-7). Even if we cannot really talk about "male" and "female" beyond the formal manifestation, these terms can be used though, because in the informal domain there still is a type of distinction and separation ("sex" comes from Lat. *seco*, "to cut, to separate"; hence the reason of gods and goddesses) The Real Marriage is the union between Shiva and Shakti (and also the union between Dante and Beatrice, after Dante covered the *Greater Mysteries*). The "Three Worlds" correspond to *Corpus*, *Anima* and *Spiritus*, and the union between *Anima* and *Spiritus* is only a virtual union in the Earthly Paradise, the real one is after the *Greater Mysteries*, when the super-individual states (governed by *Spiritus*) are assimilated. Also, regarding the symbolism of the "solar gate," there is some confusion solved by René Guénon in his article *Janua Coeli*. The real "solar gate" is the gate between Cosmos and Non-manifestation, where Cosmos contains all the "Three Worlds," including the super-individual states, which are beyond the Earthly Paradise. The real "solar gate" leads beyond the Sun, which is the Principle, leads to this neutral domain of Brahma, infinite and absolute, and the "gate" that leads to the *Greater Mysteries* is just a "determination," a "projection," or an "image" of the real gate. The problem with the modern thinking is that it is limited by an "earthly" perspective, which means that even if it admits the existence of the *Spiritus* and not only of the *Anima*, it tries to make it something extra-Cosmic, because it understands the Cosmos only as our individual world. In fact, the Cosmos contains also the super-individual states, and so, the most interesting domain is the one beyond the Cosmos, which is the Non-manifestation, and where the real "solar gate" is placed. It is true that the Occidental initiatory ways (Hermeticism, Masonry, etc) have normally as target the Earthly Paradise and the accomplishment of the *Lesser Mysteries*, but for this reason we should not be limited in reading the symbols. We should be aware that always the lesser can symbolize the greater, as the Androgyne symbolizes the neutral Brahma.

thagoras' golden relationship, a secret of operative Masonry: $3^2 + 4^2 = 5^2$. Moreover, the sum of 4 and 3 represents the universal manifestation and its principle, that is, the four cardinal points, plus zenith and nadir, plus the center.[13] Similarly, the product of 4 and 3 provides the Zodiac and its signs, that is, the universal frame.[14]

In the Hindu tradition, for example, there are four "ages" (*yugas*) and castes, but three tendencies (*gunas*), corresponding to the "Three Worlds." The total being has three main levels, three conditions of *Âtmâ*, of the universal Self: corporeal ("waking" state), subtle ("dream" state) and informal (angelic, "profound sleep" state), that is, *Corpus*, *Anima* and *Spiritus*. At the same time, there is "A Fourth" state, *Turîya*, the state of non-manifestation, the dwelling of *Âtmâ* in itself, as *Brahma nirguna* (**Mândûkya Up.** I.7). In *A Midsummer Night's Dream* there are three pairs to be married, but also there is "a fourth" one, the most important one, Oberon and Titania. In Grimm's *Cinderella*, there are four women: a mother with her two daughters and "a fourth," Cinderella; or, in a different arrangement, the mother (symbolizing *Prakriti*, the substantial pole) is the fourth and the three girls represent *Corpus*, *Anima* and *Spiritus* (Cinderella).[15]

Alexandre Dumas' most famous novel, *The Three Musketeers*, presents the same characteristic. The title refers to Athos, Aramis and

---

[13] Number seven has a special role in many traditions. The seven days of the week, the seven colors and the seven sages are well-known applications. On the seventh day, Joshua and his people went seven times round the town of Jericho, whose walls collapsed (**Joshua** 6:2-5). Plutarch tells that at winter solstice the Egyptians lead a cow seven times around the temple of the sun, the circumambulation being a spiritual journey, a quest for Osiris (Plutarch, **De Iside et Osiride**, Univ. of Wales Press, 1970, pp. 201-3).

[14] The twelve months, the twelve Apostles, the twelve Adityas are eminent applications. The "chain of union" of Masonry, mentioned before, usually has twelve knots, following a supposed Egyptian model to trace the triangle illustrating the Pythagorean theorem. The twelve knots mark the three sides ($3 + 4 + 5 = 12$). Plato and Plutarch pay special attention to those numbers (See Plato, **Republic** 546b and Plutarch, **De Iside**, p. 209). Plutarch cryptically calls Plato's diagram "his wedding figure."

[15] We may note also Poe's story, *Four Beasts in One – The Homo-Cameleopard*, where the *tetramorph* is in fact a "tri-morph": a man, a camel and a leopard.

The Four Musketeers

Porthos, the three "inseparables,"[16] yet actually the main hero is d'Artagnan, "the fourth." There is no reason to assume that Dumas was in some way "enlightened," and acquired, through some orthodox, esoteric channels, any spiritual and traditional data, which he transmitted, using his work as a cover. But he was a transmitter, an "unconscious" one, a "providential" instrument; that is a clever way the sacred kernel utilizes to survive.[17] We are aware that a hesitation between three and four musketeers is not a very solid argument. The oscillation between 3 and 4 should be more than, let's say, a result of Dumas' superficiality. It has to have a profound reason, a sacred one, which, independent of the author, should be found in his work.

In the Christian tradition, Jesus Christ himself is placed between 3 and 4. Jesus, as a newborn, is invested with the everlasting and unbroken Tradition by the *three* Magi, the wise men coming from "east" (**Matthew** 2). This Tradition, dressed in a new robe, is transmitted to the twelve disciples, and is expressed by the *four* Evangelists. The three Magi are kings and priests at the same time, as legendary king Priest John was, uniting the sacerdotal and temporal sides. They are the "powers" of the "Three Worlds" and like those Worlds, even if they seem equal, the Magi form a hierarchy, implied by their gifts: gold for kingship (temporal authority), incense for priesthood (spiritual authority) and myrrh for the supreme function ("Lord of the World"). Those gifts (treasures) represent also the consecration of Christ as king, priest and prophet, as "Lord of the World" (Guénon, **Le Roi**, p. 36).

In different traditions, as we have already seen, the symbols for these three cosmic functions were the boar (supreme spiritual master), the wolf (sacerdotal power) and the she-bear (temporal power).

---

[16] Alexandre Dumas, **The Three Musketeers**, Wordsworth Classics, 1993, p. 44. We also used the French edition, Alexandre Dumas, **Les Trois Mousquetaires**, Éd. Baudelaire, 1966. All the page indications, without other specifications, refer to the English edition.

[17] Let us remark, though, the contribution of other writers, as Maquet for *The Three Musketeers*, to Dumas' novels. It was a possible way for Dumas to receive some special influences.

Another triad was also in use: bull, ram and lion, but sometimes the lion represented the supreme function while the bull was the temporal power. The ram is an exclusive symbol of spirituality: it was an emblem of Apollo (as the wolf was), of Hermes, and of Hindu Agni; it became a sign of Christ as lamb, acquiring a central position.[18] On the other hand, the bull and the lion, together with the eagle and the winged man (Nabu, Hermes-Mercury), are the signs of the four cardinal points. Number four marks Ezekiel's vision of *tetramorph*: "Each had four faces, each had four wings ... the faces of all four were turned to the four quarters. ... As to what they looked like, they had human faces, and all four had a lion's face to the right, and all four had a bull's face to the left, and all four had an eagle's face" (**Ezekiel** I:6-11).

In the Christian tradition, the four Evangelists represent the *tetramorph*. St. Matthew's sign is the virgin or a winged man,[19] the lion is St. Mark's symbol, St. Luke has the bull as emblem, and the eagle represents St. John. The same *tetramorph* appears in the *Book of Revelation*, where the four emblems are around the lamb (**Revel.** 4 and 5). Dante, reaching the Earthly Paradise, describes a heavenly pageant with the *tetramorph* (the four Evangelists) guarding a triumphal chariot drawn by Christ as a griffon. At the right side of the chariot, dance the three theological virtues; at the left side, dance the four cardinal virtues (**Purg.** XXIX.91-132).[20]

The eagle, Vishnu, Zeus and St. John's bird, is a symbol for *Spiritus*. St. John corresponds perfectly to *Spiritus*; he is the most beloved of Christ's disciples and he transmitted the most spiritual Gospel. The eagle, a substitute for the solar ray and the thunderbolt, is also a representation of *Buddhi*, the Divine Intellect. The lion is a mark of

---

[18] Jean Chevalier and Alain Gheerbrant, **Dictionary of Symbols**, Penguin Books, 1982, p. 787.

[19] There is no contradiction between Nabu-Hermes and the Virgin. The Virgin symbolizes spiritual Knowledge; she is *Madonna Intelligenza* and *Shekinah* of the *Kabbalah*. The Virgin is also the zodiacal house of the planet Mercury. In the Islamic tradition, Jesus (*Seyid-na 'Isa*) resides in the sky of Mercury (Titus Burckhardt, **Mystical Astrology According to Ibn 'Arabi**, Beshara Publications, 1977, p. 31).

[20] Note the partition 3- 4; Christ is actually placed between 3 and 4.

The Four Musketeers

Anima, as Horapollon explained[21]; the bull, from this specific point of view, symbolizes *Corpus*.[22] That allows us to illustrate the four conditions of *Âtmâ* using the *tetramorph*: the "Three Worlds," or the corporeal, subtle and angelic states, are represented by the bull, lion and eagle; the "Fourth" state, *Turîya*, has the winged man or the virgin as sign, corresponding to Shiva-Shakti.[23]

Dumas' musketeers should match the above symbolism to convince us that their story is more than "waiting room" literature, disregarded by critics, altered by translators, and badly misinterpreted by moviemakers. In fact, there is another obvious sign, which takes the novel directly to the domain of sacred writings. The main characters are "nobodies"; they are, like Ulysses and Dionysus for example, masks or "faces" representing projections into the world of the Puppeteer.[24] The musketeers' tale becomes comparable to the religious "mysteries" of the Middle Ages, to the traditional carnivals or Shakespeare's theatre, the travesty and the mask facilitating a vivid representation of the "Three Worlds" and the pilgrimage on the spiritual path.[25] Athos, Aramis, Porthos are just nicknames, *noms de guerre* (69),[26] or "shepherds' names" (282). Even d'Artagnan is not an exact name; our hero, Charles de Batz-Castelmore, took his

---

[21] F. Portal, **Les symboles des Égyptiens**, Guy Trédaniel, 1979, p. 69.
[22] Wirth gives the following correspondences: angel-water, eagle-air, lion-fire, bull-earth. See Oswald Wirth, **Le symbolisme hermétique**, Dervy-Livres, 1981, p. 33.
[23] We have to keep in mind that the *tetramorph* is also related to the cardinal points and to the doctrine of cosmic cycles. Georgel quotes Guénon's letter in which Wirth's correspondences are linked to the cardinal points as follows: north-water, east-air, south-fire, and west-earth. See Gaston Georgel, **Les Quatre Âges de l'Humanité**, Archè Milan, 1976, p. 17.
[24] Ulysses, we saw, is called *polytropos*, "with many forms," that is, with many masks. In *Orphism*, Dionysus is "many formed" and with "various names and attributes" (Thomas Taylor, **The Hymns of Orpheus**, The Philosophical Research Soc., 1981, pp. 153-5, hymns XXVIII and XXIX).
[25] René Guénon, **Aperçus sur l'initiation**, Éd. Trad., 1992, p. 188. Guénon explains the symbolism of theatre; the mask, Latin *persona*, hides the real personality, the Self.
[26] The page references will hereafter be given parenthetically in the text.

The Everlasting Sacred Kernel

mother's family name when he came to Paris.[27] The main heroine has a "title" instead of a name; she is simply called "Milady."[28]

The three musketeers, the "inseparables," are perfect masks of the supreme triad. Athos symbolizes the spiritual Emperor, the seer, the "Lord of the World"; Aramis is the image of sacerdotal authority; Porthos represents the temporal power.

Athos is "a very extraordinary man" (245). Dumas depicts Athos in much greater depth and essence than all the other musketeers; and everything contributes to install him as the supreme head. He is the image of harmony and balance.[29] Athos, "possessed of great personal and mental attractions" (67),[30] is stronger than Porthos and more knowledgeable than Aramis (244-5).[31] Athos is the perfect noble, of extreme courage and coolness, of unimpeachable probity[32]; but his highest noblesse is not as much for his feudal rank, as for his "inner" qualities; he is the "noble man" (the Self) of Meister

---

[27] Charles Samaran, **D'Artagnan**, Auch, 1967, p. 31.

[28] *The Three Musketeers*, like *A Midsummer Night's Dream* or Rabelais' *Gargantua and Pantagruel*, is more than a novel, it is a living and endless carnival. Isabelle Jan also considers *Le Comte de Monte-Cristo* a Carnival (see Isabelle Jan, **Alexandre Dumas romancier**, Les Éditions ouvrières, 1973, p. 131). Dumas' unmistakable talent for theatre and spectacle has created a propitious décor for the sacred kernel. The fool, who has such an important role in ritual feasts and sacred plays (and Shakespeare's work), appears in Dumas' creation. In *La Dame de Monsoreau*, the fool is a Gascon named Chicot, who, like at *Saturnalia* and carnivals, takes the king's place as "Chicot the first" (III, chap. 27). Chicot is very similar to d'Artagnan in many ways. Saint Paul warns us: "if any one of you thinks of himself as wise, in the ordinary sense of the word, then he must learn to be a fool before he really can be wise" (**1 Corint.** 3:18).

[29] Athos was "admirable formed and proportioned," with "an unalterable equanimity of temper" (244). He could fight in duels "equally well with either hand" (42), or the right and left arms are the sacerdotal and temporal sides. Playing at cards, he "maintained the same impassability, whether he had won or lost" (245).

[30] In French, in the original: "d'une grande beauté de corps et d'esprit." The "beauty of body and mind" is here Platonic beauty.

[31] He is, in fact, omniscient. As a real image of the Procreator, Athos "knew all the noble families in the kingdom, their genealogies, their alliances, their arms, and the origin of their arms." He also is omnipotent: "he had the undisputed right of executing justice on his domain" (256), that is, "the right of high and low justice."

[32] Athos' ancestor, a knight of the Saint-Esprit, and the priceless sword, from the time of Francis I (68), are tokens of his supreme spiritual function.

The Four Musketeers

Eckhart (**Traités**, pp. 141 ff.). Athos is very taciturn, never laughing, like Dante never smiling,[33] and he imposed upon his valet, Grimaud, to use signs (symbols) instead of words (66-7). Silence, an important trial for the Pythagorean School, is a characteristic of the supreme center and is a mark of the non-manifestation. Moreover, Athos "never spoke of women" and "no one knew that he had ever had a mistress" (67), because he represents the One without a second, the only Principle. His nickname suggests the spiritual center, Mount Athos being the *Axis Mundi*, the saint center of Greek-Orthodox Christians. Athos' loneliness, silence, and nickname make him a saint hermit and a spiritual master.[34] The only apparent flaw is his addiction to wine (245).

The Templars were accused of the same flaw; "to drink like a Templar" became proverbial. In fact, wine is a well-known symbol for the beverage of immortality. The Templars, priests and knights at the same time, were reflections of the "Lord of the World" and guardians of the spiritual center. Athos, like the Templars, like Omar Khayyâm and other Sufis, like Little Red Riding Hood's grandmother, drinks the wine as a sacred ritual; and speaks the "language of the birds."[35]

Athos, as One-and-only, unifies the duality, but from a human perspective, he appears as Janus *Bifrons* ("two-headed"), master of the solstitial gates. He is the seer and the dragon, in the same way Saturn is king of the Golden Age and ogre; in this second hypostasis, Athos is a "child-eater" (42). For him, the summer solstice is a bad time, because then, at that crucial point, he suppresses the dual-

---

[33] It is said that Dante, after his spiritual journey, never smiled again.
[34] Dumas aids: "this nature so distinguished, this creature so beautiful, this essence so fine, was seen to turn insensibly towards a material life" (245).
[35] It is most amazing that Dumas connects Athos with the Islamic tradition. Like a veritable Sufi, Athos exclaims: "God is great (*Allâh akbar*), as the Mahometans say, and the future is in His hands" (393). We read in the **Qor'ân** (XXVII.15): "And Solomon was David's heir; and he said, O men, we have been taught the language of the birds (*ullimna mantiqat-tayri*)," and the sound of Athos' voice "was penetrating and, at the same time, melodious" (244).

The Everlasting Sacred Kernel

ity (his wife) to change the cycles.[36] "In his hours of privation Athos was extinguished as respected all his luminous nature, and all his brilliant qualities disappeared as in a dark night" (245). The "luminous nature" is his angelic side (the winter solstice); the "dark night" is his demonic side (the summer solstice). Athos is black and white, but we must insist that, from the celestial point of view, the black means not the night of chaos, but the night of super-luminous non-manifestation, the "Fourth" state, which makes Athos a proper image of *Brahma nirguna*.

Aramis represents the sacerdotal power. He unceasingly wants to become a priest, even if, momentarily, he has to fulfill other functions.[37] The church and the religious life also attract his valet, Bazin. Eventually, Aramis becomes a bishop and general of the Jesuits, that is, the chief of the most powerful Catholic organization.[38]

As for Porthos, he yearns for mundane titles and Mazarin will make him a baron.[39] Porthos represents the temporal power. He is a "king" as Athos is, but what a difference![40] Athos is the master of silence, representing the "King of the World"; Porthos, a "terrestrial" king, "had a character diametrically opposed to that of Athos: he not only spoke a great deal, but in a loud voice. ... He talked for the mere pleasure of speaking, or of hearing himself talk" (67).[41]

---

[36] "June and July were the bad months of Athos" (246). We saw in Shakespeare's play what that means.
[37] That is stressed many times in the novel; see pp. 23, 40, 70 ("musketeer by accident, but a churchman at heart").
[38] Alexandre Dumas, **Le Vicomte de Bragellone**, Robert Laffont, 1991, chs. LXXII and CXXXIV.
[39] Alexandre Dumas, **Vingt ans après**, Éditions Baudelaire, 1965, p. 760 (ch. XCV).
[40] Christ is "King of the Jews" (**John** 19:20), yet compared to mundane kings, what an immense distinction!
[41] The production of universal manifestation could be symbolized as a journey from silence to words. The silence symbolizes the non-manifestation and the supreme Principle, *Brahma nirguna*. The *Logos*, the Word (**John** 1:1), is *Brahma saguna*, God as Creator. His sacrifice, as Dragon, means cutting the Word into pieces and producing the multiplicity, the words. The more words we use the more distant from the Principle we are. Athos is the emblem of the Principle, Porthos of the world as multiplicity. The difference is plainly shown in **Mundaka Up.** (III.I.1): "Two birds that are ever associated and have similar names, cling to the same tree. Of these, the

The Four Musketeers

With d'Artagnan joining them, the three musketeers are, in fact, four.[42] Athos is Nabu-Hermes, the winged man and the Virgin, image of the only Principle. Porthos, strong as a bull, a "giant" (244), with a "Herculean hand" (54), represents *Corpus*, his sign being the Bull.[43] He, the corporeal level, is "pretentious as Narcissus" (24), fond of glittering garments and of exterior, superficial things; his baldric is of gold in the front and simple buff behind (36). Aramis, great womanizer, illustrates the emotions and sentiments, the love, and the complexity of the mind. He is the most complicated of the four musketeers. He is a master of deception and intrigues, an excellent emblem of the mental order. Aramis is *Anima* and his sign is the Lion. D'Artagnan, the youngest, with an aquiline nose, has the Eagle as emblem.[44] He is exceptionally intelligent, "the best head of the four" (80), "a well of wisdom" (172), symbolizing *Spiritus*.[45] Intelligence (*Buddhi*) is the most loved offspring of the Principle, and Athos considers d'Artagnan as his beloved son (314); similarly, St. John was Christ's most beloved disciple and His substitute as the Virgin's son (**John** 19:26).

D'Artagnan is also the neophyte. Only *Spiritus* is capable of finding absolute liberation, of transcending the Cosmos and comprehending the wedding of the Self with the supreme Principle. We have already seen that an "elected" one is usually in terrestrial order the "smallest," while the ignorant is the "greatest." D'Artagnan is

---

one eats the fruit of divergent tastes [Porthos], and the other looks on without eating [Athos]."
[42] *The Three Musketeers* was published in 1844. After 5 years, Henry Murger issued *Scènes de la vie de Bohème*, in which the main characters are four artists. Their nickname, says Murger, was "the four musketeers," the four artists being always together. Using this work, Puccini composed the famous opera *La Bohème*, hymn praising the "unity of four."
[43] Porthos, says Jan, is stubborn and devoted as a bull (Jan 155).
[44] Strange enough, the real d'Artagnan, that is, Charles de Batz-Castelmore, had a blazon with a black double-headed eagle (Samaran 33).
[45] Note that Athos is the one who asserts d'Artagnan's smartness. It is, though, a difference between Athos' wisdom and d'Artagnan's intelligence. The latter is very similar to Ulysses', who is wise, but also shrewd. Athos is a sage, an immutable seer, illustrating the Daoist *wu-wei*, the non-action of the Principle (269); *Spiritus*, that is, d'Artagnan, is active in the World.

The Everlasting Sacred Kernel

repeatedly presented as a mere boy, a child, "too large for a youth, yet too small for an adult" (6); Porthos, *Corpus*, is the giant.[46] Despite the title, the novel is, in fact, "d'Artagnan's story," his sacred fairy tale. And as a fairy tale in the very best tradition, the novel hides all three fundamental symbolic meanings: Cosmos, Year and Man. The essential triplet is mysteriously announced from the very beginning, with the first line: "Le premier lundi du mois d'avril 1625, le bourg de Meung, où naquit l'auteur du *Roman de la Rose*, semblait ..." – Dumas commences his book. Who would care about the first line? Yet after unveiling the symbolism of the four musketeers, we read with better eyes and the first line is already a source of amazement. The first line establishes with precision the spatial-temporal coordinates of the esoteric story, in the same way Dante started his epic.[47] Dumas' sacred time is "on the first Monday of the month of April, 1625," identical with Dante's time.[48] *The Divine Comedy* happens during Easter (March-April), after the spring equinox, when the sun is in the zodiacal sign of Aries (the Ram), and when, according to Christian tradition, the biblical creation has taken place. It is a crucial moment connected to the doctrine of cosmic cycles (Year), with the cosmogony (Cosmos) and with Christ's resurrection (Man); the Ram, as spiritual emblem, governs the moment.

Moreover, two years earlier, in 1623, some mysterious Rosicrucians visited Paris.[49] In 1616, *The Chemical Wedding of Christian Rosenk-*

---

[46] During the spiritual process, d'Artagnan will integrate "the three musketeers," which are his inner levels; the hero is indeed "the four musketeers." Dumas too uses animals to indicate the levels. "The four musketeers" will reach, during initiation, "no man's land," the "fourth" world, where "the bird could not pass over one's head" (Sky), "a fish jump from the water" (Hell), "a rabbit run from her burrow" (Earth) (389). Water, earth and sky are the realms of triple Hecate, as *Orphism* says: "Hecate, lovely dame, of earthly, wat'ry, and celestial frame" (Taylor 113).

[47] "Nel mezzo del cammin di nostra vita,/ Mi ritrovai per una selva oscura." ("Midway this way of life we're bound upon,/ I woke to find myself in a dark wood," **Inf.** I.1).

[48] Guénon specifies that Dante's recital begins Monday (See René Guénon, **L'ésoterisme de Dante**, Gallimard, 1981, p. 39).

[49] Frances Yates, **Giordano Bruno and The Hermetic Tradition**, The Univ. of Chicago Press, 1991, p. 446. In 1622, some manifestos of the "Brotherhood of

The Four Musketeers

reutz (Rosy-Cross) was published in Strasbourg, an initiatory ritual and a spiritual journey occurring during Easter (Bayard 41). Guénon compares the genuine Rosicrucians with the Sufis (Guénon, **Aperçus**, p. 244); also, he associates Dante with Jean de Meung and the Rosicrucians (Guénon, **L'ésoterisme**, p. 33).[50] Dumas' tale begins in "the small town of Meung, the birthplace of the author of the 'Romance of the Rose [Jean de Meung],'" around Easter. It is a very traditional and symbolical start, with a Rosicrucian tint; yet we are almost tempted to ask: we see the rose, but where is the cross?

The cross, the Easter holy cross, is present all the time. The musketeers bear this cross from one end to the other of the novel, since the tunic of the musketeers' uniform is ornate with a cross, which makes them spiritual heirs of the Templars and relatives of Rosy-Cross.[51] D'Artagnan's initiation is an ascending journey to the rank of musketeer. The Gascon has "the heart and soul of a musketeer" (46), i.e., he is an "elected" one and has the special "qualifications" required for a spiritual realization. He becomes an apprentice musketeer (54), then a musketeer (404), a lieutenant (552), and, eventually, a captain.[52] D'Artagnan acquires the cross that could be viewed as a sign of his spiritual fulfillment; he is also prized with the "vision" of a flower. It is not a rose, but an equivalent, a red lily

---

Rosy-Cross" where exhibited in Paris; see Jean-Pierre Bayard, **La Symbolique de la Rose-Croix**, Payot, 1976, p. 9.

[50] Dante's *Mystic Rose* (**Parad.** XXX) and Jean de Meung's rose announce the Rosicrucians. "The roses of Flamel, Jean de Meung and Dante belong to the same bush," Eliphas Lévi says (see Eliphas Lévi, **The History of Magic**, Samuel Weiser, 1999, p. 261).

[51] It is more than remarkable that Dumas' four musketeers have their own device, profoundly metaphysical, which consecrates them as a "brotherhood," as a "secret and traditional organization." Their device, "All for one – one for all" (84) describes the "metaphysics of *ekapâda*" and of "One and multiple." It equally suggests, from the initiatory point of view, that Athos, Aramis and Porthos are parts or levels of d'Artagnan.

[52] M. de Tréville is the actual captain and at the end of *Vingt ans après* d'Artagnan will take this position. Dumas cares to tell us that Tréville's real name was Troisvilles (17), that is, "three towns," corresponding to Hindu *Tripura*. D'Artagnan's symbolic ascent to this function is a conquest of the "Three Worlds."

(329).⁵³ The flower is worn by Milady, as expected; it is her "secret," known only by Athos, her consort; d'Artagnan, discovering it, becomes Athos' peer, and the Self (the immortal "soul") attains the Principle.

There is another symbolic journey, within d'Artagnan's ascension to the rank of musketeer, a very esoteric one, which happens actually inside his being. It is a journey "from shoulder to shoulder," each stage representing a spiritual achievement and a gradually comprehension of an "initiatory secret."⁵⁴ It begins with Athos' shoulder and ends with Milady's shoulder.⁵⁵

Just arrived in Paris, young d'Artagnan visits Tréville and becomes a silent witness of a curious scene, involving the "three inseparables." Tréville's office is a substitute for the spiritual center; the newcomer, d'Artagnan, is invited in, but no words are exchanged between the captain of the musketeers and the neophyte. It is, of course, the admittance (Latin *initium*) to *Mysteries*, the very first step. It is also a cosmic event. In the Hindu tradition, there is a fundamental text, connecting the essential triad of *Sepher Yetsirah*, Cosmos, Year and Man, and describing the cosmogony as a "Big Bang"⁵⁶: "Inside the Year, the Man (*Purusha, Prajâpati*) felt the desire to talk. 'Bhûr!' he exclaimed; and there was the Earth. 'Bhuvar!' he exclaimed; and there was the Atmosphere (the intermediary space). 'Svar!' he exclaimed; and there was the Sky" (**Satapatha Brâhmana** XI.1.6.3-4).⁵⁷ When d'Artagnan entered the office, Tréville, appar-

---

⁵³ "I am the rose of Sharon, the lily of the valleys" (**The Song of Songs** 2:1). The lily, the "fleur-de-lis," is the blazon of France and its shape represents the sign of a three-dimensional cross (the monogram of the Name of Christ).

⁵⁴ The "initiatory secret," explains Guénon, is a secret because the high spiritual knowledge is "unutterable," and has nothing to do with artificial secrets of profane organizations (Guénon, **Aperçus**, p. 89).

⁵⁵ The most sacred part of a buffalo, Black Elk says, is the shoulder (Brown 10).

⁵⁶ The sound has a pre-eminent importance in the Hindu tradition. The primordial sound, *Parasabda*, is considered the cause that produced the universal manifestation. Also, the Tradition was "heard" (*Shruti*).

⁵⁷ The three syllables correspond to the "Three Worlds." "In the beginning was the Word" (**John** I:1).

ently disregarding the young Gascon,[58] called three times: "Athos! Porthos! Aramis!" Tréville mirrors the cosmogony, but Athos is the regent of the Cosmos. D'Artagnan learns this *tremendous mystery*, which is the real goal; Athos' shoulder is just a cover-up secret.[59] The shoulder is also a "gate," and d'Artagnan violently strikes Athos' shoulder, opening the series of "initiatory secrets."[60]

D'Artagnan discovers Porthos' "secret" about his fake baldric, identifying him with *Corpus* (35); he finds out Aramis' amorous "secret," identifying him with *Anima* (167). Moreover, he reaches "the most profound" secret (165), the royal one, which includes another journey, both spiritual and cosmological. D'Artagnan is taken into the queen's confidence and has to recover her twelve diamond studs from England.[61] The purely spiritual part of the expedition comprises a double voyage. The first one, which is the trip to England, symbolizes the typical "purification rites," when the neophyte

---

[58] He only made "a sign with his hand to d'Artagnan," who became a mute spectator (25).

[59] The episode, from an exterior point of view, is non-sense. D'Artagnan, a newcomer and a stranger, is allowed to assist at a very embarrassing and intimate scene, regarding the "three musketeers." D'Artagnan *hears* that the cardinal's guards have beaten the "three musketeers," and Athos' shoulder was badly wounded, but, of course, the real secret is Athos' function. Note that d'Artagnan uses two very traditional ways to learn the "secrets": seeing and listening. We said before, the divine Knowledge is seen (the neophyte becoming a "seer") or heard. That is why Plato says that the non-initiates better "close up the doors of their ears" (**Symposium** 218b). Moreover, the final grade of initiation into *Mysteries of Eleusis* is called "watcher" (*epoptes*, "seer"), and d'Artagnan is the image of such a "watcher" (Plato, **Symposium** 210a).

[60] Athos' shoulder is comparable to Achilles' heel; Dumas actually compares Athos with Achilles (70).

[61] D'Artagnan will never betray those ritual secrets (44, 168), obeying the initiatory law. Of course, *Corpus* and *Anima* (Porthos and Aramis) would like to know the reason they are traveling to England (169), but they have to trust *Spiritus*, who is the leader of the enterprise (171). The secrecy of the *Mysteries of Eleusis*, for example, was extreme; any betrayal was punished with death or banishment (see Carl Kerényi, **Eleusis**, Princeton Univ. Press, 1991, p. 83). And Hermes says: "remember not to have seen what you have seen, and not to have heard what you have heard, and to keep silent," (Homer, **Hymn to Hermes**).

The Everlasting Sacred Kernel

suffers a ritual death.[62] Successively, Porthos, the corporeal level (172), Aramis, the psychical level (173), and Athos, the pure intellectual level (175), are sacrificed, being annihilated by adverse forces along the route Paris-Calais; the neophyte only, surpassing the "Three Worlds," and traversing the Strait of Dover, reaches the Fourth World, the "Angel-land."[63] The second voyage, following the very same itinerary from Paris to Calais, represents the rebirth and reintegration of the different levels of the total being. D'Artagnan, after delivering the diamond studs to the Queen, leaves Paris to look after his three friends lost along the route to England. This journey completes perfectly the first one, and consists of a series of "secrets," which d'Artagnan learns by *listening*[64]: the secret of Porthos' valet (226); Aramis' secret about his temporary abandonment of the priesthood (237); Athos' terrible secret.[65]

D'Artagnan *listens* to Athos' story (255-6), which reveals a metaphysical mystery: Athos is not only *ekâpada*, but also *dwapâda*. Athos is the everlasting regent, he was the regent of the previous cycle and he died resurrecting as the regent of the present cycle. But he is not

---

[62] The initiatory trials are, Guénon says, "purification rites," illustrated usually by symbolical voyages (Guénon, **Aperçus**, p. 175). But the real *katharsis* (purification) is of ignorance (Dionysius the Areopagite, **The Celestial Hierarchy** VII.3).
[63] The journey over the waters to the Farther Shore symbolizes the crossing of the River of Death; the Hither Shore represents mortality, the Farther Shore – immortality (Coom., **Metaphysics**, pp. 324-5). In this context, England, as Farther Shore, could be here "Angel-land" (German *Engel-Land*), and Meyrink used this "pun" in his occult novel about John Dee and the virgin-queen (Gustav Meyrink, **L'ange de la fenêtre d'Occident**, Rocher, 1986).
[64] Listening is very important for Dumas, as it is for the traditional symbolism. D'Artagnan uses a "solar gate," the "eye of the dome," a hole through his floor, to communicate with the lower level. The hole is similar to Shakespeare's "crannied hole" in the wall. Dumas calls this "eye of the dome" ear, "Denys' ear" (162). Through this "ear" d'Artagnan will listen; and so will "the three musketeers" (communicating with the upper level), "with their ears wide open," through a stove pipe, which is a symbol of *Axis Mundi* (373). For an extensive discussion about the "eye of the dome" as solar gate see Coom., **Trad. Art**, pp. 441 ff. Curiously, the "needle's eye" (symbol of the solar gate), is called the "needle's ear" in Romanian. See Guénon, **Symboles**, p. 340.
[65] D'Artagnan finds Athos secluded in the cellar of a hotel, where he has dwelled "all this time" (249).

The Four Musketeers

alone; he has a wife, the world not being able to exist otherwise. His consort is Milady. Milady is an angel at the beginning of the cycle and gradually, with the decay of the world, changes into a demon; she becomes the dragon that has to be beheaded to permit the Cosmos to rejuvenate.[66] Athos, the supreme king, hangs Milady on a tree (256). When d'Artagnan observes, as a silent witness, at the first appearance of the "three musketeers" (after Tréville exclaimed the three names), Athos, seriously wounded, "tomba sur le parquet comme s'il fût mort," that is, fell upon the floor, as if he was dead (28).[67] Athos suffers a ritual death and resurrects with the new cycle, which coincides with the beginning of d'Artagnan's initiation. When Athos encounters Milady again, he tells her: "You thought me dead … as I thought you dead…. Our position is truly strange" (381-2). It is strange only from a mundane point of view. From a celestial perspective, as we explained, the *ekapâda* is mother and father and hero and dragon and son and daughter; all are masks, faces of the only Principle. Athos dies, Milady dies, but they appear again in a new Cosmos, and we'll find them in any world.[68]

Milady unifies the virgin and the dragon. The Moon (*Luna*), Guénon says, is, at the same time, *Janua Coeli* and *Janua Inferni*, Diana and Hecate (Guénon, **L'ésoterisme**, p. 22). Actually, Milady is the triple Hecate, a triple mask of a "lady." As Milady, she is Hecate or Persephone (Hell); as Constance Bonacieux, she is Diana or Artemis (Earth); as Anne of Austria, the Queen of France, she is Luna

---

[66] "L'ange était un démon" (The angel was a demon"), says Athos (256); and: "You (Milady) are a demon let loose upon the earth" (381). At the end of the novel, we find out that Milady was, as a young girl, a nun (541), that is, a spiritual being.

[67] This should be compared to Dante's beautiful verse: "E caddi come corpo morto cade" ("And, as a dead man falling, down I fell"), **Inf.** V.142.

[68] The cellar, where Athos found retreat, is an emblem of a subterranean cave, a spiritual center. Herodotus tells about Dacians' god, Zalmoxis, who, from time to time, hides in an underground chamber, and then reappears in the world. It is an illustration of the cyclical cosmogony and resurrection (Eliade, **Zalmoxis**, p. 23). Zalmoxis' "cellar" is for Strabo (VII.297 f.) a cave on Mount Kogaionon. Hermes was conceived at midnight in a deep cave on Mount Cyllene (Homer, **Hymn to Hermes**). Athos' resurrection from the cellar symbolizes, beside his cyclical rebirth, d'Artagnan's high spiritual realization.

The Everlasting Sacred Kernel

or Selene (Heaven). The Queen, that is the angelic face of Hecate, symbolizes the virgin-empress, the pure Moon, with the same spiritual meaning as Queen Elisabeth I of England had for John Dee or Shakespeare.[69] She is also the Hindu Aditi, the mother of the twelve suns (the Zodiac) described as twelve diamond studs (130). Milady, i.e., the infernal aspect of Hecate, steals two studs (183), marking the abduction of the light (or luminous herd, or water) by the dragon, at the end of time. Constance, between angel and demon, mediates the recovery of the light; she will ask d'Artagnan, on the queen's behalf, to undertake the voyage to England. D'Artagnan's spiritual journey has, thus, also a cosmological significance, providing the reappearance of light and the birth of a new world.[70]

Milady hides the ultimate "secret" that d'Artagnan reveals, unveiling her body and learning the "naked truth," the fleur-de-lis marked on her shoulder. At the same time, d'Artagnan consummates the sacred union with the everlasting Bride (Milady as *Shakti*), taking Athos' place and fulfilling the spiritual realization[71]; d'Artagnan ends by dressed in women's clothes, like Hercules, indicating his supreme achievement, the androgynous state.[72] But the spiritual and cosmological journey is not yet complete; the hero

---

[69] Elisabeth I was mostly praised as chaste as the Moon. See Frances Yates, **Astraea**, Penguin Books, 1975, pp. 59-76. Porthos clearly states "Let who will talk about the king and the cardinal, but the queen is sacred" (24). Tréville too has a special veneration for the queen. The queen symbolizes *Madonna Intelligenza*, the spiritual light of Chivalry.

[70] D'Artagnan, retrieving the studs (*Fiat Lux*), is allowed, as a reward, to kiss the queen's hand, but he can not see her face (194). Only after a complete spiritual realization can someone see the Principle face-to-face.

[71] It is suggested that this is a kind of incest, Athos being d'Artagnan's spiritual father and Milady's consort. In fact, the incest, which appears in diverse traditions (as in well-known Oedipus' story), is non-existent from a spiritual perspective, Milady, for example, being at the same time mother and sister and wife, various masks of the same Principle. In the Hindu tradition, Aditi is Daksha's daughter and Daksha is Aditi's son; and Sûrya, the sun, is Aditi's son and husband.

[72] Inexplicably, this episode is cut from the English edition we used. It appears, though, in the Pyramid Books edition, 1974, pp. 365-6 (unfortunately, this version has other flaws).

The Four Musketeers

(neophyte) must die and resurrect, and the dragon has to be immolated.

Eventually we comprehend that, in a sacred story, all the characters, angelic, terrestrial and demonic, have the main task of helping the hero in his spiritual journey. They are all masks of the Puppeteer, who is the real, absolute, and only "spiritual master." The angelic faces will guide, the terrestrial will mediate and the demonic faces will oppose, in order to provoke and force the neophyte to develop a spiritual effort. At the end, the majority of the characters will disappear, absorbed and united in the totality of the neophyte's being.

Rochefort is the principal demonic character. He generates the first trial, in the town of Meung, and oddly, from now one he will be for d'Artagnan "the Man of Meung" (122), a man without name, a "nobody."[73] He is marked with a scar, as Milady is marked, suggesting an infernal affiliation.[74] Constance is the terrestrial character. She is d'Artagnan's substitute lover until Milady replaces her. Actually, Milady (as dragon) kills (absorbs) Constance (the mundane aspect), provoking d'Artagnan's ritual death: it is the death of the *ego*.[75] At the same time, the dragon itself has to die, simultaneously with the neophyte's resurrection.

Milady is beheaded by the "four musketeers," that is, by the hero. The dragon's sacrifice is not only the neophyte's spiritual rebirth, but also the revival of the world. The old world is dying and the sacrifice will bring a new one. Dumas presents an infernal vision of the agonizing world. It is midnight. The river Lys "rolled along its waters like a river of molten fire" (symbolizing Styx, the River of Death); "A silence as of death weighed down all nature" (543). And Milady is forced to cross the river and the executioner beheads her on the Farther Shore (546).

---

[73] He is the counterpart of Jean de Meung.
[74] Rochefort is "the cursed man, my evil genius," says d'Artagnan, "the devil," says Athos (504). Rochefort and Milady are "two kinds of demons" (516) and Rochefort will salute Milady saying "My compliments to Satan!" (520).
[75] "D'Artagnan ... uttered a cry, and fell beside his mistress, as pale and motionless as herself" (529).

The Everlasting Sacred Kernel

Now the initiation is completed. With Constance and Milady dissolved, the triple Hecate is again One – the only Queen. D'Artagnan finds out Athos' real name (541), but also Rochefort's name (548)[76]; he becomes lieutenant of the musketeers and realizes the *coincidentia oppositorum*, embracing Rochefort (552). The spiritual voyage ends. Interestingly, the journey began at midday and ended at midnight, suggesting in this case the ascension from summer solstice to winter solstice, from the mundane to the spiritual sun.[77] The initiates to the *Greater Mysteries*, specifies Guénon (**Symboles**, p. 243), "contemplated the sun of midnight." Reviewing the scene of Milady's execution, we find the "stormy sky, covered by large copper-coloured clouds, which created a sort of twilight in the middle of the night" (543): the light of the spiritual Sun.[78]

Dumas' novel proves to be a sacred story. We even stressed that it is a fairy tale. There are many beautiful fairy tales, which could confirm our assertion. We chose just one, a most amazing fairy tale, profoundly spiritual and symbolic, *The Story of Harap Alb*. It is a Romanian tale, barely known to the Western reader, but so completely sacred, so faultless, that we have to mention it.[79] "Harap" comes from *Arab* and indicates a Moor, a "dark face"; "Alb" comes from Latin *albus*, "white." *Harap Alb*, the hero of the fairy tale, is then the "White Moor" or the "White Black." The name alone is extremely significant. It refers to midday-midnight, to Athos, with his bright and dark sides, to the spiritual center, which is simultane-

---

[76] "The angel of the Lord replied, 'Why ask my name? It is a mystery.'" (**Judges** 13:19). The Principle is "far above ... any name that can be named, not only in this age but also in the age to come" (**Ephes.** 1:21). D'Artagnan, finding the names, *hears* the supreme revelation.

[77] D'Artagnan meets the "three musketeers" for the duel at noon (42). Milady is beheaded at midnight. Midday and midnight are both crucial points and the two sides of the same "gate," accepting different meanings.

[78] This night is not the infernal night, even if Milady is a demonic creature; it is "the super-luminous darkness" of Dionysius the Areopagite (**The Mystic Theology** I.1).

[79] "The Story of Harap Alb" was translated into English under the name of "The Story of the White Arab" (Folk Tales, pp. 1-60). Some symbolic elements of the tale were discussed in "Études Traditionnelles," 1936-1937, and translated into Italian (Geticus).

The Four Musketeers

ously black and white.[80] Of course, *Harap Alb* is not the real name of the hero; it is a sacred nickname. *Harap Alb*, like d'Artagnan, starts his spiritual journey from home; he gets his father's horse, an old, hidebound jade, as d'Artagnan gets his father's old, yellow steed (6).[81] The king, *Harap Alb*'s father, creates the first trial[82]; dressed in a bearskin, he tries to scare his son, but *Harap Alb* is unbeaten.[83] D'Artagnan's duel with Athos (who is the spiritual father) represents the same trial (45).[84] During the spiritual process, *Harap Alb* brings a miraculous stag's head, ornate with precious stones, like d'Artagnan brought the diamond studs.[85] One of the last trials takes place at midnight, when *Harap Alb* "quests" for the Red Emperor's daughter.[86] Eventually, *Harap Alb* is beheaded (the ritual death, the dissolution of the individuality) and resurrected. D'Artagnan's ritual death is corroborated by Constance's extinction and by Milady's decapitation.[87]

There is no more to say. Milady, who was hanged by Athos and then beheaded, will revive again, that is sure. Some people will think that Milady is a ghost. Or is Milady's beauty different from that of our entire world? "Hell has given you (Milady) new life," specifies Athos (381). Is Milady a ghost from hell or from the "other world"?

---

[80] Hermes is considered the god of dawn (white) and crepuscule (black). Gemini, besides the Virgin, is the zodiacal house of the planet Mercury; usually, the twins are figured one white, the other black.
[81] In fairy tales, the old horse is, in fact, a supernatural animal.
[82] The first trial always unveils if the hero is an "elected" one, having the required "qualifications."
[83] The bearskin has a long history in Romania. It is said that a bearskin was thrown over Zalmoxis at his birth (Porphyry, **Life of Pythagoras**, 14).
[84] It is the only time when d'Artagnan crossed his rapier with Athos'.
[85] *Harap Alb* beheads the stag at midday; and he wears a mask.
[86] Note that cardinal Richelieu was nicknamed by Aramis the "Red Duke" (23). The Red Emperor is described as evil and bloodthirsty; his daughter as a terrible witch and a demon. Nonetheless, *Harap Alb* will marry the Emperor's daughter, which proves the universal role of Milady.
[87] *Qui non bis nascitur, in regnum caelorum non ascendit* ("He who is not twice born will not ascend to the Kingdom of Heaven"), the Islamic tradition says. See **The Mysteries**, Eranos Yearbooks, Princeton Univ. Press, 1978, p. 153.

Chapter Seven

DRACULA'S CASTLE

DUMAS, no doubt, knew how to charm his reader: mysterious atmosphere, a lot of secrets, and apparitions or ghosts wandering through the story, all form the unbeatable recipe, guaranteeing success. It is also a perfect cover for the sacred kernel; so perfect that sometimes the kernel gets lost and its cover is mistaken for the only existent reality. Especially during and after the Renaissance, when the fall from spirituality to materialism started to accelerate, it was more and more difficult to see with the "eye of the heart," or to listen with "Denys' ear." Hermes Trismegistus' teachings, for example, became for the Western world just magic; the same way the *Yi Jing* became a "book of divination" only, the spiritual meaning being forgotten (despite the traditional commentaries attached to it).[1] With the "solidification" of the world, the doctrine of cosmic cycles was reduced to our human cycle only; the three-dimensional helix became a closed circle. This made it possible to consider Milady a ghost. The divine functions projected as masks, and appearing again and again in each cycle (greater or lesser), were misunderstood as "apparitions." While the "Three Worlds" were compressed

---

[1] Virgil's spiritual status was also misinterpreted; Dante's guide was praised as a magician, his work being used for divination (Guénon, **L'ésoterisme**, p. 39). In the same way, when the esoteric significance of the carnivals and feasts was lost, witchcraft and the Sabbats – strange imitations, started to flourish (Guénon, **Symboles**, p. 164).

into one - the lowest (the corporeal level), the everlasting functions were confounded with material bodies; angels or demons, all became very corporeal and "human." The spiritual level's name was abducted and converted into "spiritism" or "spiritualism," the "science of ghosts."[2]

Dumas published *The Three Musketeers* in 1844. In the same year, he published *Le château d'Eppstein*, having a ghost as main character, a benefic one, but still a ghost. The count of Monte-Cristo is a ghost, too. The novel itself contains many symbolic and sacred elements, yet ghostly characters and events mark the "mystery," enveloping the whole story and hiding the essential kernel. "Monte-Cristo" is another sacred nickname; in fact, the count of Monte-Cristo is a "nobody," wearing many masks and names.[3] He is the Principle's reflection, God's arm; he possesses the alchemical elixir of life (a mysterious red liquid), obtained, at the same time with a lot of knowledge, from his spiritual master, Abbot Faria. Despite his spirituality, he is presented as a ghost, coming back, like Milady, into the world from the tomb. Dressed in black, very pale ("deadly pale"), Monte-Cristo is called a "vampire" and compared with Byron's vampires.[4] Dumas also presents Pyramus and Thisbe's story, not as a tragic double death, like in Ovid's *Metamorphoses*

---

[2] It is not the place to discuss the real meaning of "ghosts," which have a long history. Knight took the trouble to study the Greek and Roman beliefs regarding "ghosts" (see Jackson Knight, **Elysion**, Rider & Co., 1970); and Guénon wrote an entire book about this subject (René Guénon, **L'erreur spirite**, Éd. Trad., 1984).

[3] "Monte-Cristo," an island and a mountain, is obviously an emblem of the spiritual center, similar to Mount Athos. The cascade of names in Dumas' novel deserves a special study. Edmond Dantés is not only Monte-Cristo, but also Lord Wilmore and Abbot Busoni and M. de Zaccone and Simbad le Marin. His real name is whispered as a sacred ritual. At the end of the novel, Morcerf erupts: "You called yourself in Paris Count of Monte-Cristo; in Italy, Simbad le Marin (Sinbad the Sailor); in Malta, what do I know? I forgot it. But it is your real name that I ask for, it is your real name that I want to know, from your thousands of names," Alexandre Dumas, **Le Comte de Monte-Cristo**, Éd. Baudelaire, 1966, chap. XCIII.

[4] See chap. XXXV (Dumas, **Le Comte**, I, p. 429), which is called, suggestively, "Apparitions," and p. 517. Dumas insists in presenting him as a vampire; even his horse has an eloquent name, "Vampa" (I, p. 687); in another chapter (XC), significantly called "The Night," Monte-Cristo says: "but I, betrayed, murdered, thrown in a tomb, I arose from that tomb, by God's mercy," (II, p. 393).

The Everlasting Sacred Kernel

(IV.55-169) or in *A Midsummer Night's Dream* (and *Romeo and Juliet*), but as death and resurrection, Valentine being buried and then revived by Monte-Cristo's elixir; nonetheless, Valentine is a ghost, coming from a tomb.

Le Comte de Monte-Cristo was published in 1845-6. *Les mille et un fantômes* was printed in 1849.[5] With this work, Dumas pushes the "ghost" theme to an extreme, and actually describes a vampire in action. Romania is chosen as the homeland of vampirism, a strange choice from Dumas' part because vampire tales are not specific to Romania.[6] Moreover, Transylvania, a province of Romania that is usually considered Dracula's homeland and mistakenly associated with vampirism, is never the central place of the plot.[7] Dumas' location is a very traditional one. It is a sacred region, Moldavia (an eastern region of Romania), where during the Middle Ages and after, a famous fortress and a monastery with the same name, Neamtzu, coexisted.[8] Both, fortress and monastery are symbols of the spiritual center. Dumas also talks about two other monasteries, Sahastru and Hango, emphasizing the spirituality of that area. The Carpathian Mountains constitute the background.

The mountains hide a castle: the Carpathian Castle, residence of Brankovan, a princely Romanian family.[9] The castle is, as we already know, a central emblem, angelic ("holy city") or demonic ("city of Dis"), and represents not only the "heart" of the Cosmos, but also of the total being, the dwelling of the Self. The immortal "soul" (the Self) has a "roommate," the *ego*, the mortal "soul": they are the two birds of *Mundaka Upanishad*. In the Romanian traditional cosmol-

---

[5] The book was translated and adapted into English as a horror story, *Horror at Fontenay*.

[6] Andrew Mackenzie, **Dracula Country**, Arthur Barker Ltd., 1977, p. IX.

[7] In fact, the occultists promoted Transylvania as a "vampire-land" and a "ghost-land." Annie Besant and other theosophists also helped with this image.

[8] Dumas says "Niantzo" (Alexandre Dumas, **Les Mille et un fantômes**, Petite Bibl. Ombres, 2001, p. 171).

[9] Dumas, well informed, mentions the rivalry between Brankovan and Cantimir families. A member of the Cantimir (in fact, Cantemir) family, Dimitri, was of high erudition and a Rosicrucian follower (like Leibniz, with whom he was in written contact).

ogy, the two are brother and non-brother,[10] but it is crucial to understand that any duality is so only from a mundane, limited point of view. The symbol of *yin-yang* explains it perfectly: the white half has a black point inside and the black half a white point, to remind us that, beyond the duality of the manifestation, there is the only Principle, the White-Black.[11] Spiritual realization transforms the *ego*, which is absorbed into the Self, which is absorbed into the only Principle. But until then, duality seems very concrete, not an ephemeral, relative reality, and surely not an "illusion."

Two stepbrothers inhabit the Carpathian Castle: Grégoriska, the master of the castle (the Self, the "brother"), and Kostaki, the master of the forest (as Dumas stresses), an outlaw, a bandit (the *ego*, the "non-brother"), the forest being the "outside darkness."[12] The Helen of Troy theme is used to depict the spiritual realization, the conquest of the virgin being here converted into a fight of contraries. The virgin is a young Polish woman, a stranger. The Self and the *ego*, both are in love with her, but the supreme Knowledge is only for the *Spiritus*, not for *Anima* or *Corpus*. The "non-brother" (the "devils" of our *psyche*, the individuality) dies, pierced by his brother's sword[13]; and the "brother" marries the virgin, attaining divine wisdom and liberation.[14]

It is a typical sacred story, but the non-initiate Dumas hides (debases) it with a thick profane veil. Kostaki becomes a ghost and a vampire. Grégoriska, instead of functioning as the regent of a new

---

[10] We talked already about a Romanian legend that calls the God "brother" and the Devil "non-brother," God illustrating the Oneness and Devil the multiplicity, the "outside darkness."

[11] The *yin-yang* is an explicit duality (explication) of an implicit unity (complication), and not an irreconcilable Manichaean opposition.

[12] Grégoriska is "God's servant" and Kostaki "Satan's minion" (**Horror at Fontenay**, Sphere Books Ltd., 1975, p. 187). Like Athos, Grégoriska owns the spiritual sword of an ancestor, a Crusader who conquered the saint-center Constantinople (Dumas, **Horror**, p. 179).

[13] In fact, Kostaki kills himself: he throws himself onto Grégoriska's sword. It is a subtle way to say that the *ego* melts into the Self, but Dumas introduced suicide as a moral issue to explain the vampirism.

[14] Though married, the young woman remains a virgin (Dumas, **Horror**, p. 187).

cycle, fights the vampire and dies with him. The spiritual meaning is altered into magic and horror.[15] Note that a year after, in 1850, Dumas published another strange novel, *La femme au collier de velours*, in which Hoffmann, the main character, spends a night of love with a beheaded ghost.[16]

Although Bram Stoker became the celebrated classical writer of vampires, his fame being surpassed only by his hero, count Dracula, Dumas is the one who provided the prototype. Stoker's novel (published in 1897) happens also in Romania and Dracula's castle is also a Carpathian castle.[17] Again, Transylvania is not the mythical area, but Bukovina, a beautiful region, north of Moldavia (Stoker 13, 19). Count Dracula strongly resembles the count of Monte-Cristo: he doesn't eat (Monte-Cristo barely ate), and is dressed in black and very pale (Stoker 25-7).[18]

---

[15] Kostaki, a perfect precursor of Dracula, comes from his tomb and bites the virgin's neck and drinks her blood. And Grégoriska knows that a vampire is killed with a wooden stake, sharp-pointed, hammered through his heart at a crossroad. But for this ghost that is not enough (Dumas, **Horror**, pp. 173-8). The holy sword is the weapon that will definitively kill the vampire (Dumas, **Horror**, p. 185).

[16] Hoffmann's gruesome stories, written thirty years earlier, made him an interesting character not only for Dumas, but also for Barbier and Carré who wrote a comedy about Hoffmann, and then Barbier composed a libretto for Offenbach's opera, *The Tales of Hoffmann*, performed in 1881. E. T. A. Hoffmann (1776-1822), an artist, musician and successful writer, substantially influenced the writers to come, and, implicitly, modern mentality. His attraction for tenebrous and devilish subjects, including vampirism (in 1821 he published a vampire story, *Der Vampyr*), could be more than an expression of his talent for imaginative, emotional and fantastic. However, Dumas, who used Hoffmann's stories about music and violins, was also influenced by this satanic side. In 1823, when Dumas came to Paris, he went to watch Nodier's play, *The Vampire*, and in 1851 he himself wrote a play called *The Vampire* (the vampire is Lord Ruthwen, the same to whom is compared the count of Monte-Cristo).

[17] Bram Stoker, **Dracula**, Signet Classsic, 1965, chap. 1.

[18] Jean Robin associates count Dracula with count Rákóczy, prince of Transylvania, who was considered a "manifestation" of the mysterious count of Saint-Germain. See Jean Robin, **La véritable mission du comte de Saint-Germain**, Guy Trédaniel, 1986, p. 71. Undoubtedly, due to the identification of Saint-Germain with Rákóczy (See Paul Chacornac, **Le comte de Saint-Germain**, Chacornac Fréres, 1947, pp. 18-20), Transylvania became famous for occultists. Helena Blavatsky, the founder of the Theosophical Society, was considered "Saint-Germain of the XIX century" and even identified with Saint-Germain (Chacornac 249, 253).

Dracula's Castle

Stoker, whose novel kept no sacred symbolism at all, tries though to motivate the preference for a Romanian landscape, covering his "occultist" inspiration. "I read," he says, "that every known superstition in the world is gathered into the horseshoe of the Carpathians" (Stoker 12). But even in this case he had a predecessor. "The Transylvanian land is still much attached to the superstitions of the early ages," observes Jules Verne, the famous author of *Around the World in Eighty Days* and of *The Mysterious Island*.[19] Jules Verne wrote those words at the beginning of a very curious novel, published in 1892, which has a title reminding us of Dumas' Romanian vampire story: *Carpathian Castle*. Again, the plot takes place in Romania.

For the Western world, Romania was an exotic country, a kind of "Far East." It was a magic land, ideal for strange tales. Verne, and then Stoker, weren't mistaken much about the "superstitions"; but those "superstitions" became such only when the sacred kernel was completely lost. And for a long time, in that part of the world, tradi-

---

For the theosophists, the count of Saint-Germain was the most brilliant messenger of the Grand White Lodge (Chacornac 254). Annie Besant, who in 1907 became president of the Theosophical Society, wrote a book about Saint-Germain's "incarnations"; besides Rákóczy, prince of Transylvania, she considers John Hunyadi, the governor of Transylvania, also an "incarnation" of Saint-Germain (Chacornac 256, Geticus 64). John Hunyadi, whose father was a Romanian, is a well-known historical figure, a brave Christian knight of Transylvania; under his orders Vlad, the historical Dracula, fought against the Turks. Some occultists called John Hunyadi "the white knight of Wallachia" and suggested that he was an incarnation of Christian Rosenkreutz (Chacornac 256). Interestingly enough, for her "secret doctrine" Helena Blavatsky used information about Asia from the work of a Transylvanian (Hungarian) explorer, Alexander Csoma de Körös (René Guénon, **Le Théosophisme**, Éd. Trad., 1982, p. 97). In the same way, Bram Stoker used another Hungarian source, Arminius Vambery, also a fervent explorer of Asia (Robin 58); the English word "vampire" was even considered (wrongly) Hungarian (Robert Hendrickson, **Word and Phrase Origins**, Checkmark Books, 2000, p. 696). We may add that Stoker was a member of the "Golden Dawn," which had close links with the Theosophical Society (André Nataf, **The Occult**, Chambers, 1991, p. 121, Robin 58); significantly, when Stoker publishes his novel, the grand master of the "Golden Dawn" is the black magician and satanist Aleister Crowley, who will be expelled in 1900, after which A. E. Waite will try to reform the Order.

[19] Verne adds: "Transylvania is one of the most superstitious (countries in Europe)."

tional data remained alive as vestiges of a spiritual past. On that territory, the Dacians built their traditional society, praising Zalmoxis and his doctrine of immortality. Georgel even assumes that Dacia was an important secondary spiritual center (Georgel 262). Until the Renaissance, the Romanians[20] appeared as "nobodies," keeping a curious anonymity, resembling the non-manifestation. And when they surfaced into the historical world, their first king – says the legend – was "The Black Prince," an aspect of *Harap Alb*. The multitude of fairy tales, ballads, carols, legends, symbols and other vestiges of sacred rites have been guarded untouched until modern times. The richness of Romanian "superstitions," as stated by Verne and Stoker, is precisely a sign of the ampleness of this traditional and spiritual past. Jules Verne caught a glimpse of this "lost world" and used some traditional data in his novel. But he was also influenced by Dumas' story about Romania, as Stoker was by Dumas and Verne.[21]

Jules Verne wrote five novels with Romania as background: *Mathias Sandorf*, *Claudius Bombarnac*, *Kéraban le Têtu*, *Le Pilote du Danube* and *Le Château de Carpathes*. The last one, *Carpathian Castle*, is very interesting from our point of view. Dumas' influence is plainly detectable[22]; yet Jules Verne prefers, instead of ghosts and vampires, to use the other option of the profane world – science fiction,

---

[20] The Romanians, says Stoker, "are the descendants of the Dacians" (Stoker 12).
[21] Even the name "Dracula" has a sacred history. It comes from Romanian *drac*, meaning devil; but the Romanian devil (*drac*) reminds us etymologically that what we now call devil is actually the Dragon (*drac* derives from Latin *draco*, dragon). The Dacians' banner represented a *draco* with a wolf's head. Romula, the mother of the Roman emperor Galerius, was a Dacian priestess whose consort, says the legend, was a dragon, a "Dracula" (Sextus Aurelius Victor, **Épitome**, Panckoucke Éd., Paris, 1846, p. 389). After many years, in the Middle Ages, a Romanian prince became a Knight of the Order of the Dragon, and got the name *Dracul*. His son, Vlad the Impaler, was identified with Stoker's Dracula (Mackenzie 27). There are many "fantasies," more or less innocent, about Romanian tradition. Occultism, for example, considers Romania a "land of the Dragon" in an infernal sense, and regards the Order of the Dragon as dwelling in a "vampires' initiation" (Robin 58, 72).
[22] Jules Verne comes to Paris in 1848 and meets Alexandre Dumas who becomes his mentor and substitute father. Mathias Sandorf, confesses Jules Verne, is an image of Monte-Cristo.

also a daughter of materialism. "High-tech" discoveries replace the "occult" phenomena, but both are anti-traditional, burying the sacred kernel.

As in Dumas' case, despite the material envelope of Verne's work, there are signs of spirituality hiding silently inside. Mircea Eliade in 1957 already indicated the strong symbolism in Verne's creation; it was also suggested, erroneously, of course, that Verne wrote "initiatory" novels.[23] However, there are traces of the sacred kernel in Verne's work, and we intend to find them. The first signal could be the name of an important character that is present in two major novels: Captain Nemo. Nemo belongs to the medieval feasts and carnivals and was considered in folklore a saviour and a divine creature (Bakhtin 413 ff.). The name comes from Latin *nemo*, meaning "nobody." Nemo strongly relates to the Hindu doctrine of negation (*neti, neti*) and to Dionysius the Areopagite. He is an expression of the super-rational world of principles; in that world, the biblical expression *Nemo Deum vidit* ("nobody saw God") changes into "Nemo saw God," stressing that only Nobody sees God face-to-face. Jules Verne uses this character as a model for his providential Captain Nemo; even if Verne's Nemo is a master of technology, he is an encouraging sign for our quest.

Carpathian Castle bases its plot also on technology. But beyond this materialistic cover there is a sacred scenario, which, like Nemo,

---

[23] See Simone Vierne, **Jules Verne et le roman initiatique,** Éd. du Sirac, 1973. Vierne finds in Verne's stories a "heroic" initiation. We must keep in mind that Verne wasn't an initiate as Dante was, for example. He didn't think about sacred meanings in his work; those are there as a natural heritage of the past. However, they impressed Eliade who confessed in his *Journal*: "I'm reading Jules Verne's *Journey to the Center of the Earth*, and I'm fascinated by the boldness of the symbols, the precision and richness of the images. The adventure is, properly speaking, an initiation, and, as in every adventure of this sort, one can find the wanderings through the labyrinth, the descent to the underworld, the crossing of the waters, trial by fire, meetings with monsters, trial by absolute solitude and by darkness, and finally the triumphant ascension, which is nothing other than the apotheosis of the initiate. How right these images of the underworlds are – the other worlds – how admirably precise and coherent, too, the mythology, which is hardly camouflaged by Verne's scientific jargon" (Mircea Eliade, **No Souvenirs,** Harper & Row, 1977, pp. 2, 48-9); but we know how Eliade deviated from the traditional way.

comes from a spiritual heritage. The novel is a strange story, very different, if not unique, from anything Verne's wrote: a love story. The high-tech part is unimpressive and the plot seems barely motivated. In fact, Jules Verne tries to recreate Dumas' vampire story, combining it with Dumas's tale about Hoffmann, and adapting it to his science fiction style.[24]

Jules Verne chooses Romania as a background for his novel. It seems this time that Transylvania is the place of the plot, but Verne imperceptibly moves south towards Wallachia, like Stoker did later, shifting to Bukovina. In fact, the region selected as décor for the Carpathian Castle is the oldest sacred place to Romanians, called in medieval documents *terra Harszoc*, "the Hatszeg-land."[25] Here, the Dacians, and then the Romans built their capital-city, *Sarmizegetusa*; here, the Dacians raised their amazing temples. The oldest Romanian churches of early medieval times and those strange fortresses with a central tower are to be found in the Hatszeg-land. Verne describes this land as "the ancient land of the Dacians" and "the wildest part of Transylvania."[26] He repeatedly affirms that Werst, the village where the action takes place, is one of the most backward villages in the region (18), meaning that here the ancient traditions had been guarded alive better than in other places; it is also a natural thoroughfare between Transylvania and Wallachia (31), i.e., a passage (gate) between two worlds.

The beginning of the novel is almost a sequel to Dumas' vampire tale. Jules Verne introduces his first character, an old shepherd, Frik, as "a sorcerer, one who could call up fantastic apparitions.

---

[24] There are other sources that provided information to Jules Verne, including those containing Romanian traditional data. As the science fiction literature itself, Jules Verne owes a lot to fairy tales, initiatory journeys and other sacred writings.

[25] The Hatszeg-land is situated south of Transylvania, connecting it with Wallachia and with the western province, Banat.

[26] Jules Verne, **Carpathian Castle**, Ace Books, 1963, p. 10. The page references will hereafter belong to this English edition. We corroborated the English version with the French edition, and made the proper corrections if necessary. We used Jules Verne, **Le Château des Carpathes**, Presses Pocket, 1992. This French edition has also a rich appendix containing commentaries about the novel and quotations from Verne's sources.

Dracula's Castle

Some people said that the vampires and stryges obeyed him" (12). The first chapters (almost a quarter of the entire novel) are meant to create a "country of dreams," filled with supernatural entities, similar to Shakespeare's play. A telescope – a scientific instrument – bought by Frik from a pedlar,[27] opens the gate of this "other world," suggesting magic and illusion (20). Jules Verne, well-read, describes "that vampires known as stryges, because they shrieked like strygies, quenched their thirst on human blood; that 'staffii' lurked about the ruins. In the depth of the forests, those enchanted forests, lurked the 'balauri,' gigantic dragons, the 'zmei' with vast wings, who carry away the daughters of the blood royal" (27).[28]

The Carpathian Castle is "a fitting refuge for the creatures of this Romanian mythology" and its inhabitants are dragons, fairies, stryges and ghosts (27); "A castle deserted, haunted and mysterious" (26), which "nobody dared visit."[29] "It spread around it an epidemic of fear as an unhealthy marsh gives forth its pestilential emanations" (27). It is the Devil's residence (39).[30] The castle is presented as a "city of Dis," but, at the same time, it is connected with the summer solstice and its "country of dreams."[31] The ghostly atmosphere is proper for the end of time, and Frik, the sorcerer, knows how to read the signs. He laments: "Old castle! … Old castle! … Three years more and you will have perished, for your beech-tree has only

---

[27] "These vendors, says Verne, seem to be a people apart, with something Hoffmanesque in their appearance" (15). It is a transparent allusion regarding one of Verne's sources.
[28] *Balauri* and *zmei* are dragons populating the Romanian fairy tales; the *zmei* are equivalent to Hindu *asuras*. *Staffii* are ghosts guarding ruins and abandoned walls; they represent psychical influences, benefic or malefic. Stryges, in fact *strigoi*, are not exactly vampires, but doomed people who wander after death, dancing together during specific nights; they can turn into animals (Mackenzie 97).
[29] That means only Nobody dares to enter the castle.
[30] Jules Verne uses the name *Chort* for devil, but this one comes from Slavic, not Romanian mythology. As we mentioned, in Romanian the devil is *Dracul*. It would have been more accurate to say that the Carpathian Castle is Dracula's Castle.
[31] Verne specifies the starting time: May 29; the novel ends just before the summer solstice.

three branches left.... There were *four*, but the fourth has fallen during the night."[32]

A ghost will prove to be the key character, Stilla, matching the macabre environment. She died, like Milady, before the story started, but she remains a luminous angel, a singing bird and a star, a good symbol for *Madonna Intelligenza*.[33] Yet she is a devilish illusion and, because of Verne's attraction for mystery, magic and phenomena (specific to the mentality of his century), the story unveils an interesting side of the initiatory process: failure.

As Grégoriska and Kostaki were in love with the Polish virgin, so baron Rodolphe de Gortz, the master of the Carpathian Castle (25), and count Franz de Télek, the master of the Castle of Krajowa (108), were in love with Stilla.[34] Rodolphe represents the dragon and the dark face; Franz is the initiate and the luminous face. They are the two masks of the same and only personality. Like Grégoriska, Franz was ready to marry Stilla (115), which would have represented the spiritual wedding, the union with the Principle. But Stilla, who was a famous opera singer (109), dies on stage: "a blood-vessel has broken in her chest" (118).[35] This unexpected death is a

---

[32] "The beech-tree had lost one of its main branches every year. So every branch that fell meant a year less in the castle's life" (28). The beech-tree is the *Axis Mundi* and also the "Tree of Life" and the "Tree of Knowledge." The English word "beech" (German "Buche") became *book* (German "Buch"). Losing the branches illustrates perfectly the descent of the world to its end. In Siouan mythology, we find something similar: every year the sacred buffalo loses one hair, and every age he loses one leg (Brown 9). The Carpathian Castle, strongly linked with the beech-tree (28), is an image of the Cosmos and of the Center of the World.
[33] Stilla, in fact Italian *Stella* and Romanian *steaua*, means "star."
[34] Note that Gortz (in fact Gorj) and Krajowa belong to Wallachian and not Transylvanian toponymy.
[35] The idea of a singer dying on stage is not new. It was used by Dumas in *La femme au collier de velours*, in which Hoffmann loves "a singing bird" and "an angel," Antonia, whose mother, a professional singer, died on stage (something broke inside her). At the same time, Hoffmann falls in love with a ballerina, Arsène, who will be guillotined, becoming a ghost. A small doctor dressed in black, representing evil, guides Hoffmann. Offenbach had composed an opera in 1877 using Verne's story, *Doctor Ox*, in which a character is called Stella. Offenbach's famous opera, *The Tales of Hoffmann*, has as its main character a *prima donna*, named again Stella. She has many faces, and appears in each act as a different woman. First, she is a mechanical

profanation of the sacred story and announces simulacrum of initiation. It also shows on Verne's part incomprehension of the traditional data used, much alike the ignorance of Dumas when he decided to make a vampire of Kostaki. But it is, despite all these things, a lesson about the spiritual process of initiation. The sacred kernel is so powerful that, even if a profanation takes place, it cannot destroy the hidden wisdom.

Frik notices, through his telescope, smoke coming out of the Carpathian Castle (29). Werst's inhabitants are convinced the fire is Devil's fire (39) and the village's schoolmaster, Magister Hermod, who teaches the kids all the Romanian legends and fairy tales, is sure that supernatural beings (spirits, goblins and lamias), are populating the castle (45). Only Nic Deck, the forester, doubts it. He is a brave young man, Miriota's fiancé.[36] Nic decides to investigate the Carpathian Castle, pushed by curiosity. He represents the profane and materialistic world, the ignorant, and the princes of *The Sleeping Beauty*.

There are two initiatory journeys, two attempts to accomplish a spiritual realization, which could be compared with *The Sleeping Beauty*. The first attempt is of *a prince* (Nic Deck), the second one of *the Prince* (Franz de Télek), yet finally the "prince" (Nic) will marry the girl (Miriota). Miriota symbolizes spiritual Knowledge in the vestiges of the Romanian tradition; she is the divine messenger and would be a perfect emblem of the Virgin. But she plays no role in the novel. Stilla, not Miriota, is the equivalent of Helen of Troy or Beatrice. Yet Stilla is a ghost, a "puppet" like Olympia, an (optical

---

doll, Olympia, a singer, and magic glasses (similar with Verne's telescope) make Hoffmann think she is real. Then, she is a courtesan, Giulietta, who captures Hoffmann's soul or reflection (as in a mirror). Finally, she is Antonia, an innocent singer, whose mother died due to an evil character, Dr. Miracle. The same evil doctor forces Antonia to perform and she dies singing. Note the important role played by devilish influences and magical illusions, both in Dumas and Offenbach's works; they are signs of the end of time.

[36] Miriota is Judge Koltz's daughter. The judge is also Mayor of Werst, observing a very old Romanian medieval social structure. The name Koltz is interesting; the ruin of a real castle with a central tower, located in Hatszeg-land, is called Koltz.

and electrical) illusion.[37] Verne, consistent with his beliefs, dresses the incomprehensible (for him) initiatory goal with technical clothes. Here electricity is the "hidden treasure," the castle's guardian and archangel. From a traditional point of view, Frik is right: it is Devil's castle, not a "holy city." The Technology is the Devil's domain. The wedding of Nic and Miriota at the end of the story, just before the summer solstice, is a mockery of the spiritual wedding.

It is interesting. In *A Midsummer Night's Dream*, the chaos, the confusion and the upside-down world were stressed by mixing the lovers. In the *Carpathian Castle*, the same chaos of the end of time appears due to Verne's involuntary mis-match of names and situations.[38] Verne says Stilla instead of Stella, Miriota instead of Miorița (the Romanian real name), and reverses the names of Rodolphe and Franz.[39] He reverses the lovers too, and culminates by describing the descent to Hell, as an ascent of the Mount of Purgatory towards the Earthly Paradise, which makes the picture of the agonizing world very credible.

We find, otherwise, all the elements of the spiritual journey to the saint center ("holy city"): the "outside darkness," the labyrinth, the "cutting," the punishment for trying to cross the wall, the counter-current ascent along the river to the Source, the inferior psychic-physical components trying to pull back and tempt the neophyte. The story follows a fairy tale model, in which the two elder brothers (*Corpus* and *Anima*) fail the initiatory trials and only *Spiritus*, the child and youngest brother, succeeds. Nic Deck and

---

[37] The spiritual revelation is heard and seen. As a demoniac parody, Stilla's phantom combines her voice and her image.
[38] Jules Verne, unconsciously, illustrates a traditional rule: when a revolt takes place and a society is replaced by another, more inferior (according to the doctrine of "fall"), the symbols, names, and words, are changed or acquire opposite meanings. At the end of time, when everything is a mockery and a monkey-like parody of the Golden Age, these signs appear very clearly.
[39] Franz de Télek, a Romanian from Wallachia (Krajowa is an important city of Wallachia), carries a German-Hungarian name, specific to Transylvania. Rodolphe de Gortz, a Romanian from the south of Transylvania, bears a Wallachian name (Gortz is a Wallachian county, and Rodolphe is a distortion of the traditional name Radu).

Dracula's Castle

Doctor Patak, his companion, form the "individuality," *Anima* and *Corpus*. Doctor Patak is obviously the corporeal level, the most materialistic part. He ridicules the ancient legends and beliefs about supernatural beings (47), but in spite of his bluster Patak is a coward (49), and he is forced by the others to accompany Nic on his journey to "Dracula's Castle" (54).[40]

The old passage linking the village with the castle is, after so many years, no longer visible; instead, a "labyrinth of woods" obstructs Nic and Patak's journey (57). The "outer darkness" and chaos replaced order ("cosmos") and the luminous way. Verne's woods, similar to Dante's or Little Red Riding Hood's forest, illustrate, very traditionally, the obstacles as temptations, appetites and wanderings.[41] Patak, symbolizing the corporeal and inertial elements of being, is another important obstacle; he tries, over and over, to tempt Nic to return (60-1). Nic is almost a genuine neophyte: he doesn't give in to temptations and doesn't look backwards.[42] But the real temptation – the Devil's, is in front of him. To go through Hell successfully, a spiritual guide is needed, as Dante had Virgil. Nic takes as a guide the river Nyad, an Ariadne's thread, to escape the labyrinth of woods and, climbs upstream, to reach the castle (63).[43] The Carpathian Castle appears described as being similar to the "city of Dis," and the "cutting" is manifested: "a crenellated wall defended by a deep moat, whose only drawbridge was drawn up against a gate surrounded by a gateway of stone" (65-6).[44] Nic, the

---

[40] Doctor Patak says "the Chort's Castle" (47), but we saw that the correct name is "Dracula's Castle."
[41] Elms, beeches, mighty oaks, birches, pines and spruces (58) are part of the initiatory "obstacles." "Enormous masses of trees blown down by the storm" and "enormous trunks" (59) stress the symbolism. Black storks, like Poe's black birds, suggest an infernal atmosphere.
[42] His fiancée here plays Eurydice's role, trying like a Siren to stop him, but Nic forgets the village and Miriota, and, similar to a true initiate, looks only forward.
[43] The symbol is a very spiritual one: going "counter-current" or "upstream" means reaching the divine world, as Hindu tradition says that the heavenly world is counter-current (Coom., **Metaphysics**, p. 324). Here the Nyad is a parody: it is "Dracula's river," leading to the "city of Dis." The ascension is, in fact, a descent.
[44] It is, no doubt, "Dracula's Castle." At midnight sharp, Patak sees a "spectral light" (70), similar to the flames Dante saw (**Inf.** VIII.1-6), projecting monsters,

unworthy initiate (the *ego*), tries to trespass the "cutting" and is put to death.[45]

Franz de Télek should be *Spiritus*. After Nic and Patak's failure, he will resume the sacred journey. The spiritual Love of Dante and of the Grail knights, not Nic's curiosity, moves Franz to enter the castle. Franz easily reaches the "cutting," and his enterprise starts from there. It is a typical descent to Hell. The *avatâra*, the hero of the fairy tales, goes downward into the "other world" (the world of darkness), to liberate the Light (royal daughter, virgin, sun or stars) abducted by the dragon (Hindu *asura*, Romanian *zmeu*), in order to generate a new *Fiat Lux*, cosmic and spiritual. In these kinds of sacred stories, the two nights, infernal chaos and the non-manifestation, coincide; when chaos represents only Hell, the descent is compulsorily followed by ascension. The essence of ancient *Mysteries* is nothing else. The descent to Hell is part of their sacred ritual. Demeter went down to bring back her daughter, Persephone. Hercules rescued Alcestis from Hell, who sacrificed herself for her husband Admetus' immortality. Dionysus descended underground to liberate his mother, Semele. Orpheus visited the realm of Hades to release his wife, Eurydice.

The last two, Dionysus and Orpheus, are very closely related. Both die torn to pieces, like Prajâpati or Osiris, a cosmogonical and spiritual sacrifice. Dionysus plays a major role in *Orphism*, and Orpheus appears connected to the Bacchic mysteries (**The Mysteries** 67).[46] Dionysus and Orpheus, including their *Mysteries* and *Orphism*, come from Thrace (**The Mysteries** 66, 84, West 4), which is not surprising. A doctrine of immortality, equivalent to the Hindu doctrine of liberation (*moksha*), belonged to ancient Thrace. The Thracians, the "greatest nation on earth after the Indian," mourned the newborn, considering life as suffering, and rejoiced over death

---

dragons and vampires (71). "Then a light shot from the central donjon, an intense light, which leapt flashes of penetrating clearness and blinding coruscation" (72); the light is not, alas, the divine Light, but the infernal fire of Dis (**Inf.** VIII.73-75).

[45] Nic is electrocuted (77); the traditional "powers" are replaced with physical energy. It is a simulacrum death, and Nic and Patak will return safe to Werst.

[46] See also M. L. West, **The Orphic Poems**, Clarendon Press, 1998, p. 15.

(Herodotus V.3-4), regarding it as a "liberation" and a gate to immortality. The Dacians (Getae), "the bravest and most law-abiding of all Thracians," says the same Herodotus, "claim to be immortal" (IV.93-4).

Orpheus was regarded as being closely related to Zalmoxis (West 20). They were considered magicians and even connected to theories like "reincarnation" and "return of the dead." But only the loss of the true spiritual meaning could facilitate such an error. Zalmoxis' disappearance underground and his return after three years (Herodotus IV.95) don't make him a ghost and surely he is not a reincarnation.[47] Dumas, Verne and Stoker are in good company: scholars degraded the *Mysteries*, mistaking the spiritual realization and the doctrine of immortality with the "cult of the dead."[48] Franz's descent to Hell to find Stilla is Orpheus' descent to release Eurydice, yet Verne's Stilla is a ghost, an illusion created by a magician, as a central part of a strange cult of the dead.

To consider Orpheus just a magician and his wife, Eurydice, a ghost, would be a serious error.[49] In fact, Eurydice is the abducted Light or the hidden Knowledge, and her return is a *Fiat Lux*, not at all a "return of the dead." Orpheus is an *avatâra* and an initiate. A master of celestial music, he tames birds and animals, as Ramana

---

[47] For the whole discussion and bibliography see Eliade, **Zalmoxis**, chap. 3. Greek rationalism exaggerated the "cult of the dead," forgetting what immortality really means. Herodotus himself seems to have a profane mentality already; he says that the Dacians "*claim* to be immortal." *Orphism*, relating Dionysus and Hermes with the realm of Hades (See Taylor 179, 188, hymns XLV and LVI), increased the confusion. But, an attentive reading reveals that Persephone (in *Orphism* Dionysus' mother) is more than Hell's Queen, she is *Shakti*, the energetic aspect of the Principle, dwelling in the super-luminous night of non-manifestation. Her function is "Life to produce, and all that lives to kill" (Taylor 154, hymn XXVIII), illustrating the Hermetic *solve-coagula* and the "inspiration-expiration" of Brahma.

[48] See, for instance, Walter Otto, **Dionysus**, Indiana Univ. Press, 1965, pp. 115 ff. and Jackson Knight. "In Thrace there was certainly among the Getae (Dacians) a strong cult of the dead centered on the Dionysian god Zalmoxis... These Getae lamented at a birth and rejoiced at a death, firmly believing that their lives would be far happier after death than before" (Knight, **Elysion**, p. 77).

[49] "Orpheus, a famous lyre-player of Thrace ... went down to Hades to bring back his *dead* wife," says Knight (**Elysion**, p. 75), disregarding any spiritual symbolism.

The Everlasting Sacred Kernel

Maharshi, the great sage of our times, did. With his music, Orpheus saved the Argonauts from the Sirens' temptations (West 4), proving to be a spiritual guide. Beheaded, his head continued to sing and became an oracular head, a symbol of divine wisdom. On the other hand, Orpheus is the model for initiatory failure. He goes underground to regain the Light, the *Madonna Intelligenza*, but he surrenders to the Sirens' temptations and looks backward. The initiation fails and Eurydice disappears as an illusion (emblem of the whole ephemeral manifestation itself). Stilla is the same illusion. She symbolizes not the spiritual Light, but a reflection of the primordial Sound as Music, illustrating celestial harmony. A scientific genius, Orfanik, Rodolphe's companion, recorded her last song and, after her death on stage, this recording and an optical projection of her picture, created a phantasmal Stilla, a devilish illusion.[50]

The *Carpathian Castle* mixes the main Orphic elements. Stilla is an angelic singer,[51] a disciple of Orpheus' divine music.[52] Franz is Or-

---

[50] Orfanik uses a system of mirrors (188) to project Stilla's image. The mirror is a very old symbol used in different traditions. Verne follows E. T. A. Hoffmann's example who, in *Klein Zaches genannt Zinnobar* and *Kater Murr*, presents the mirror as a magical and infernal object. In *Kater Murr*, Hoffmann describes an "invisible girl," an illusion of sound and image, a plausible model for Verne's Stilla.

[51] She played on stage the role of Angelica (143).

[52] In Dumas' *La femme au collier de velours* (chap. 3), Hoffmann's musician master says about music: "the art with which *Orpheus, our supreme master*, attracted the animals, moved the stones and raised cities." Stilla's equivalent, Antonia (musician master's daughter), has a name reflecting the two greatest violinmakers: *Antonio* Amati and *Antonio* Stradivarius. The violin is a substitute of Orpheus' magic lyre and Dumas compares it with Ulysses' divine bow (as an initiatory trial). The violin, says the musician master, hides under its humble aspect the most amazing treasure of harmony, allowing access to the beverage of immortality; yet the violin is Satan's invention to tempt and make people lose their soul. The two sides, angelic and demonic, specific to any symbol, are well described by Dumas. Like Ulysses' bow, the violin "kills" the ignorant (the "princes") and saves the "elected" one (the Prince). Antonia is compared to Dante's Beatrice (chap. 4). Her mother died on stage singing Gluck's opera *Alceste*; it is an obvious allusion to Hercules' descent to Hell to bring back Alcestis. Note that Gluck's other opera is called *Orpheus and Eurydice*. Dumas calls the musician master "maître Gottlieb Murr," which was considered another evidence of Hoffmann's influence (in 1820-2, Hoffmann wrote a strange novel, *The Life and Opinions of Kater Murr*); yet a Rosicrucian Gottlieb von Murr truly existed,

pheus as a neophyte descending to Hell. And Orfanik, the magician who took possession of Stilla's voice, has almost Orpheus' name.[53] Among various etymologies, two are interesting here: one connecting the name Orpheus to Greek *orphanos* ("orphan") and the other relating it to Greek *orphna* ("dark, night"). The former projects Orpheus into the company of divine beings, like Melchizedek, who was an orphan too; the latter is not just an image of Orpheus' connection with Hell, but also with the super-luminous blackness. In Verne's story, Rodolphe de Gortz and Franz de Télek are both orphans and with an irresistible passion for music (25, 107). They are "twins," yet appear in the world as hero and dragon.

The dragon tempts the hero, first using Stilla's recorded voice (131) to attract Franz at the castle, then projecting Stilla's image to make him enter the castle (142). Franz doesn't have to force the "cutting": the door opens for him (149). The castle's "geometrical plan was as complicated as those of the labyrinths of Porsenna, of Lemnos, or of Crete" (150) and Verne compares Franz with Theseus "pursuing the daughter of Minos." Without a spiritual guide,[54] the hero wanders in the darkness, lost "in the depth of this maze" (151). The dragon lures Franz into a circular crypt having two opposite doors (153-4), an image of Zalmoxis' underground chamber or, better, a replica of Homer's cave of Nymphs (**Odyssey** XIII.102-112).[55] Forcing the second door of the crypt, Franz passes gate after gate, a cascade of gates,[56] and arrives at the "center,"

---

and he died just ten years before Hoffmann published his *Murr* (See Arthur Edward Waite, **The Brotherhood of The Rosy Cross**, Univ. Books, New York, p. 41).

[53] In the same way, magister Hermod has a name related to Hermes. Note that Orfanik is "one-eyed" (113).

[54] Jules Verne asks: "Would he find Ariadne's thread which had served to lead the Greek hero?"

[55] Zalmoxis' chamber refers to the super-luminous Night and not to infernal chaos. Meister Eckhart describes the same chamber: "the chamber is the silent darkness of the hidden Paternity," it is "the secret treasure chamber of the eternal Paternity where he [the Son, Zalmoxis] has slept eternally, remaining unexpressed. *In principio*" (Eckhart, **Sermons**, I, p. 195).

[56] The movie *The Ninth Gate* (1999), based upon the novel *The Club Dumas*, used the infernal and parodical symbolism of the gates.

meeting the Devil itself, and Stilla. He is still deceived and thinks he has found his fiancée, but soon the truth is uncovered (183-4). Stilla is a ghost, a shadow, and the Devil's "puppet."

Franz's initiation is a monkey-like initiation. At the end, the mirrors, which created Stilla's image, are smashed, the cylinder with her recorded voice destroyed, and the castle itself blows up. Franz becomes insane. This is very interesting. The story actually warns us about the perils of such a trial. Without a divine guide, a spiritual master, the neophyte will be beguiled and misled by the Devil. What he thinks to be a spiritual realization is, in fact, a mockery, a "fall" into the inferior psychical domain, and there are many examples of such cases in different traditions. It is interesting because the Devil, no matter how malicious and cunning it is, always betrays itself. In this case, even if the spirituality is hiding and profanity is triumphing, Jules Verne exposing the victories and achievements of materialism, the story unveils the real meaning: the Devil's realm is an illusion.

Dracula's Castle became a ruin. "For many years the younger generation of the village will still believe that spirits from Another World are haunting the ruins of the Carpathian Castle" (190). The ruins could be dangerous, working as "supports" for infernal forces. On the other hand, they can be "supports" for beneficial influences; for that reason, gothic cathedrals and traditional edifices were built over sacred ruins of ancient sanctuaries. A Romanian legend describes how the great mason Master Manole, accompanied by the Black Prince, looked for such sacred ruins upon which to build a temple.

In the Romanian traditional vestiges, three characters are on top: Miorita, Master Manole and the Black Prince.[57] All three are well known by Verne. Miorita, who in Romanian tradition is a "clairvoyant lamb," becomes Miriota, the "little sheep" (35); the other two are mentioned in relation with the Carpathian Castle. Wondering "what architect could have built it", Jules Verne says: "Nobody knows, and the bold builder is unknown, unless it was the Roma-

---

[57] For a detailed description of these legends see Eliade, **Zalmoxis**, chap. 5 and 8.

nian Manoli, so gloriously sung of in Wallachian legend, who built at Curte d'Argis the celebrated castle of Rodolphe the Black" (24).[58] Rodolphe the Black is a historical reflection of the Black Prince. The traditional ballad doesn't say Rodolphe the Black, but the Black Prince. We have already met the color black several times. Superficially, black is considered to symbolize something malefic, infernal darkness, in comparison to white and the daylight. But would it be possible for a people to base its existence on a malefic hero, as the Black Prince for example?

The Wallachians were called the "black faces" and a Romanian medieval chronicler considers that, because they lived in the south part of Romania, the sun burned their faces. In fact, the ancient Wallachians were "burnt faces" like the Ethiopians, but the sun that blackened them was the spiritual Sun. In medieval times, the Romanian provinces were known as "Black Wallachia" and "Black Moldavia." Also, the first and legendary blazons of these provinces were ornate with Moor heads (Hasdeu 233). Not surprisingly, the traditional founder of Romania is the "Black Prince." Even black, this Prince is not a Dracula, an infernal king, but a supernal one, image of the "Lord of the World."

---

[58] Oddly, Verne's commentator of the French edition has no idea about these legends, being much less informed than Verne himself. He thinks Miriota, Manoli and Rodolphe the Black are Verne's inventions. For the occultists, the Carpathian mountain close to *Curtea de Arges* is "the Mount of Assembly in the recesses of the north" (**Isaiah** 14:13), Lucifer's mountain (Robin 63).

Chapter Eight

BLACK AND WHITE

"I AM BLACK, but lovely," sings the Bride of *The Song of Songs* (I:5). In the Christian tradition, similarly, the Virgin Mary is sometimes worshipped as a Black Virgin and scholars tried to explain this symbolism.[1] Oddly, nobody seemed to notice the important fact that Jesus, sitting in the Black Virgin's lap, is also black. Shakespeare, in *Lover's Labour's Lost*, extremely praises the love for black Rosaline, a spiritual love for which "day would turn to night." This black virgin gives everlasting youth; she is felicity (Sanskrit *ananda*) and the supernal Sun (Act IV, scene III).[2] Guénon warns us against the error of considering black an infernal color only. In ancient times, people were called "black heads" or "black faces," like the Chinese, the Sumerians and the Ethiopians. It is hard to believe that such a designation was used in a deprecating sense (Guénon, **Symboles**, pp. 134-5). On the contrary, the color black is related to the supreme state, the supernal night as a dwelling of the Principle. Black is the color of the super-luminous darkness of Dionysius the Areopagite. It is the color of Krishna who represents the Self (the immortal "soul") and the everlasting non-manifestation, while Arjuna (meaning "white") symbolizes the mortal *ego* and the ephemeral

---

[1] Jean Hani, **La Vierge Noire**, Guy Trédaniel, 1995.
[2] In the Celtic tradition, the "black maiden" is Peredur's cousin and she appears also with golden hair; note that her father is "one-footed" (**Mabinogion** 185-7).

manifestation (Guénon, **Symboles**, p. 308).[3] The Center of the World is both black and white, black in itself (*ab intra*) and white *ab extra*. Hermes reveals to Ulysses the powers of a miraculous plant called *moly*, which is black and white. In Masonry, the "tessellated pavement" consists of alternating black and white squares; superficially, it represents the light and the darkness, the day and the night, like *yin-yang* or *moly*. But profoundly, it signifies the non-manifestation and the manifestation, the invisible (eternal, immortal world) and the visible (temporal, mortal world).[4]

Hermia and Helena, from *A Midsummer Night's Dream*, one short and black (an "Ethiope"), the other tall and pure white (III.II.144), were considered the emblems of midsummer, when the day is the longest and the night the shortest, their conflict being the battle of day and night.[5] It is a very profane interpretation, which surprisingly maintains the old error of taking the symbols *ad litteram*.[6] Hermia and Helena are twins, "two seeming bodies, but one heart and crowned with one crest" (III.II.212-214), a perfect illustration of *yin-yang*, and clearly indicating that black and white come from the same

---

[3] The zodiacal twins and the Greek Dioscuri bear the same meaning. The fairy tale hero, *Harap Alb* (the "White Moor"), is a perfect emblem of this symbolism.

[4] In Iranian Sufism, "all beings have a two-fold face, a face of light and a black face. The luminous face, the face of day, is the only one that, without understanding it, the common run of men perceive. Their black face (is) the one the mystic perceives" (Henry Corbin, **The Man of Light**, Omega Publications, 1994, pp. 112-3). The "black face" corresponds to the "black light" and to the "divine Night," which is the super-luminous Night of *superconsciousness*, in opposition to the dark night of *subconsciousness* (Corbin 7, 111).

[5] David Wiles, **The Carnivalesque in *A Midsummer Night's Dream*** (Knowles 76).

[6] Guénon and Coomaraswamy already explained, years ago, that a physical phenomenon doesn't need to be symbolized. On the other hand, a corporeal thing or phenomenon is apt to symbolize elements of a superior order. That is actually the reason for existence of a symbol: to express things of higher levels. Therefore, the physical sun is a symbol of the supernal (spiritual) Sun and the couple day-night illustrates the manifestation and the non-manifestation, or the Cosmos and the Chaos, and so on.

and only Principle. They are, in the highest perspective, the "Ethiopian Albino" or *Harap Alb* (the "White Moor").[7]

In modern times, Edgar Allan Poe was very interested in the symbolism of black and white. Jules Verne wrote an essay about Poe, appreciating his work and comparing him with Hoffmann.[8] Verne also tried to continue Poe's only novel, *The Narrative of Arthur Gordon Pym of Nantucket*, composing a sequel called *Le Sphinx des glaces*. But for Verne, Poe's creation is about imaginary, strange and fantastic things, nothing more. Another author inspired by Poe's *Pym* was Herman Melville.[9] *Moby Dick*, published in 1851, is about black and white and depicts the famous sacred theme: the hero fighting the dragon. But here the dragon is a real monster, not a dark human character like Kostaki or Rodolphe. There are some striking similarities between *Pym* and *Moby Dick*. In both cases, the sea voyage starts from Nantucket Island and Pym's ship *Grampus* is mentioned in Melville's novel.[10] But the major resemblance is the mystery of black-and-white.

---

[7] In the physical order, Hermia (the Ethiope) is the smallest and Helena the biggest; in the spiritual order, they will appear exactly reversed. In Islam, black is a spiritual color, since saint Kaaba is black. Regarding the epithet "Ethiope" for Hermia, note that in the time of the Crusades (and after) the mysterious king Priest John was located in Ethiopia. The medieval chronicles subjecting the quest of his kingdom describe strange people living in Ethiopia: "sciapods" ("one-footed" persons) and white-haired children – "Ethiopian Albinos" (Silverberg 153). We should note also that Shakespeare in *The Winter's Tale* compares pure white with the "Ethiopian's tooth" (IV.III), which stresses the unity of black and white.

[8] In fact, it is admitted that E. T. A. Hoffmann influenced Poe, and Dostoevsky considers Hoffmann even greater than Poe. We may note that in *Kater Murr*, Hoffmann describes the "invisible girl" as an Ethiope, a gypsy girl with dark skin, but her name is Chiara, which in Italian means "bright, white."

[9] The studies on Poe and his *Pym* are abundant. About Poe's "major influence" on Melville, both considered "Gothic" writers, see Ronald C. Harvey, **The Critical History of Edgar Allan Poe's *The Narrative of Arthur Gordon Pym***, Garland Publishing, 1998, pp. 83, 159 and Sidney Kaplan, **The Narrative of Arthur Gordon Pym of Nantucket**, Hill and Wang, 1966, *Introduction*, p. X.

[10] Herman Melville, **Moby Dick**, Wordsworth Classics, 1993, pp. 6, 11. Nantucket is comparable to Ulysses' Ithaca. The island is a central place in any symbolic sea voyage.

Black and White

At the very beginning of the novel, Ishmael, the young "hero" (child) resembling Pym, enters an inn and is strongly impressed by a large, "besmoked" oil-painting. What "most puzzled and confounded" him "was a long, limber, portentous, black mass of something hovering in the center of the picture" (Melville 8-9). The black "center" could represent, says Melville, "the Black Sea in a midnight gale" or "a Hyperborean winter scene" or "the breaking-up of the ice-bound stream of Time" or "even the great Leviathan himself" ("an exasperated whale").

The "marvelous painting" is an image of the unimaginable inner blackness of the Center of the World. Melville's hints come from a rich, ancient and medieval heritage. He talks in the same tone as Ovid, who was exiled on the shore of the Black Sea, in Dacia, and has described the region as "polar" and being situated under the North Star. A traditional symbolic perspective locates the primordial Center at the North Pole, correlating it with the winter solstice and the "gate of gods."[11] The Hyperborean region, situated up north, was considered primordial land, Paradise.[12] In time, the location descended towards south, some ancient and medieval writings suggesting the Dacians' country and Scythia as substitutes for the Hyperborean primeval land.[13]

---

[11] Melville suggests this crucial gate mentioning its emblems: midnight, winter, and eternity. The breaking-up of the stream of Time happens only in the Center, which is the North Pole as a gate towards immortality. Boethius compared eternity with the center, and time with the circumference of a circle (Boethius, **The Consolation of Philosophy**, Harvard Univ. Press, 1990, p. 363).

[12] In the Hindu tradition, the north is *uttara*, "the highest" (Coom., **Trad. Art**, p. 484). The North Pole combines the immanence (as Center) and the transcendence (as the Highest) of the Principle, which dwells at that Pole. Besides this sacred geography, Tilak tried to prove that the origin of humankind is the terrestrial North Pole. See Lokamanya Bâl Gangâdhar Tilak, **Origine polaire de la tradition védique**, Archè Milan, 1979.

[13] The Dacians' region was considered one of the locations for the Hyperboreans (Geticus 19-21). Strabo says, for example, that the Hyperboreans live north of the Danube and of the Black Sea (**Geography**, XI, 6.2). In early medieval times, the Dacians were called Scythians, which increased the confusion. The ancient authors mention the Scythian Abaris, a Hyperborean and Apollo's priest. Iamblichus tells how Abaris recognized Pythagoras as Hyperborean Apollo, and how the Dacians'

The Everlasting Sacred Kernel

The Black Sea of Melville's painting is another polar allusion, but can also be related to an ancient tradition regarding Apollo the Hyperborean. Diodorus Siculus (**Bibliotheca Historica** II.47) describes the land of Hyperboreans, following Hecataeus, as a Nordic mythical island where Apollo was born; on the island, a spherical temple is dedicated to Apollo. The location of the island was a challenge for many. From a traditional point of view, the location is not important. It is plausible to assume that such an island, symbolizing the Center of the World, has many projections as secondary spiritual centers for different traditional societies. The same thing happened with *Thule* or with the realm of Priest John.[14] The "one thousand feet" of the manifestation have developed from the "one-footed" Principle; in the same way, from the unique island of the North Pole other islands were projected in many directions. In fact, there is only one island, which is not only the Center of the World but also the center of our heart, where the Heavenly Kingdom is. "For as this appalling ocean surrounds the verdant land, so in the soul of man there lies one insular Tahiti, full of peace and joy, but encompassed by all the horrors of the half known life" (Melville 228).[15]

Pausanias (**Itinerary of Greece** III.19.11) describes an island, very similar with Apollo's Hyperborean island, situating it at the Danube's mouth, in Dacians' Black Sea. The island is called *Leuke*, "the White Island" (Greek *leuke* = "white, bright") and represents "the land of immortality" where Achilles continued to live after his death and married Helen of Troy. Pausanias also remarks on a tem-

---

god Zalmoxis, like Abaris, received the Pythagorean knowledge (Iamblichus 72-75, 92). That makes Guénon identify Abaris with Zalmoxis (**Symboles** pp. 192-3).

[14] The realm of king Priest John was located in medieval times in Tibet, India and Ethiopia. The locations are not only symbolical, but they reflect the multiplication of the primordial center into secondary centers. The chronicles about the quest of Priest Johns' kingdom continue Herodotus' heritage and present strange and mythical beings like one-footed or one-eyed people, establishing a good model for the modern writers. Interestingly, Priest John's royal standard is depicted as a white flag bearing a black cross (Silverberg 169), stressing his function of the "Lord of the World."

[15] The island of peace and felicity should be Melchizedek's realm, Salem ("Peace").

Black and White

ple dedicated to Achilles. Ancient authors (Pliny the Elder, Pindar, Lucan, Quintus of Smyrne) tell that white cranes or herons, living on *Leuke* island, look after Achilles' temple, and describe a city in Dacia, on the shore of the Black Sea, called Geranos, "the city of cranes" (Greek *geranos* = "crane").

Leuke is an image of Apollo's Hyperborean island, symbolizing the only Center. The whiteness superimposes the blackness. The White Island in the middle of the Black Sea is a perfect picture, illustrating the manifestation (white) emerging from non-manifestation (black), but also the pure and luminous spiritual center as the "land of immortality," surrounded by the mundane passions and ephemeral agitation.[16] In the Hindu tradition, the present cycle of manifestation is called *Shwêta-varâha-Kalpa*, "the cycle of the white boar," and the polar land, residence of the primordial spiritual center, is named *Vârâhî*, "the boar's land" (Guénon, **Symboles**, p. 178). The boar, we saw, is an emblem of the "Lord of the World." The white color symbolizes spiritual light, purity and heavenly aspiration. The Hindu *sattva*, the *guna* (tendency) corresponding to the celestial World of *Tribhuvana*, is white, like *yang*, while *tamas*, the *guna* corresponding to the terrestrial World, is black, like *yin* (**Bhagavad-Gîtâ** XIV.11-13).

White is the Principle manifested in the Center of the World as *Logos* and One; black is the Principle *ab intra*, hidden in non-manifestation as a barren Dragon without eyes and ears and feet, as Zero (Void and Silence).[17] Yet from a mundane point of view, black is chaos, infernal darkness, ignorance, and white is illumina-

---

[16] A Slavic ballad speaks about a hawk perching on a *white* rock in the middle of the *Black* Sea (bordering Romania at east). The hawk watches a terrible storm coming and covering the sun and the moon, and pushing the Cossacks' boats into the Danube's mouth and towards *Bilarapsiku land* (Hasdeu 239). *Bilarapsiku land* means "The White-Black land." Homer places the White Rock in front of the Sun-door (**Odyssey** XXIV.11).

[17] The White One is the Sun of manifestation, "thousand-eyed," "thousand-rayed" and "thousand-membered," his light being "the progenitive power." For this reason in Navaho mythology the virgin is a "non-sunstruck girl." See Coom., **Trad. Art**, p. 372.

tion, the light of wisdom and of spiritual realization.[18] Therefore, in different traditions the supreme land of immortality and felicity is designated as a white or a solar (luminous) island (Guénon, **Le Roi**, p. 84). Aztlan, for example, the Aztecs' primordial center, means "place of whiteness" or "place of (white) herons" and was described as an island in the middle of the water.[19] The initiation, depicted as a spiritual journey, is often presented as a sea voyage towards an island or a mountain or a divine land, which symbolizes the initiatory goal, while the ocean with its continuously changing waves and its agitation represents the "sea of passions." The greatest Hindu spiritual master, Shankarâchârya, says: "Having crossed the ocean of illusion and having killed the demons of likes and dislikes, the Yogi, now united to peace, finds delight in the Self."[20] Melville, regardless his mentality, doesn't say less when describing the island of joy and peace surrounded by the appalling ocean.[21]

The ocean as "Black Sea," on the other hand, symbolizes the non-manifestation, the Origin and End of all Existence, the superluminous darkness.[22] In the Hindu tradition, the non-manifestation is presented as "the night of Brahmâ" during which the giant Vishnu reposes in the Ocean on the coils of an immense Dragon, the serpent Ananta ("the Infinite"). Vishnu, the Dragon and the

---

[18] "What is night for all beings is the time of awakening for the self-controlled; and the time of awakening for all beings is night for the introspective sage" (**Bhagavad-Gîtâ** II.69).

[19] Mary Miller and Karl Taube, **The Gods and Symbols of Ancient Mexico and the Maya**, Thames and Hudson, 1997, p. 42. Aztlan is a perfect replica of *Leuke* island.

[20] *Atmâ Bodha* translated by Ramana Maharshi (**The Collected Works of Ramana Maharshi**, Venkataraman, Tiruvannamalai, 1979, pp. 191-2).

[21] In the *Bible*, the "sea of passions" is the "sea of evil" and the abode of the Dragon. At the end of time, the Sea (Romanian "He-Otter") and the Dragon (Romanian "She-Otter") will be dissolved; "the first heaven and the first earth had disappeared now, and there was no longer any sea" (**Revel.** 21:2). God, creating the cosmos from chaos, holds the Sea and the Dragon in control; "Am I the Sea, or the Wild Sea Beast, that you should keep me under watch and guard?" (**Job** 7:12).

[22] The immersion into the Ocean (symbolizing *Nirvâna*) is the Buddhist's final goal (Coom., **Trad. Art**, p. 406). See also Coom., **Yaksas**, pp. 107 ff.

Black and White

Ocean are one and the same (Zimmer 37-8).[23] Vishnu asleep is the Dragon containing the whole Cosmos in a synthetic mode. The holy man Mârkandeya wanders inside Vishnu like Jonah in the Leviathan. Escaping through Vishnu's open mouth, Mârkandeya sees the archetype of Melville's mysterious painting: a Black Sea, an enormous shape resembling a mountain and a dreadful darkness (Zimmer 41). Yet the whiteness is present too. The Hindu cosmogony describes the Principle as *Hamsa*, a solar bird (a luminous swan or gander), floating on the primordial Ocean and incubating the "World Egg" (Chevalier 955).[24] The swan, as we have already discussed, is the "Feathered Serpent," emblem of the supreme Principle, uniting the bird and the serpent, Heaven and Earth. The crane, the heron, the gander and the stork belong to the same symbolism, their shape being similar.[25]

Aztlan and *Leuke* are white islands populated with white herons and cranes. The Hyperborean island of Apollo is populated with white swans. In the Hindu tradition, the swan is Brahmâ's vehicle. It is Apollo's vehicle, too. A flock of swans assisted Apollo's birth, rotating seven times around the island and singing a hymn of praise. In the fall, they carry Apollo in a golden chariot to the Hyperborean land, up north, where behind a barrier of ice reigns a perpetual summer; in the spring, the swans bring the solar god back south (Charbonneau-Lassay 245). Apollo follows the Migratory-Bird's

---

[23] "Ananta" means *ad litteram*, like the equivalent kabbalistic *Ein-Sof*, "without end." In the Romanian traditional vestiges, the infinite Ocean is called, in a ballad, "the He-Otter" and the Dragon, dwelling in the Ocean, "the She-Otter." Such a "duality" is needed only for our discursive mind; in fact, the Infinite is One-and-only. The Ocean is the Abyss as reservoir of all the "seeds" of the invisible (non-manifestation) and visible (manifestation) orders. It is the supreme Principle as Source or Well (**Zohar** II.63b), and should not be confused with the infernal abyss, the devilish whirlpool, which is the dark night in opposition to the super-luminous Night.

[24] *Hamsa*, the Migratory-Bird, dwells within the heart and within the sun (**Maitrâyanîa Up.** M). The Swan (Gander) is a symbol of the Self and of the Principle as spiritual Sun. Zeus, changed into a swan and producing the egg with the Dioscuri, illustrates the same cosmogonic pattern. See also **Satapatha Brâhmana** XI.1.6.

[25] Interestingly, in Greek, the stork is called *pelargos*, meaning "the black-white."

itinerary north-south, expressing the evolvement of cosmic cycles and suggesting the initiatory course between the poles.[26]

Mârkandeya listens to the "Song of the Immortal Gander" (Zimmer 47-8): "Many forms do I assume. And when the sun and moon have disappeared, I float and swim with slow movements on the boundless expanse of the waters. I am the Gander. I am the Lord. I bring forth the universe from my essence and I abide in the cycle of time that dissolves it." For Melville, the Principle is not *Hamsa*, swan or gander, but the whale, the Leviathan, a monstrous fish similar to Vishnu's first *avatâra*.[27] Yet the symbolism is the same. Like *Hamsa* floating on the surface of the primordial Ocean, like Vishnu sleeping on Ananta in the black waters, so Melville's

---

[26] The Hindu *Hamsa*, like the Chinese dragon or the Christian Holy Spirit, is an emblem of divine freedom and omnipresence: it flies into the sky, it floats on the waters, it walks on the land, and it dives into the sea. It is the Master of the "Three Worlds." Migrating south and north with the seasons, it is the homeless free wanderer between the upper celestial and the lower terrestrial spheres, symbolizing divine essence (Zimmer 48). It is also a symbol of the Self, and its migratory journey illustrates the ascendant and descendent spiritual realization. A famous legend says that "when the swan becomes aware that death is about to release it from its ties with the earth, the swan sings a beautiful song of liberation, with the light of another life shining before its eyes," this pre-death song symbolizing the joyful death of the saints (Charbonneau-Lassay 250). The swan's death song is identical to the joy of the Dacians and Thracians in the face of death and represents the liberation of the Self. The swans, which are Apollo's birds, Plato says, sing stronger than ever when they die, expecting full of joy to go to their god (**Phaedo** 85a, b); in the same way, for the Dacians "to die" meant "to go to Zalmoxis." Note that Jules Verne's Stilla ended her life singing, being an image of the swan. In the Hindu tradition, linguistic roots imply at the same time "light" and "sound"; the supernal Sun, or the Self, is not only shining but also singing (Coom., **What is Civil.**, pp. 42-3). Therefore, the spiritual realization is not only "seeing" but also "hearing." It means to discern the Real from the unreal, to listen to the Song of *Hamsa*, not hearing the tempting songs of the Sirens. It means to achieve the spiritual power of discrimination (Sanskrit *viveka*) between the truth of Brahma and the illusion of the world, as Shankarâchârya explained in a whole book (Shri Shankarâcârya, **Vivekachûdâmani**, Advaita Ashrama, Calcutta, 1974). *Hamsa*, the Hindu tradition says, is the symbol of *viveka*, because from a mixture of water and milk he is able to drink only the milk, the spiritual white beverage (Coom., **Pour comprendre**, p. 104).

[27] Melville identifies Moby Dick with Vishnu's first manifestation as *matsya-avatâra*, and with the sea-dragon killed by Perseus (Melville 217).

whale represents the supreme Dragon in the middle of the Ocean.[28] The oil-painting at the beginning of the novel suggests the Dragon as a huge black whale, the Principle *ab intra*. But the whole story is about the quest for a *white* whale, white like the immortal *Hamsa*, the Principle *ab extra*. In fact, Melville's dragon is a white-black whale, the "Albino whale," the white color increasing the terror that the whale usually creates (Melville 148, 161).[29]

The quest for the white whale starts at Christmas (Melville 85), at the winter solstice, suggesting the North Pole as a symbolical departure point and reminding us of Dante. Dante's spiritual journey evolves from the North to the South Pole, constituting an admirable archetype. It is an initiation along the "spiritual axis," the initial point being crucial and considered simultaneously the "middle of time" (or the "center" of a cycle) and the "middle of space" (or the "Center of the World" as Jerusalem, the "spiritual pole" situated

---

[28] Guénon compares the whale with Noah's Ark. The Ark symbolizes the "World Egg" containing the seeds of the future manifestation, and Jonah's whale or *matsya-avatâra* of Vishnu plays the same role. Jonah or Noah represent the divine germ, and the period of time during which Jonah is inside the whale symbolizes the non-manifestation between two cosmic cycles and also the interval between the neophyte's death and his rebirth. At the same time, the whale's symbolism contains not only a benefic meaning but also a malefic one. If, from a sacred point of view, the whale's womb represents the way of resurrection and spiritual achievement, from a mundane point of view it represents Hell and Death (Guénon, **Symboles**, pp. 172-176).

[29] Melville presents the white, not the black color, connected with death, ghosts and fear (157-160). Yet the sea-monster, the dreadful dragon as a white whale, has all the characteristics of the Prime Mover (the Principle as *Brahma saguna*). God, says Melville, came into a whale to Jonah (39). Moby Dick is eternal, immortal and ubiquitous (149, 379-380), and its manifestation is the zodiacal route of the sun (164). He is the Light, his spermaceti feeding the lamps and the candles, and whale hunting being a quest for Light (247, 350). The whale's shape is an excellent illustration of the indefinable Principle: "you see no one point precisely; not one distinct feature is revealed; no nose, eyes, ears, or mouth; no face"; "you feel the Deity and the dread powers more forcibly than in beholding any other object in living nature" (286). He is the Sphinx and his beheaded head represents the primordial wisdom, like Ganesha's head or Orpheus' head (256-7). "That head upon which the upper sun now gleams," says Ahab, but the head is the sun. In the Hindu tradition, the beheaded head of the dragon becomes the sun.

The Everlasting Sacred Kernel

symbolical at North Pole).[30] Dante, lost in the dark woods, tries to climb a luminous mountain toward the sun (*Oriens*), but the "short way" to liberation is only for sages. Therefore, he has to follow the "long way," descending first to Hell, instead of climbing straight to Heaven (**Inf.** I.28-93, II.120). The mountain is "the blissful mountain, the cause and first beginning of all joy" (**Inf.** I.77-8), marking the spiritual and paradisiacal center, the Pole. It is the *Axis Mundi* having the divine Sun on top.[31]

The North Pole, specifies Edgar Allan Poe, is represented by a black rock, towering to a prodigious height.[32] This black rock is comparable with Melville's "black mass," as well as with Dante's mountain and with the white rock in the middle of the Black Sea. In the Islamic tradition, Qâf is the "polar mountain" on which perches the solar bird Rukh (Guénon, **Symboles**, p. 118).[33] Qâf is also the name of letter Q (*qâf*), and the Arabic letter *qâf* is the initial of the word *qutb*, "pole," thus being a "hieroglyph of the Pole" symboli-

---

[30] See the diagram in Sayers' translation of *Inferno* (p. 70), and Guénon, **L'ésoterisme**, pp. 64-5.

[31] There seem to be two different symbolisms: a "solar" and a "polar" one. But *Oriens* is not only the common east of the rising sun, it is also the Pole, where dwells the "Midnight Sun." (Corbin 45-6).

[32] See Poe's note at the end of his story, *Ms. Found in a Bottle* (**The Complete Tales and Poems of Edgar Allan Poe**, Barnes & Noble, 1992, p. 136). The black rock marking the North Pole (*Ruper nigra et altissima*), is what Mercator labels it on his map of 1569 (Kaplan XIV).

[33] Rukh is the equivalent of the Hindu Garuda and of the hawk perching on the white rock; it is related to the symbolism of *Hamsa* and other birds. Note that the first "historical" Wallachian blazon represented a raven on a helmet, later the raven being replaced with a hawk. The helmet illustrates the polar mountain and the raven is, as we saw, an emblem of spirituality. Ovid tells that the raven was white at the beginning and then changed into black (Ovid II.539 ff.). Raven is Apollo's bird and the ancient Greeks illustrated the Center of the World as Delphic *omphalos* (an oracular stone) on which perches a holy bird, with Apollo at its side (See Jane Harrison, **Themis**, Merlin Press, 1989, pp. 99-100). Related to this, we should mention the image of the two eagles, one black and one white, feeding on a hare (Aeschylus, **Agamemnon** 104-139).

cally situated above the black Kaaba (Guénon, **Symboles**, pp. 132-3).[34]

Even if Poe ends *Ms. Found in a Bottle* with that odd note about the North Pole, the story depicts a journey towards the terrifying and mysterious abyss of the South Pole, towards "some exciting knowledge – some never-to-be-imparted secret" (135). In *Pym*, the same South Pole is the target of Pym's symbolical sea voyage. Poe follows Dante's example[35] and therefore his novel, *The Narrative of Arthur Gordon Pym of Nantucket*, becomes attractive for its possible symbolism. Dante descends to Hell, along the polar axis of the Earth, and comes out on the other side, ascending to the South Pole. There he faces the Mount of Purgatory (situated on an island in the middle of the Ocean), which is in fact not different from the *bel monte* ("beautiful mountain," **Inf.** II.120) of the North Pole, suggesting the fundamental identity of the solstitial gates.[36] After a long odyssey, Pym will reach the far south around the winter solstice (812) and will be "completely hemmed in by the ice" of Antarctica (813-5). The "bottom" of Dante's Hell is frozen and icy, but arriving at the South Pole, Dante finds a paradisiacal climate, mirroring Apollo's Hyperborean land, and the same one Pym discovers beyond the ice ring. Poe's South Pole is a good replication of the Center and Pym's adventure ingeniously imitates an initiation. Moreover, the Center is black and white.

Poe's *Pym* is a "sea voyage" and it is well known that often spiritual initiation was symbolized by such a journey; Ulysses' odyssey

---

[34] In Hebrew, the corresponding letter, *qoph*, has a shape which reminds us of the Latin letter P (See William Harper, **Hebrew Method and Manual**, Amer. Soc. of Hebrew, Chicago, 1886, p. 26). In Masonry, the cubic stone is shown in old documents crowned by an upstanding axe, which was identified with the Hebrew letter *qoph*, marking the Pole (Guénon, **Symboles**, p. 131). Curiously, the Latin letter P, having the shape of *qoph*, is the initial of the Pole. In the Christian tradition, the *chi-rho* monogram (representing the first two letters of Christ's name) contains a vertical P (Greek letter *rho*), which later, in the imperial figure of the "Globe of the World," indicated the Pole. Maybe it is not a coincidence that Poe's main characters of his novel, Pym, Peters and Parker, all have names starting with the letter P.
[35] Poe knew Dante's work in Italian (Kaplan XIX).
[36] See Sayers' commentary (**Inferno**, pp. 75, 83). See Dante **Purg.** I.23-30.

and the Argonauts' voyage were most famous, but not the only ones. Poe's work was analyzed from many angles, and always labelled as strange and mysterious, and more recently, as a "horror" masterpiece.[37] We already explained that in Poe, Dumas and Verne's times, spirituality became hidden, while magic and witchcraft, demonology and spiritualism took its place. Poe's work has to be located in this kind of environment. Pym's sea voyage has plenty of evil, being mostly a voyage through Hell, and in some respect, it is a voyage within us, where our devils dwell. Nevertheless, it is worth trying to find a sacred symbolism, even if misused.

Pym's initiation starts at a temporal crucial point, the summer solstice (748), and has as its goal the matching spatial crucial point, the South Pole. Pym represents Poe, as Dante himself was the voyager. The name "Pym" could be even the short form for "pilgrim," the spiritual *peregrinus*, as Dante is an abbreviation for Durante (as Boccaccio suggested).[38] Pym's guide is at the beginning his best friend Augustus, as Virgil was for Dante in Hell.[39] Augustus is a guide, but like Virgil in front of the city of Dis, he is incapable of dealing with all the evil forces, and God's help is continuously needed. Augustus' name also suggests a spiritual ascendance (Latin *augustus* = "sacred, highness") and Pym's endeavour to escape from Hell and reach Augustus illustrates *ad augusta per angusta*. However, after the end of the first set of trials, a higher guide is needed and that will be Dirk Peters, a deformed dwarf, symbolizing a cosmic and a psychical force. Augustus will end his role and eventually will disappear. On the other hand, of all the evil people, representing the demons, only one will survive, Richard Parker, who symbolizes the dragon defeated by Pym. Parker and Peters are aspects of Pym himself.

---

[37] *Pym* is Poe's only long piece of prose. About different opinions see Sidney Kaplan's introduction.
[38] Carol Peirce and Alexander Rose also assume that Pym may come from "pilgrim." They relate Pym's first name Arthur to legendary king Arthur and compare Pym's voyage to the Grail's quest. See **Poe's *Pym*: Critical Explorations**, Duke Univ. Press, 1992, pp. 62-3.
[39] We may note that Virgil lived during Roman emperor Augustus' reign.

Black and White

Like the Trojan War, Pym's voyage, we can assume, took ten years, Pym returning to the United States and accepting the publication of his narrative in 1837, ten years after its beginning (724, 733). Similarly to Samson's tale or the Trojan War, there is a repetition of the voyage. At first, Augustus guides Pym in the middle of the night to sail their boat *Ariel*. The name *Ariel* unveils Poe's second great inspiration source, beside Dante: Shakespeare. The airy spirit Ariel from *The Tempest* is famous. Shakespeare's play (the most obvious symbolical one) starts with a sea voyage involving a tempest (provoked by Ariel), a wreck and the fear of death. Prospero's cave and island symbolize the spiritual center, in spite of Ferdinand's opinion that "Hell is empty and all the devils are here" (Act I, scene II). Poe uses all these elements in his *Pym*, where the deformed ("not honour'd with a human shape") Caliban is converted into Dirk Peters.

Pym's first voyage is marked by "a kind of ecstasy" and drunkenness, which illustrates a state of "non-rational," a Bacchic trance typical for some sacred rituals, wine being the "beverage of immortality" (725 ff.). Pym and Augustus are both "beastly drunk" with wine. Even if Augustus is the providential instrument that brings Pym into this one-night voyage, he becomes powerless and the real help and guidance is God. During the whole novel, God will always be mentioned as the supreme guidance and saviour.[40] The end of this short "adventure" is marked by a yell "from the throats of a thousand demons." It is the yell of Hell, when the ritual death and rebirth take place. Augustus and Pym die and resurrect, being tied to the cords of the "Golden Chain."[41]

---

[40] "I recommended myself to God," Pym says (728).
[41] "I was resuscitated from a state bordering very nearly upon death," Pym declares (731). A large whaling-ship passed over *Ariel*, demolishing the little vessel, but the two boys remained fastened to the wreckage. A rope binds Augustus, while a bolt nails Pym (730). Their salvation is due to what "the wise and pious" considers being the "interference of Providence" (729). On the other hand, if we regard this episode not a "preview" of the whole initiation, but an illustration of Pym's decadence, the rope represents the mundane "ties" and the bolt is Plato's bolt which nails the soul to the body, to the corporeal appetites and passions (Augustus' drunkenness), preventing him to become pure (**Phaedo** 81c, 83d). That motivates the second sea voyage.

The Everlasting Sacred Kernel

The second voyage is much longer and more complex. Pym is presented as "melancholy," a sign of his "election" for the initiatory process.[42] The sea journey starts at the summer solstice (733, 748), and we have already seen this gate opening not only to salvation, but also to Hell and dreams and demons. The first part of the journey is a descent to Hell and Augustus is the guide. The brig *Grampus*, under the command of Augustus' father, leaves "for a whaling voyage" (732) and Augustus helps Pym to embark clandestinely aboard. Augustus makes all the arrangements and guides Pym to his hiding place (a box into the brig's after hold), that is, down into Hell (733-735). Augustus guides Pym "through innumerable narrow passages," a labyrinth (735), and Pym descends "holding on to the skirts of my friend's coat." Augustus provides a "dark whipcord" as link between him and Pym, the "cord of salvation" being black in Hell; the cord is supposed to replace Augustus' guidance and help the hero, like in fairy tales, to climb back up and reach the light (736). Pym remains "buried" alive for a long time.[43] He suffers infernal trials; he sleeps a lot and for long periods of time; Pym says:

---

[42] Agrippa explains the power of melancholy, connecting it with the divine order. Melancholy has the force to draw celestial spirits into men's bodies and men will learn the secrets of divine things. See Cornelius Agrippa, **Three Books of Occult Philosophy**, Llewellyn Publications, 1998, pp. 188-9. Melancholy has a "black face" (*facies nigra*) and corresponds to Saturn (Yates, **The Occult**, pp. 51-7). Because of that, melancholy was considered the lowest and most hateful of all the four humours; in fact, it is the highest, the emblem of spirituality, melancholy, like Saturn or the black color, accepting a two-faced symbolism. Poe uses both meanings, insisting upon the tenebrous side. Pym's melancholy generates hellish images and passions. Pym's "visions" and "desires" are Saturnine and demonic, about shipwreck and famine, death and captivity among barbarian hordes, sorrow and tears (732), this inclination toward Hell being a part of Poe's perception of salvation.

[43] Pym seems to be the sacred germ, similar to Eleusis' wheat grain. The brig is Noah's Ark, yet also the Leviathan. In fact, Pym is inside the Dragon's womb, which for him represents Hell. Like the holy man Mârkandeya inside Vishnu, like Jonah inside the Leviathan, Pym copies the traditional symbolism of the hero swallowed by the monster in order to suffer the ritual death. Indeed, the brig's name, *Grampus*, is an old term for the killer whale, but also for the grey dolphin (the dolphin is Apollo's emblem and contains a valuable symbolism). Nonetheless, the ritual swallowing accepts a double meaning, like the double meaning of the black color. The monster's jaws symbolize the Sun-door. For the neophyte, the Sun-door is the

I fell into a state of profound sleep, or rather stupor. My dreams were of the most terrific description. Every species of calamity and horror befell me. Among other miseries I was smothered to death between huge pillows, by demons of the most ghastly and ferocious aspect. Immense serpents held me in their embrace.... The scene changed; and I stood, naked and alone, amidst the burning sand-plains of Sahara. At my feet lay crouched a fierce lion. (738)

His dream[44] describes not only the journey through Hell but also suggests the end of time, the end of the cycle. Augustus, who is supposed to come and liberate Pym from the hiding place, is missing, and Pym tries hard to climb upwards to reach him. God is the only salvation. "My brain swam," Pym continues; "Making a last strong effort, I at length breathed a faint ejaculation to God, and resigned myself to die." Poe's Hell is a labyrinth as Minos' labyrinth, "the narrow and intricate windings" (740). Thirst, famine, suffocation and lack of light are present as infernal powers (741), representing the primary elements: water, earth, air and fire, typical for initiatory journeys and symbolizing the purification according to each element. With desperate efforts, Pym tries to climb from Hell through "the narrow passage" but like Dante who couldn't climb the luminous mountain alone, he cannot succeed by himself, re-

---

Gate of Liberation; for the ordinary man, it is the Jaws of Death. The whale's womb is Hell and chaos, but also the non-manifestation as a principle of rejuvenation and spiritual rebirth (Guénon, **Symboles**, pp. 356-360, and Coom., **Trad. Art**, pp. 486-490). See also Grace Farell Lee's interpretation of Pym's descent to Hell (Harvey 93).

[44] Poe, like others, uses the dream as a "hellish" gate. The dream could be also a "human" and a "divine" gate. René Guénon said: "un songe dans lequel s'exprime quelque inspiration « supra-humaine » est véritablement symbolique, tandis qu'un rêve ordinaire ne l'est nullement, quelles que puissent être les apparences extérieures" (**Articles et comptes rendus**, tome I, Éd. Trad., 2002, p. 89).

The Everlasting Sacred Kernel

maining "entombed" (740-1).[45] Eventually, Pym's dog, playing the dragon's role, with his mouth as solar gate, simulates the swallowing of the hero and only then does Augustus appear, saving Pym and guiding his ascension from Hell (747-8). Pym doesn't forget to thank God for his escape (759).

A new stage starts, still an infernal one. The demons are now human beings, the most abject ones, evil elements of the end of time, "the most ruffianly of the brig's company" (749). They are the demons dwelling in our *anima*, they are the most inferior appetites and desires. Poe presents them as mutineers taking possession of the vessel (the vessel is a substitute for the "city of Dis"), then fighting and killing each other, in continuous mutiny, and creating chaos. The mutiny prevented Augustus from coming sooner to rescue Pym, yet for this stage Pym has a new guide, Dirk Peters, a strange dwarf. "His arms, as well as legs, were bowed in the most singular manner, and appeared to possess no flexibility whatever. His head was equally deformed, being of immense size" and covered with a bearskin (751). Peters saves Augustus from the mutineers' hands and protects Pym, and he wants to sail south (756, 763). But most of all, Peters leads Pym and Augustus in overcoming the devils. They fight them during a terrible tempest, at midnight (773). The human demons will be defeated one by one, but the definitive victory is due to Pym himself who, disguised as a ghost, a carnival travesty (769-771) suggesting his "revivification" (772), scares the villains to death.[46] And Pym crushes the dragon, represented by Parker, who is the only one Pym fights: "(Pym) felled Parker with a blow on the head" (772). Yet Parker doesn't die, he is tamed

---

[45] Ulysses, says Dante, couldn't reach at all the Mount of Purgatory; he didn't have a spiritual guide. From this perspective, we could say that Pym fails the first voyage because his guide, Augustus, was "beastly drunk" and "could not longer stand, speak or see" (727). Pym's attempt to climb through the narrow passage is a close replica of the Lover's final trial in Jean de Meung's *The Romance of the Rose* (99.230-280); unlike Pym, the Lover succeeds in reaching the Rose.

[46] Pym impersonates Rogers, a mutineer who died from being poisoned. Pym's appearance as Rogers alive in front of the other thugs should be compared with Dante's infernal journey, the Florentine poet being the only one alive among devils and sinners (**Inf.** XII.82-87, **Purg.** I.77).

("transformed"), and will be the fourth survivor, beside Augustus, Peters and Pym.

Now, after the demons' defeat, the next initiatory stage commences. Because of the tempest, the ship turned into wreckage. "By the mercy of God, however, we were preserved ... and about midday were cheered by the light of the blessed sun" (777). This solar light is, though, just a reflection of the spiritual Sun, and Pym doesn't reach yet the Mount of Purgatory. He will dream[47] "in a state of partial insensibility" a kind of Paradise, described as the Wheel of the World, Pym's dream predicting the joy to come, yet indicating that he is still in the "country of dreams." The new stage of initiation requires an active role from Pym, after Augustus and Peters have fulfilled their mission. Pym's companions are fastened to the ship's wreckage with ropes and couldn't move. Pym rescues them from their ties, a symbolic gesture illustrating the hero's liberation from the "ties" of inferior passions and appetites, and his leading position. The four survivors are in fact "four beasts in one" representing Pym's own levels that have to be purified and integrated into spiritual unity. The new sufferings will be those of hunger and thirst, suggesting the ritual fasting, which tames the body and the inferior urges (779). And of course, again they ask God's help: "Throwing ourselves on our knees to God, we implored His aid in the many dangers which beset us" (781).[48] Pym continues to travel through Hell, redeeming his inferior levels. That is why Poe introduces the episode of the *Flying Dutchman*, the painted black, ghost-brig,[49] stressing that the infernal journey is not finished yet and that, as Dante says, in Hell there is no hope (*lasciate ogni speranza*). Pym loses the "visions of deliverance and joy" (783); "There seemed now to be no longer any room for hope" (785). There is only one way to revive hope and purify Hell. The moment has come to initi-

---

[47] We notice the dream again!
[48] Pym's "desire" to suffer is the medieval monk's desire to expiate his sins by sufferance.
[49] The sea-gull "busily gorging itself with the (human) flesh" on the *Flying Dutchman* (783) should be compared with Dante's Ugollino eating Ruggieri's brain, both frozen into ice (**Inf.** XXXII.127).

ate the sacred sacrifice, which ends a cycle and starts a new one, which rejuvenates the world and resurrects the Self. And Pym is the hero. They are trying to find some provisions left in the hull, but only Pym finds a bottle of wine, nobody else could, and the sacrifice of wine, as in Christian Eucharist, is accomplished, "giving thanks to God" (785). And only Pym understands the meaning of the sacred ritual, the others (representing, in a way, inferior parts of Pym), getting drunk and talking incoherently (as the Apostles did, but here is rather a reaction of the inferior forces of the Babel tower), eventually falling asleep (786). The dragon itself suggests the second part of the Eucharist, again Parker playing this function. Parker proposes immolation in order to provide nutriment for the others and he will be chosen by destiny to be sacrificed. He is cut into pieces, like Osiris or Purusha or any other dragon,[50] as Christ parted the bread saying that he is parting his body (**Luke** 22:19-20). Parker's sacrifice mirrors his previous one, which ended the prior stage, and symbolizes, in the same way, the end of an initiatory degree and the start of a new one.

Parker is a substitute for Pym, as Peters is his vicar (as Peter was for Christ). The sacrifice of Parker is the mystery of One changed into multiplicity, and for Poe this is a ritual action meant to provoke a strong reaction, helping the return to God. Immediately after the immolation, Pym finds provisions and is once more a saviour. Again Peters and Augustus, as inferior parts of Pym (*psyche* and *corpus*), prove to be greedy, eating a lot, "not being able to restrain their appetite"; Pym instead ate a small portion (793).[51] *Corpus*, represented by Augustus, will be eventually tamed and transformed, that is why he will die on August 1, his month, at noon (crucial point) (798). Soon after that, on August 7, salvation comes from the East (*Oriens*), "a sail to the eastward, and evidently coming towards us!" (801). Pym and Peters will be rescued by the Jane Guy, a schooner going "south" (802).

---

[50] The others cut Parker's head, feet and arms (792), obeying a traditional ritual.
[51] To be compared with the two birds of *Mundaka Up.*

Black and White

The last stage now starts, an intermediary one between Hell and Purgatory, aiming for the Earthly Paradise. It is important to understand that Poe's point of view is a restricted religious one, which means that Pym's voyage has as target at best the center of human integral individuality and the accomplishment of the *Lesser Mysteries*. The best part is missing. Heavenly Paradise is the reward for the *Greater Mysteries*, representing the Hindu liberation (*moksha*), but Poe apparently cannot surpass the common theological perspective and his hero's endeavour is not a full realization.[52] Therefore, Poe is obsessed with the duality of good and evil, and especially with the problem of evil.[53] Hell will be present in Poe's novel from the beginning to the end.

After a long voyage, from island to island, Pym reaches the far south and the icy fields of Antarctica (815). Yet crossing the barrier of ice, farther south, "the temperature of the air, and latterly of the water, became milder" (818), indicating the proximity of the paradisiacal region, the entire picture duplicating the Hyperborean land description.[54] Pym arrives at the Black Sea ("the sea being of an extraordinarily dark color"), which stresses the "polar" image as a "preview" of Melville's mysterious black painting. Actually, Pym attains the purpose of his voyage, the Center, which is, as we already know, black *ab intra* and white *ab extra*. The hero discovers a group of islands constituting the "realm of black." People, animals, birds, rocks, trees, everything is black (820).

Poe, from his religious point of view, sees black primarily as an infernal color, and Tsalal, the island where Pym lands, is the city of Dis, the core of Hell. The white color scares the dark people to death (822, 839), the apparently irreconcilable opposition between

---

[52] "Poe was a Biblical fundamentalist of the most orthodox sort" (Kaplan XXIII).
[53] In a similar way, Wiles refers to the Manichean division of Devil and God within the human individual (Knowles 63), which is a mundane point of view and limited to the relative duality governing the terrestrial world.
[54] Like in *Ms. Found in a Bottle*, Poe warns us that "one of the most intensely exciting secrets" (819) is to be found at the South Pole. An aspect of this "secret" is the symbolic and essential equality of the two Poles, like the equivalence of Dante's mountains.

white and black suggesting the devil's rejection of the divine light. The inhabitants of the black islands are presented as "the most barbarous, subtle, and bloodthirsty wretches that ever contaminated the face of the globe" (830) and again as "the most wicked, hypocritical, vindictive, bloodthirsty, and altogether fiendish race of men" (848); they are the devils, the demons. Pym and Peters, once again become prisoners of Hell. They fall into an infernal hollow (841), "being thus entombed alive" (832), and Pym thinks "that the day of universal dissolution was at hand" (832), which is true in a way, this episode representing the final ritual death of the neophyte before his illumination, and the change of cycles.[55] Pym and his companion discover a series of mysterious chasms (842-3) and with great difficulty succeed in escaping from this infernal trap and from the devils' hands.[56] They sail southward into a canoe (848), entering a "region of novelty and wonder" (850): it is *Leuke* or *Shwêta-dwîpa*, the "white land," the counter-face of the black region. Like Dante, Pym is now purified of ignorance and demonic darkness, and receives the paradisiacal and intelligible light. A huge shrouded human figure of pure white arises and the novel ends abruptly. Pym's initiation is accomplished. He reaches the Earthly Paradise exactly at spring equinox (852), which corresponds to *Oriens* – the source of spiritual Light and to the Garden of Eden situated at the East (**Gen. 2:8**).[57]

---

[55] "I firmly believed," says Pym, "that no incident ever occurring in the course of human events is more adapted to inspire the supremeness of mental and bodily distress than a case like our own, of living inhumation" (832). This is a perfect remake of the early episode when Pym was buried in the brig's hold.

[56] It is the end of time, the reign of chaos, and Poe describes accordingly the landscape: "The place was one of singular wildness, and its aspect brought to my mind the descriptions given by travelers of those dreary regions marking the site of degraded Babylon. Not to speak of the ruins of the disrupted cliff, which formed a chaotic barrier" (846).

[57] We have to be cautious. The "shrouded human figure" having the hue "of the perfect whiteness of the snow" (852) could easily be misinterpreted as a ghost, an apparition. Theosophism calls its supreme center "Grand White Lodge" (Guénon, **Le Théosophisme**, pp. 46, 299), and the Occultism excessively used the terms "white" and "light" in opposition with "black" and "dark." From a traditional point of view Poe's shrouded human figure has to be compared to the Chief of Days

Black and White

It seems obvious that Pym's symbolic journey is a voyage from black (the infernal pole) to white (the divine pole), as unveiled in this last stage.[58] Nevertheless, the supernal meaning of black is also present, even if unwittingly, which allows us to affirm that the black island is similar to Apollo's Hyperborean island and to *Leuke*, the White Island. The black island is encircled by a reef (820) that represents the symbolic "cutting," and thus illustrates the Center of the World. It is populated with black albatross (825) and, more importantly, with black herons (837), being a precise replica of Achilles' island and of Aztlan. Yet the most curious thing is the description of the chasms; their figures, says Poe, constitute the Ethiopian verbal root "dark" and the Arabic root "white" (853).[59] We may note that both these words, suggesting black and white, are together on Tsalal, which as a veritable Center contains them united. Tsalal represents, as black island, Ethiopia, the legendary land of Priest John and of Hermia. A common king governs the group of black

---

whose "head was white and pure as wool, and his raiment indescribable" (Matthew Black, **The Book of Enoch**, Leiden, 1985, 71.10), or to the Ancient of Days, whose "robe was white as snow, the hair of his head as pure as wool" (**Daniel** 7:9), or, of course, to Jesus Christ during the transfiguration (**Matthew** 17:2), when "his face shone like the sun and his clothes became as white as the light." Note that associated with the white color is the idea of purity. A spiritual initiation is composed of a series of purifications, which eventually succeed to purify the "ignorance" and transform it into divine knowledge. The shrouded figure has the perfect whiteness of the snow, or the snow is a symbol of purity. For Shakespeare, Helena is "pure white," more pure than "pure congealed white, high Taurus' snow" (III.II.142). Perdita's hand is "as soft as dove's down, and as white as it, or Ethiopian's tooth, or the fann'd snow that's bolted by the northern blasts twice o'er"; and Hermione, Perdita's mother appears in dream dressed "in pure white robes" (**The Winter's Tale**, IV.III and III.III). The Medieval Catharians had their name from the Greek *katharos*, "pure"; the Sufis' name comes from an Arabic root meaning "wool" and "pure" (Martin Lings, **What is Sufism?**, Univ. of California Press, 1977, p. 46), and we saw the Ancient of Days with his hair white and pure as wool. The spiritual center is "the pure land" as Plato states it. The ignorant people dwell inside the Earth's chasms and cavities, and cannot climb up to the "pure land," a land of light and bliss (**Phaedo**, 109b, d, 111a, d); Plato's cavities could be the archetypes of Poe's chasms.

[58] Melville follows this scenario, Ishmael's adventure being comprised between the black mass (whale) and the white whale.

[59] For a discussion of these roots see Kaplan XVII- XX.

The Everlasting Sacred Kernel

islands; his name is *Tsalemon* or *Psalemoun* (850), i.e., Solomon, the Lord of Peace, a name of the "Lord of the World."[60]

The white region is noticeably *Leuke*. Everything is white, and gigantic and pallidly white birds fly continuously (852). The water is very warm and has a milky color (850), which is a direct allusion to Paradise.[61] But the white is not alone, and Poe tells about "a sullen darkness" hovered above Pym (851), a darkness that increases and contrasts the white birds (852), again the black and white being together.[62]

Like Hermia and Helena, Poe's two regions, black and white, are twins and the screams of the black bitterns and of the giant white birds stand for Shakespeare's "one heart and one crest" unifying them.[63] Even if Tsalal is the realm of black, some white is also present, and, in the same way, in the white zone some darkness is in site, including a black inhabitant of Tsalal. It is an illustration of *yin-yang*'s profound meaning. "The Divine Dark is the inaccessible

---

[60] The odd chasms should be related not only with the profane cavities of Plato, but also with the subterranean kingdom of the "Lord of the World," described by Ossendowski (Ferdinand Ossendowski, **Beasts, Men and Gods**, Blue Ribbon Books, 1931, pp. 301-306). The Hopi cosmogony states that during the destruction of the First World the chosen people hid safely underground where they had homes like those destroyed on the earth-surface (Frank Waters, **Book of the Hopi**, Ballantine Books, 1977, pp. 17-20). The *Popol Vuh* affirms that Maya originated in seven womb-caves or ravines, at Tulan (See **Popol Vuh**, Maisonneuve, 1980, p. 85, and Waters 142). We see again the coexistence of two opposite meanings (supernal-infernal) of the same symbol.

[61] There is a striking resemblance with Diodorus Siculus' story about the sea voyage of two Ethiopians (Pym and Peters) to the "islands of eternal happiness," a group of seven islands located at the South Pole (II.58). Diodorus also describes another "Isle of the Blessed" (i.e., a spiritual center), where the sea is white and all the animals are completely white (III.47), Poe's description exactly.

[62] When Edmond Dantès escapes from the island (château d'If) where he was incarcerated (representing his journey through Hell), he swims ("sea voyage") towards the island of Monte-Cristo (the Paradise) and he sees "huge white birds shown on black clouds" (I, p. 239).

[63] The strange words, *Tsalemon, Tsalal* and *Tekeli-li*, which Pym heard on the black island, belong to the "language of the birds," that is, they belong to the primordial and divine language; the first two imitate the scream of the black herons (850), the third one is the scream of the gigantic white birds (852). About the Hebrew origins of these words see Kaplan XVII-XX.

Black and White

Light," Dionysius the Areopagite says; "And the deep of the darkness is as great as the habitation of the light; and they stand not one distant from the other, but together in one another," Jacob Boehme adds (Coom., **Trad. Art**, p. 490). The essential brotherhood of black and white is stressed by their two-fold symbolism. On the one hand, Poe's birds, white and black, have a precedent in the Christian and Islamic traditions where white birds represent the angels and black birds the sinners thrown in Hell and the demons (see Miguel Asín Palacios, **L'Eschatologie musulmane dans la Divine Comédie**, Archè Milan, 1992, pp. 295-7, 337, 355-7). On the other hand, Poe's birds have a model in the tales of the Holy Grail. During his Quest, Bors has a dream in which he experiences a vision of two birds: one white and big as a swan, the other black and small. The white bird offers all the riches of the world to Bors; the black bird asks for his services. A fake hermit, representing the devil, interprets the dream: the white bird means "love" and the black one means "sin." We see the mundane (inferior) and exoteric point of view. A holy hermit tells the reverse: the white bird symbolizes "the enemy" (the devil), the white color being a hypocritical and a false one; the black bird represents the Holy Church, in accordance with the biblical saying "I am black, but I am beautiful."[64]

The black-and-white symbolism appears also connected to that of the twins, Hermia and Helena being a particular example of this association. Yet the twins' symbolism is interesting in itself and would be worthy of elaboration. The next chapter gives us this opportunity.

---

[64] See **The Quest of the Holy Grail**, Penguin Books, 1969, pp. 183 ff.

Chapter Nine

THE TWINS

THE TEMPLAR seal represents two knights mounted on the same horse.[1] This enigmatic figure is an exact duplicate of the Hindu Asvins, the twin-gods, riders on a horse or in the same chariot. Krishna (the black, the Self, the spectator) and Arjuna (the white, the *ego*), ride too the same chariot. Hopi tradition depicts the twins (a boy and a girl) as two sides of the same body, the boy – black, and the girl – white; the center (the navel) is marked by a circle, black on the white side and white on the black side (Waters 91), suggesting, as *yin-yang* does, the primordial unity.

Black and white symbolize the duality of the world. The Cosmos exists only as duality. A "perfect world," with faultless harmony and unity, is impossible in manifestation. The planets are not perfectly round, as a sphere, the most perfect Platonic geometric form; the planetary orbits are elliptical and not circles. Absolute perfection is beyond our world, beyond the whole "Three Worlds"; even the angels are not perfect, that is why Lucifer could fall. One finds perfection by entering the Sun-door and actually realizing the *coincidentia oppositorum*. Otherwise, living within the Cosmos, everything is subject to a dual influence: the supernal, essential influence of *Purusha* (Heaven) and the infernal, substantial influence of *Prakriti* (Earth),

---

[1] Malcom Barber, **The New Knighthood**, Cambridge Univ. Press, 1994, pp. 180-1. Barber offers only an "exoteric" explanation, that by riding the same horse the Templars show humility.

The Twins

illustrated by the two serpents of Hermes' *caduceus*. For our human mind, which belongs to this duality of the world, it is difficult to understand that, beyond all the pairs of contraries, a common Principle contains the black and the white united. To comprehend it, the mind has to surpass its own limits, to rise to the super-rational order, and to appear seized by drunkenness and madness; or it has to use shocking illogical terms, like *Harap Alb* (the "White Moor"), "Ethiopian Albino" and "white whale." There is another way, which maintains the duality, so dear to human mentality, yet plainly indicates the unity within which the dyad could coalesce: the symbol of twins.

The twins are duality but also unity. Though separated, they ride the same horse, they act together and their likeness makes them one person. The symbol is so fit for our rational mind that it was universally used to explain the cosmogony and the spiritual realization. The twins are the two hemispheres of the "World Egg" and the two poles of Existence.[2] They represent the two arms of the "Lord of the World," the spiritual authority and the temporal power.[3] They also are the two natures of Christ, the divine and the human one, coexisting in unity (in the same "body").[4]

Aditi is in the Hindu tradition the super-luminous Mother, the feminine aspect of the Infinite, "the infinite Light" (Aurobindo 423), giving birth to Adityas, the suns (gods) that govern the cosmic cycles.[5] The Adityas are sometimes twelve (**Brhadâranyaka Up. III.9.5**), sometimes eight, when they are four pairs of twins

---

[2] In the Hopi tradition, the primordial twins contribute to the creation of the Earth; they will be placed, one at the North Pole, the other at the South Pole, to keep the world properly rotating (Waters 4-5).

[3] See Ananda K. Coomaraswamy, **Autorité Spirituelle et Pouvoir Temporel**, Archè Milan, 1985, pp. 52-3.

[4] The Greek Dioscuri were born from the Swan's egg – a cosmogonic image; at the same time, one is immortal (Pollux), the other mortal (Castor), representing the Self and the *ego*. *Harap Alb* has to choose, as an initiatory trial, between two twin girls, and he points out the emperor's genuine daughter (the Self).

[5] Adityas correspond to the ten suns of Chinese tradition and to the five suns of Aztec mythology, each sun governing a cosmic era (Miller 88).

The Everlasting Sacred Kernel

(**Maitrâyanî Samhitâ** I.6.12).[6] Another sacred story tells about Sanjnâ, Sun's wife, who gives birth to solar twins Manu, Yama and Yamî (**Vishnu Purâna** III.2). Manu is the prototype of the "Lord of the World"; Yama and Yamî are the explicit duality of Manu, the twins symbolizing Heaven and Earth, *Sacerdotum* and *Regnum*, Day and Night, similar with the Asvins or Mitrâvarunâ (Coom., **Autorité**, pp. 52-5).[7] Other traditions corroborate this picture: *Popol Vuh* narrates about the Hero Twins (Miller 134); the Greek mythology presents the Dioscuri; the Romans have Romulus and Remus as ancestors; the biblical Esau and Jacob, the ancestors of Israel and Edom, are twins (**Gen.** 25:24)[8]; and the Gnostics affirm that Apostle Thomas is Christ's twin brother.[9]

The twins' theme, charged which such a powerful symbolism, remained a very tempting subject during the centuries. Two famous ancient stories should be mentioned first: Plato's myth about Atlantis, in which he states that five pairs of twins, Poseidon's children, became the first rulers of the island (**Critias** 114a), and the love story of king Nala and Damayantî, a sacred initiatory tale, in which the twins represent the seeds of the new Cosmos (**Mahâbhârata** III.50-57).[10] Afterward, the twins' theme is subtly transmitted along

---

[6] The famous Hindu gods, Mitra and Varuna, represent such a pair; occasionally, they are melted as Mitrâvarunâ reminding the unity of the twins. Evidently, all different pairs of twins are just aspects of the primordial and unique pair (Coom., **Autorité**, p. 55).

[7] In Sanskrit, *yama* means "twin." Note the solar nature of the twins. In fairy tales, the twins are a boy and a girl with golden hair or totally gilded (Ispirescu 54), gold being the sun of minerals; interesting, the twins appear in the 19th card of the Tarot, "the Sun."

[8] A parallel could be made between the seven kings of Rome and the seven Edomite kings of Hebraic *Kabbalah*, both series developing from a twin; the Jews gave to Rome the name Edome (Guénon, **Le Roi**, p. 58).

[9] "Brother Thomas ... since it is said that you are my twin and my true friend," Christ says in *The Book of Thomas* (See **The Secret Teachings of Jesus**, Vintage Books, 1986, p. 41). Note that Apostle Thomas' name means "twin" (in the Gospel he is called "Thomas the Twin," **John** 20:24).

[10] The twins are Nala and Damayantî's children, a boy and a girl, named significantly Indrasena and Indrasenâ. To marry Nala, Damayantî has to choose (like *Harap Alb*) between five identical "Nalas" and find out who is the genuine one (the

The Twins

the ages as a sacred heritage. Dante, for example, strongly praises the zodiacal constellation of Gemini before entering Paradise.[11] Shakespeare uses twins in *Twelfth Night* and *The Comedy of Errors*. Mozart suggests a twin couple, Papageno-Papagena, costumed as birds in his Masonic opera *The Magic Flute*.[12] Alexandre Dumas develops the twins' topic in his well-known stories about the *Iron Mask* and the *Corsican brothers*. Yet another author, who wrote an entire novel about the twins, deserves special attention: Mark Twain.

Mark Twain publishes *The Prince and the Pauper* in 1882.[13] He presents the novel as "a tale for young people of all ages," insisting that it is a tale and, of course, it remained labelled as "children's literature." Indifferent to Twain's intentions in using the twins' theme, the fact that his story is a tale already tells a lot. As a tale for children and having children as main heroes, there is a fair chance that the story inherits a sacred kernel, undamaged by the author's interference and his distorted mentality. It is not important if Twain was aware or not about a symbolism in his tale. The fact that we can discover that symbolism is all that counts. The sacred kernel has its

---

five "twins" are Nala and the gods Indra, Agni, Varuna and Yama who took Nala's appearance).

[11] "O glorious constellation! O lamp imbued/ with great powers, to whose influence I ascribe/ all my genius, however it may be viewed!/ When I drew my first breath of Tuscan air/ the Sun, the father of all mortal life,/ was rising in your rays and setting there./ And then when I was granted Heaven's grace/ to enter the great wheel that gives you motion,/ I was led upward through your zone of space" (**Parad.** XXII.112-120, Mentor Book, 1970, tr. John Ciardi). Dante was born under the sign of Gemini, which guided his destiny towards a spiritual realization. Passing the same constellation in his initiatory celestial flight means that he is born again. Note that for Dante the Sun as Principle is our real and only father.

[12] Mozart composed in 1768, when he was only twelve years old, a short opera called *Bastien and Bastienne*; Bastien-Bastienne, Papageno-Papagena, are "twin" pairs reminding of the Hindu couples Yama-Yamî and Indrasena-Indrasenâ. *The Magic Flute* (first performance in 1791) is charged with symbols of Freemasonry and apparently a high Mason, baron Ignaz von Born from Transylvania, played a significant role in its creation (See Jacques Chailley, **The Magic Flute unveiled**, Inner Traditions International, 1992, pp. 15-17).

[13] For page references we are using Mark Twain, **The Prince and the Pauper**, Signet Classic, 1964.

own ways to survive over the course of ages, and the twins' theme is a striking example.

There are two boys in Mark Twain's novel: a very poor one, Tom, with horrible father and grandmother (17), the Devil's exponents, very active at the end of time; and a prince, the future king of England, Edward. Tom has two sisters, twins (16), who enhance the theme and remind us of Greek Dioscuri who also have twin sisters (Helen of Troy being one of them). Of course, Tom symbolizes the *ego*, the mortal "brother," and Edward represents the immortal one, the Self. Tom and Edward are perfectly alike, twins, the two halves of the "World Egg," Heaven and Earth.[14]

The cosmic cycle is close to its end and a sacred initiation is required to rejuvenate the world and change the old era with a new one. Edward has reached his royal position without any effort from his part, which means that he cannot be yet a true king for the new era. We have to understand that in a genuine and perfect traditional society, the "Lord of the World," represented by an emperor or a king, is not any man; the man who is invested with this function has to be an "elected" one, therefore he has to embark on a spiritual path to match the function. That was the problem in Europe during the Middle Ages: too often the human individuals didn't match the sacred functions they were designated for. For that reason, Dante placed popes and nobles in Hell. The pope as a function represents the "sacerdotal power" with all the divine influences transmitted in uninterrupted continuity since Christ. Unfortunately, the individual occupying the function was often just an ordinary, profane man, instead of a truly "elected" one who passed the initiatory trials and accomplished spiritual realization. The same discrepancy appeared in the case of the kings, who frequently couldn't satisfy the sacred qualifications of the royal function. In Twain's tale, on the contrary, before being crowned king, Prince Edward follows a sacred initia-

---

[14] Heaven and Earth, like the North and South Poles, they mirror each other as twins. "Whatever is below is like that which is above, and whatever is above is like that which is below," the Emerald Tablet of Hermeticism states (Burckhardt, **Alchemy**, p. 196).

The Twins

tion. That is the perfect situation when the individual strives to match the function.

Mark Twain has an illustrious model: Shakespeare's *The Winter's Tale*, which deserves a chapter by itself. Note the title suggesting a "tale" and the winter solstice; Twain's title is also present: when Hermione is blamed for mistaking Polixenes for Leontes, in the same paragraph another warning is stated against the lack of discrimination between "the prince and beggar" (II.I). The main characters are Leontes, the king of Sicilia, and Polixenes, the king of Bohemia, "twinn'd lambs that did frisk i' the sun" (I.II).[15] They are the twin poles: "they have seemed to be together, though absent; shook hands, as over a vast; and embraced, as it were, from the ends of opposed winds" (I.I). Yet at the end of the cycle Leontes, the immortal twin, appears as an unworthy king, a tyrant who doesn't match his sacred function anymore, and he suffers an initiatory transformation, which restores the Self and rejuvenates the world, bringing a new cycle and retrieving the "Lost Tradition."[16]

---

[15] In Romanian fairy tales, the twins change into golden lambs. Leontes and Polixenes are the solar twins; though presented both as kings, Leontes is the "prince" and Polixenes the "pauper."

[16] Hermione is Leontes' wife and she symbolizes the Tradition (Hermetic tradition). It is the end of the cycle, when apparently the tradition (Hermione) is no longer the "bride" of the Self (Leontes) but of the *ego* (Polixenes), the unworthy, mortal husband being mistaken for the immortal one. Leontes himself no longer matches the supreme function. He is "in rebellion with himself," illustrating the chaos of the dying cycle. He wrongly accuses Hermione of having an affair with Polixenes and he considers the newborn girl as Polixenes' daughter, condemning her to exile in a wasteland. The girl, with a suggestive name (Perdita, Latin "lost"), represents the divine germ of the new cycle, but also the "Lost Word" of Masonry, that is, the "Lost Tradition," which has to be recovered to start a new reign and a new age. She is the same as her mother, Hermione. Shakespeare's play is basically a fairy tale using, beside the twins' theme, two other major symbolical elements. The first one is the daughter's exile (same thing happens to Snow-White or to Hansel and Gretel); the second one is the "petrified" world. Leontes condemns Hermione to death and she supposedly dies, illustrating the end of time. In fact, she is "petrified" (symbolizing the "solidification" of the world at the end of the cycle) and considered a statue, which at the same time with Leontes' spiritual rebirth and transformation, becomes alive. Many fairy tales present the end of the world as a "petrifaction" or as in *The Sleeping Beauty*, as drowsiness or sleepiness. As the Prince kisses the Sleeping Beauty, resurrecting her (and the Cosmos), so Leontes wants to kiss the statue.

The Everlasting Sacred Kernel

In Shakespeare's play, Leontes' son, Mamillius, dies and the old king takes his place as neophyte. Normally the old king dies and his son, a perfect copy of his father, accomplishes the spiritual initiation and becomes the new king. That is what happens in Mark Twain's story: the old king Henry is dying and Edward should become the new king, but in a traditional sense, which implies a spiritual realization.

Tom is the *ego*. Like Polixenes, he is not the "evil" inside us, but a normal *ego*, with dreams and desires, an unworthy "prince" dreaming of being in charge instead of the Self. With the world running to its end, the *ego* becomes more arrogant. For a while, Tom is in command and is the only master of the Great Seal, in the same way as Polixenes is the host of Perdita, but neither one knows the real meaning of their treasure. Anyway, Tom likes his position, of course, and becomes so "egocentric" that he rejects his own mother, feigning that he doesn't know her. On the other hand, the Little Prince, Edward, as a neophyte, has to become poor and hum-

---

Paulina commands: "Music, awake her: strike! 'Tis time; descend; be stone no more; approach;/ Strike all that look upon with marvel.... Bequeath to death your numbness, for from him/ dear life redeems you" (V.III). And Hermione "descends," as the Primordial Tradition did at the beginning of the World, and resurrects from stone, symbolizing the commencing of a new reign. "Turn, good lady," adds Paulina; "our Perdita is found." Hermione's revival means the recovery of the "Lost Word." Note the role of Apollo in Leontes' initiatory process and Paulina's ambivalent function (she is the Initiatress, Platonic Diotima or Beatrice, but also the "stepmother," the inferior pole controlling the superior pole at the end of time). Finally, we should remark Shakespeare's expansion of the twins' theme. Not only Leontes and Polixenes appear as twins, but also accordingly to the creation of man in the likeness of God the whole manifestation is the Principle's image and Shakespeare stresses it again and again. "He (God) of whom all this world is but the copy" and "In every figure He has been the model; by his Mâyâ (art of illusion) Indra moves multiform" *Rig Veda* says (II.12.9, VI.47.18). Mamillius, Leontes' son, is a copy of his father, they are "as like as eggs"; Florizel, Polidexes' son, is his "father's image" and has "his very air" (in fairy tales, the hero is a young image of the old royal father, illustrating the similitude of the cycles and the common and only Origin). The newborn Perdita is a perfect copy of Leontes (II.III). That is the sport of the Principle, suggested by Leontes' words: "Go, play, boy, play: - thy mother plays, and I play too" (I.II), and by a series of travesties; Perdita, also in travesty, states: "I see the play so lies that I must bear a part" (IV.III).

ble, a spiritual way of all traditions; he has to pass through Hell first, to suffer a ritual death, and then to be born again in the paradisiacal center.[17]

The plot takes place at the end of a cycle, just before the old king, Henry VIII, dies. Tom's terrible habitat and his awful father and grandmother, connected with the lowest class of thieves, beggars and villains (17), illustrate the chaos of the dying world[18]; but Tom and his sisters' profound ignorance is also a "sign of the times." The knowledge is hiding, and only secretly could Tom have access to some lore, from a priest. Father Andrew, similar to Verne's magister Hermod, is the sacerdotal *guru* who teaches Tom "the old tales and legends about giants and fairies, dwarfs and genii, and enchanted castles, and gorgeous kings and princes" (17), making the "soul" (*jîvâtmâ*) longing for the "Self" (*Âtmâ*). Tom lives in a dream world; he is the "mock prince" (19), behaving and acting as a real prince, and yearning for the royal palace (the heart, the center). Diverse spiritual methods recommend this way: the neophyte should simulate the bliss, peace and serenity of the final stage, taming the mind and the psyche, emptying them of thoughts and emotions, silencing the words, this "mock realization" being gradually replaced with a real one, when this sublime state will come in a natural way as part of the transformed being. "We become what we think of," says the Hindu tradition (Coom., **La doctrine**, p. 212); and "A man becomes what he loves," affirms St. Augustine (Eck-

---

[17] About humility see, for example, the Gospels' words: "For everyone who exalts himself will be humbled, and the man who humbles himself will be exalted" (**Luke** 14:11), and "anyone who wants to be first among you must be your slave" (**Matthew** 20:27). Meister Eckhart's commentary stresses that "the deeper the humility abyss the higher the supreme exaltation" (**Traités**, p. 85). "(Jesus Christ) was divine, yet he did not cling to his equality with God but emptied himself to assume the condition of a slave" (**Philipp.** 2:7). In the same way, *Harap Alb*, son of an emperor, becomes at the beginning of his initiation the slave of the "beardless one," a character representing the *ego* with all the devils.

[18] In opposition with Ulysses as "beggar," Tom's father and his companions are the evil aspects of the dragon, corresponding to the dark night and not to the superluminous Night of Ulysses.

hart, **Sermons**, II, p. 64). In the same way, Tom's dream is an "upwards" dream, preparatory for a spiritual ascension.

After a "melancholy day," Tom decides to initiate the journey from his hell and misery to the royal palace (19-21). This voyage is only a "preview" of Edward's initiation, because even if the "soul" desperately yearns for immortality, only the awakened Self could accomplish the divine voyage. "The eye with which I see God is the same eye with which God sees me: my eye and God's eye are one and the same eye, and the same one vision, and the same one knowledge, and the same one love" (Eckhart, **Sermons**, I, pp. 123-24). Only *Spiritus* sees the Kingdom of Heaven; *Anima* has no access there.[19] Nonetheless, Tom, in front of the palace's gate, has the vision of the "little prince," who says: "Open the gates and let him in!" Psyche is allowed to enter into the "cavity of the heart" and "the little Prince of Poverty passed in ... to join hands with the Prince of Limitless Plenty" (22-3). That is a "religious" union, not a metaphysical one, because the duality still exists and, in fact, after this short "vision" of the Self, the soul will lose it and will start to believe that there is nothing else beside the *ego*.

Tom and Edward change their clothes, functions, and places; they look miraculously alike, they look like twins (25), but they are

---

[19] "*Samsâra* is just one's own thought; with effort he should cleanse it, then. What is one's thought, that he becomes; this is the eternal mystery" (**Maitri Up.** VI.34). "What we are today comes from our thoughts of yesterday" (**Dhammapada** I.1). Tom dreams to become a prince, and he becomes. But his "upwards" dream stops at the mind level and cannot pass to the "super-rational" order. We'll see later that Mark Twain himself, in his "dark" stories, reduces everything to a "thought," rejecting the supernal world. "When unto mindlessness one comes, then that is the supreme estate!" (**Maitri Up.** VI.34), and the neophyte attains spiritual bliss. Only the Self escapes the ties of the mind. As a preparatory method, thinking of God is good, but it is not enough to be free from the wheel of rebirths. A silent *sannyâsi* transmitted us once, on the shores of Gangâ: "if someone remembers God ten million times, he is able to see God," but here "ten million" symbolizes immeasurability and totality. As Meister Eckhart says, we have to cut even the (measurable) ties of God.

The Twins

not.[20] Tom is just the *ego*, the mortal soul trying to reach the Divine, but only the Divine can do it, that is, only the immortal part, *Spiritus*, the Self, the real prince, can do it. Edward, "the little prince" (27), has to come down into chaos, into Hell, to purify himself and the world, and take possession of the inferior levels, before to ascend and conquer the superior levels. However, Tom's most precious desire comes now true. He asks the prince: "And if that I could clothe me once, sweet sir, as thou are clad, just once," and Edward answers in a godlike manner: "Then so shall it be" (25). They exchange clothes and then "went and stood side by side before a great mirror, and lo, a miracle: there did not seem to have been any change made! They stared at each other, then at the glass, then at each other again" (25-6).

This is a crucial episode and deserves our special attention. First of all, looking at each other, and also at the mirror (which is the same thing), symbolizes a fundamental spiritual concept of the "vision eye to eye" (Coom., **Trad. Art**, p. 233). Tom and Edward's vision of the miraculous resemblance is just a gross and corporeal expression of what anyone experiences when looking in somebody else's eyes; "the face of one who looks into another's eye is shown in the eye over against him, as if in a mirror, and we call this the 'pupil' (*korē*)" (Plato, **Alcibiades** I.132f). The twin image in the other's eye is for the seer his "self's immortal Self," but "the eye that does not 'know itself' will see nothing but itself (this man, So-and-so)" (Coom., **What is Civil.**, pp. 51-2).[21] While looking at each other, Edward sees himself as *ego*, the So-and-so as individual, while Tom sees the Self; yet they think of no difference, and the outside

---

[20] We find something similar in the Celtic tradition. Pwyll prince of Dyfed changes place, appearance ("form and semblance"), and function, with Arawn king of Annwn for one year (**Mabinogion** 4).
[21] In Arabic, the pupil of the eye is called "the person in the eye," identical with the Hindu tradition where is called also person (*purusha*). The great seer Muhyddin Ibn 'Arabi says that "the man is to God what the pupil is to the eye," yet the "man" is the Universal Man (the Self, the immortal Person). See Titus Burckhardt's translation of Muhyddin Ibn 'Arabi, **La sagesse des prophètes**, Albin Michel, 1973, p. 27.

ignorant world will not discern any difference either. A sacred initiation is required to awaken and reveal the shining Self, the immortal Person.

"This shining, immortal Person who is in this sun and this shining, immortal Person who is in the eye – he is just this Self, this Immortal, this Brahma, this All" (**Brhadâranyaka Up.** II.5.5). The dictionaries define the "pupil" as "the opening in the center of the eye which looks like a black spot." Looking into somebody else's eye we can see a small image of ourselves, there, in the pupil of the eye. For that reason in Latin "pupil" is *pupilla* (*pupa*), meaning "little girl" (corresponding to Greek *kore*, Sanskrit *kanînakâ*, Chinese *tóng*,[22] etc.), and illustrating that miniature twin image; note that Latin *pupa* means not only "little girl" but also "puppet" (word derived from the Latin form). Therefore, what we see in the pupil of the eye are ourselves as God's puppets but also, if we can really see, the immortal solar Person, the Self as child. The blackness of the eye, where the "child-like" Self dwells, signifies the super-luminous Night, and it is no surprise that the ancient Egyptians praised the solar Horus as Harpocrates, a child "weak in his lower limbs," imperfect, and mute (Plutarch, **De Iside**, pp. 147, 225). The Self as a little child in the blackness of the eye is equivalent to Horus the child, and corresponds to Godhead as midnight Sun and Dragon without feet and eyes, mute and inactive, the emblem of the Principle resting within the supernal blackness.[23]

Osiris, Harpocrates' father, is black, affirms Plutarch, and the bull sacred to Osiris is also black. "Again, they call Egypt, since it is mostly black, Khemia, like the black part of the eye, and they liken it to a heart" (Plutarch, **De Iside**, pp. 169-171).[24] Plutarch's statement

---

[22] See Martin H. Manser, **Concise English-Chinese Chinese-English Dictionary**, Oxford Univ. Press, 1999.
[23] The black pupil is the only place where the light can enter the eye: the supernal blackness is also the supreme lightness. It is interesting to note that, despite the diverse colors of the eyes, the pupil is always black; in the same way, despite the different colors of the cows, the milk is always white.
[24] See also Guénon's commentary in René Guénon, **Écrits pour Regnabit**, Archè Milan, 1999, p. 113.

The Twins

is most interesting, and its meaning has a universal value. Any traditional kingdom is a "central" land and an image of the Center of the World, which makes it comparable to the divine blackness and also to the pupil of the eye; as we already saw, the Egyptian Thebes was built having the shape of God's eye (Knight, **Vergil**, p. 220). The kingdom and, all the more, its capital-city, represent not only the Eye, but also the Heart of the World, yet we have to keep in mind that the kingdom or the city can also be within us. Egypt is compared to a heart, not so much in shape, but as sacred significance; the immortal Person within the spiritual Sun is the same immortal Person within the pupil of the eye, and is the same immortal Person within the heart: "that golden Person who is within the sun is even He who dwells within the lotus of the heart" (**Maitri Up.** VI.1).[25]

The royal palace is that heart and Edward is the immortal Person (as a child), but only after the completion of his spiritual journey could the little prince actually reign as shining Person; right now, at the end of time, the Self is hiding and nobody can discern between the wheat and the darnel, between Tom and Edward. The two boys look at each other and they see a miracle, not the real Person. There is another "heart," the "heart of the heart," which enhances the picture of the dying cycle: the Great Seal.[26] A special story points out the Great Seal, the token of the royal power, as a spiritual

---

[25] This immortal Person, child and dragon, is also the "Feathered Serpent," another emblem of the supreme Principle, which for the ancient Egyptians is a black-and-white bird, the ibis. Thoth, the lord of wisdom (identified later with Hermes Trismegistus), is described having an ibis head, the head of knowledge and wisdom, similar to Ganesha's elephantine head. A legend tells that when the ibis hides its neck and head under its wings, it looks like a heart, and therefore the Egyptians consider it a sacred bird; there is a Western representation too of a stork as a heart (Guénon, **Écrits**, p. 114). The ibis, the stork, and other similar birds, symbolize the Principle as "Feathered Serpent," and their assimilation with the heart only stresses more this symbolism.

[26] The "heart of the heart" is identical with the pupil of the eye, which Philo calls "the eye of the eye." Philo considers the Intellect as "the soul of the soul" and equal with the pupil, "the pupil which is the eye of the eye" (Philo 10). The Intellect is not the rational mind; between them it is the same difference as between the sun and the moon.

The Everlasting Sacred Kernel

"treasure" comparable to the Holy Grail.[27] Immediately after the two boys changed their clothes, Edward hides the Great Seal, a gesture stressing the ending of the world. While the real prince follows his spiritual journey, the Great Seal remains hidden and lost, illustrating the "Lost Word" of Masonry, and the vanishing of the sacred kernel at the end of time. When Edward, after his spiritual realization, comes back as king and a new cycle starts, the Seal is found. The divine and immortal heart of the new world shines again in the center of the Cosmos. Significantly enough, Tom knows the hiding place of the Great Seal, but he has no idea what the Seal represents, or its value (50, 92): the *ego* has no power to comprehend the celestial treasure. Edward is the one who will remember the hiding place of the Great Seal, this remembrance symbolizing his illumination; because of that, he is eventually recognized as the real and only king, as the immortal Person.[28]

The episode of the clothes exchange bears not only a spiritual meaning, but also reveals an "anti-cosmogony," a mirrored image of the original cosmogony. At the beginning of time, the Principle as Creator (the Godhead as God) desires to become multiple and produce the beings and the worlds. In the Islamic tradition, God says: "I was a Hidden Treasure and *I wished* to be known, and so I created the world" (Lings, **Sufism**, p. 15); the same divine desire appears in the Hindu cosmology: "Prajâpati *desired*, 'May I become multiple, may I be reproduced!'" (**Satapatha Brâhmana** VI.1.1.8). In the

---

[27] The Holy Grail is equivalent to Christ's heart. On the other hand, a legend tells that the Grail's vessel was carved by the angels from an emerald that fell from Lucifer's front, the emerald representing the "third eye" of Shiva (Guénon, **Ecrits**, p. 4). The Holy Grail is heart and eye at the same time, and so has to be understood the Great Seal.

[28] For the Islamic tradition, Muhammad is the "Seal of the prophets" (*khâtam al-nabiyyîn*). See Muhyddin Ibn 'Arabî, **L'Arbre du Monde**, Les Deux Océans, 1982, p. 36. The Universal Man (*al-insân al-kâmil*, the immortal Person) is not only the pupil of the eye but also the "royal seal" which seals the king's treasure chest. When this "seal" disappears the world ends (Ibn 'Arabî, **La Sagesse**, pp. 27-8). Moreover, the heart (*qalb*) of the Universal Man is identical with the "seal" (Ibn 'Arabî, **L'Arbre**, p. 141); see Charles-André Gilis' translation of *Kitâb Fusûs al-Hikam* (Ibn Arabî, **Le livre des chatons des sagesses**, Éd. Al-Bouraq, 1997, I, p. 315).

The Twins

ancient Greek theogony, Eros, the Desire (Love, Mercy), is born ahead of the Cosmos and the gods (Hesiod, **Theogony** 120). This divine love and desire, dwelling within God's heart, unveils as *Logos*, the Word that in the Hebrew and Christian traditions operates the cosmogony: "God said, 'Let there be light,' and there was light" (**Gen.** I.1).

It is understandably hard for a modern mind to accept such a "legend," though modern science copied it emitting the "Big Bang" theory, which is nothing else than the traditional Hindu doctrine of *Parasabda* (the "supreme Sound") and the biblical doctrine of *Logos*. In the divine order, the thought (or desire), the word and the deed are one and the same, a perfect match that illustrates the absolute Truth and makes possible the cosmogony. With the decay of the cycle, these three elements become more and more discordant, which means "with a divided heart" (Latin *dis, cor*), and describes the "lie" and the "falsehood" governing the end of time, when people think one way and talk the other way, or talk one way and act the other way. We also have to comprehend the divine desire as an intellectual love, which the Hebraic *Kabbalah* calls the Thought (*mahshavah*).[29] This Thought dwells in the cavity of the heart, which is the traditional abode of the Intellect, and represents the primeval determination of the Principle as "silent *Logos*," as Word *ab intra*; the immediate next determination is the Thought *ab extra* as Word (*meimra*) in act.[30]

From a profane point of view, the heart lost any intellectuality and remained the dwelling of sentiments and emotions, and human desires and love; "with all one's heart" means profane enthusiasm and desire, and "by heart" refers to memory and mind not to Intel-

---

[29] Gershom Scholem, **Kabbalah**, Meridian, Penguin Books, 1978, p. 93. The elder Horus, "born maimed in the darkness," represents this Thought: "for he was not the world, but only a picture and a vision of the world to come (Plutarch, **De Iside**, p. 205).

[30] There is a close relation between heart and word. Thoth is called "the heart of Re" but also "the tongue of Ptah." "Of the plants found in Egypt they say that the persea is especially sacred to the goddess (Isis) because its fruit is like a heart and its leaf like a tongue" (Plutarch, **De Iside**, p. 225).

lect. Tom's desire to change clothes and Edward's biblical statement, "Then so shall it be," reflect the cosmogony but in a reverse manner. The "discordance" is present by the simple fact that there is duality, even if this is apparently a twin one; moreover, the "thought" belongs to Tom, the "mortal" twin and it leads to a parody of reign, specific for the carnival at the end of time.

At the end of a cycle, the world is upside down: Tom now occupies Edward's place and vice versa. Edward, dressed like a beggar, as Tom's image (but only superficially), tries again and again to state the fact that he is the real prince (as essence). Everybody laughs at him, nobody believes him, nobody recognizes him (28). The profane and ignorant people, at the end of time, have no ability to recognize the sacred kernel and the *avatâra*; when ignorance reigns, the Self is not remembered, it is neglected and forgotten. In the same way, Christ was put to death because he wasn't believed to be the Messiah. Edward is now Tom o' Bedlam (30), a fool, a mad boy. This madness is concluded about Tom too, when playing his royal role (the nobles and King Henry think that he lost hid mind) (32, 44). It is the sacred madness typical of initiation.[31]

The real prince, chased from his own palace, is the same beggar as Ulysses. He starts the journey through Hell: misery and hunger overwhelm Edward, and Tom's father abuses him (57). But we have to understand that all the life's vicissitudes and trials are just sym-

---

[31] This madness is often present in Shakespeare's plays. In *King Lear*, Edgar is disguised as Tom o'Bedlam (III.IV) and simulates demoniac possession (Yates, **The Occult**, p. 156); yet he is the spiritual guide and seer (Martin Lings, **The Sacred Art of Shakespeare**, Inner Traditions, 1998, p. 111). The king's Fool affirms: "This cold night will turn us all to fools and madmen" (III.IV). We deal here with a "problem of discrimination." Edward and Tom's madness are related, but gradually a real folly is uncovered, an infernal madness, regarding Tom's acceptance to be a king. Shakespeare always has in mind "the sacred radiance of the sun,/ The mysteries of Hecate, and the night" (**Lear** I.I), and it is the reader's task to discriminate the wheat from the darnel, the light from darkness. The same thing happens with the symbolism of melancholy. Melancholy can be celestial ("melancholy of inspired vision") or demonical ("melancholy of witchcraft and evil"). Hamlet's melancholy and madness are divine and his father's phantom is not an infernal ghost but a prophetic vision (Yates, **The Occult**, pp. 153-4). Tom's melancholy (19) is an inspired one that starts the whole initiatory process.

bols for the initiatory trials. It would be a great mistake to think that some individual, who has to suffer and overcome a lot of difficulties and troubles, accomplishes a sort of initiation and reaches a higher spiritual level.

The little prince has, of course, a guide, who will protect him during the infernal trials, a noble knight named Miles Hendon. Miles shows up exactly when the old king dies and Edward has to complete his journey to the throne (66). The knight plays a special role: on the one hand, he is a "divine presence" and a "guardian angel"; on the other hand, Miles himself achieves an initiation, in parallel with Edward. As "guardian angel" he is Edward's rescuer, who helps to liberate Edward from the power of evil forces (70, 75). Miles considers himself as "a knight of the Kingdom of Dreams and Shadows" (77), the king being Edward, and we see the similarity with "A Midsummer Night's Dream," but also Twain's attraction for the "country of dreams."

The little prince is for a while in the power of the most abject gang of burglars, thieves, vagabonds and beggars, but he will resist all pressure and will not beg or steal: that is the "English hell," as Twain says (112). Similar to Christ, Edward suffers a mockery coronation as "Foo-foo the First, king of the Mooncalves" (113-4), the villains crowning him with a tin basin, and using a barrel as throne. He escapes though, and continues his journey; like Pym, Edward is hungry and chilly, and tired and drowsy (119). He finds shelter for the night in a stall, beside a calf, like a newborn Jesus. "He was free of the bonds of servitude and crime, free of the companionship of base and brutal outlaws ... he was happy" (121). Next morning, the little prince will say: "when a king has fallen so low that the very rats do make a bed of him, it surely meaneth that his fortunes be upon the turn, since it is plain he can no lower go" (122. That means he reaches the bottom of Hell and is prepared for his ascension to light. The little prince becomes humble, the humblest, matching Meister Eckhart's saying, "the deeper the humility abyss the higher the supreme exaltation"; in all humility, he will wash the dishes in the house of a very humble peasant woman (126).[32]

Before ascending to the paradisiacal center, Edward has to suffer a ritual death. The little prince wanders into the dark and dense forest (the labyrinth) and finds a hermit's hut as center (127). But it is the dragon's center. A fake holy hermit claims to be an archangel, yet he is the "fallen" angel, the devil, which has to perform the sacrifice and kill the royal neophyte. The little prince is completely tied up and threatened by the hermit's knife, and we have to assume that he is ritually killed, and resurrects after (129-136); again, Miles Hendon helps the boy to escape the evil forces, which have made a last attempt to keep Edward within the infernal darkness (142, 149).[33]

The last trial that follows shows openly that there is a parallel initiation and a double spiritual realization. Not only the little prince but also Miles has embarked on a spiritual path. The king and his guardian knight, seek refuge at Miles' castle, which has become the city of Dis, under the power of Miles' brother, Hugh (155-156). Of special interest are Miles Hendon and his evil brother Hugh. They represent also the Self and the *ego*, similar to Dumas' Charpatian brothers, Grégoriska and Kostaki. In this case, Hugh is, unlike Tom, the very inferior *ego* with all the greed and demons and low appetites, and the "melancholy of witchcraft." Hugh is "a mean spirit, covetous, treacherous, vicious, underhanded – a reptile" (74); he is the dragon at the end of time and the regent of the dying world, who has abducted the divine Knowledge, that is, the Virgin represented by lady Edith. Lady Edith is the virgin betrothed to Arthur, the eldest brother, yet Arthur is in love with another maid,

---

[32] "The humble man and God are one." The height of the Godhead is the depth of the humility (Eckhart, **Sermons**, I, 135).

[33] The wandering into the forest and the encounter of a fake hermit is an episode that we can find in the Arthurian tales. *The Trials and Temptations of Bors* represents a good example. Bors, during the Quest of the Holy Grail, meets a false hermit, signifying the devil ("the enemy"). Twelve maidens, who are similar to the twelve serving women who betrayed Penelope (**Odyssey** XXII.465), tempt the hero, but Bors overcomes the trials and, after that, he meets the genuine hermit (**The Quest**, pp. 190-9).

The Twins

and Edith loves Miles who also is madly in love with her. Due to Hugh's intrigues, Miles is banished from England for three years and he suffers "hard knocks, privation," and eventually captivity for another seven years (75). Like the little prince, Miles has his own journey through Hell, which takes ten years, as the Trojan War. Meanwhile, Arthur dies (163) and Hugh becomes the unworthy husband of Lady Edith. Hendon Hall is now the city of Dis, where the Virgin is captive (159).

Hugh rejects his brother, pretending he doesn't know him, and sends Miles and Edward to prison (160). There, a last purificatory trial takes place: Edward is punished by being whipped, like Christ was, but Miles becomes the "whipping boy," the scapegoat, and takes the lashes (171). They are released after, which means that the infernal trials come to an end, and the paradisiacal center is nearby.[34] Edward and Miles arrive in London (175), just in time for the Coronation Day. Tom appears now as pure *ego*, enjoying his royal position "more and more every day," and hoping to be crowned king (176-8). Yet when "the Archbishop of Canterbury lifted up the crown of England and held it over the trembling mock king's head," Edward shows up (188). The Self becomes visible and the *ego* has to admit him and recognize him: "Loose him and forbear! He *is* the king!"[35]

---

[34] The prison is a typical symbol for the mundane bondage. Platon uses it and *Maitri Up.* (IV.2) compares the soul (*bhûtâtman*) with "a lame man – bound with the fetters ... like the condition of one in prison."

[35] Tom and Hugh are the two criminals, the good and the evil thief, crucified with Christ, on the right and on the left. Hugh is the lower part of the soul, he is the evil *ego*, which rejects the Self and fails to recognize it. Tom is the upper part of the soul; he is the good *ego*, which doesn't hesitate to proclaim the Self as real king. He still is a "criminal" because on Coronation Day, just before admitting his imposture, Tom rejects his own mother: "I do not know you woman!" (182). This rejection is identical with Peter's triple rejection of Christ, and awakes the "remorse" and the "penitence"; also shows the difference between the *ego* and the Self. In the Celtic tradition, there is such a theme of "filial disobedience." Peredur leaves for adventure disobeying his mother, who dies of dismay (**Mabinogion** 160). The same thing happens with Cú Chulaind (**Early Irish** 136) or with Percivale, knight of the Round Table. Yet here the rejection of the mother is a sign of cutting the corporeal ties, as illustrated by Christ himself and more recently by Ramana Maharshi. Related to this,

The Everlasting Sacred Kernel

Edward's spiritual voyage is almost complete. The supreme trial, which brings Liberation and makes the neophyte match his royal function, occurs: the little prince solves the enigma of the lost Great Seal and unveils its hiding place. At the king's command, Lord St. John brings back into view the "hidden treasure" (193), and Edward is, consequently, recognized as the true king (194); with the spiritual essence recovered, a new cycle can begin.[36] In parallel, Miles' initiation ends also. Miles Hendon is recognized as Edward's noble knight and takes his normal place (200), while his brother, Hugh, is punished and dies (203); Miles obtains the Virgin and the "kingdom." The darkness is replaced by light and the chaos by order.[37]

Thetis' attempt to make her son, Achilles, invulnerable by dipping him in the river Styx, presents a "countercurrent" meaning. The mother tries to protect the *ego*, or Achilles obtains Liberation precisely due to his "vulnerable" heel, where the divine Ray penetrates, against his mother's "will." Same story with Balder, the famous god of the Norsemen. Frigga, his mother, makes Balder invulnerable by asking all the animate and inanimate things to swear not to injure her son. Yet Hodur kills his brother, Balder, with a twig of mistletoe, the only thing that wasn't asked to swear. In the Celtic and Norse traditions the mistletoe symbolizes the spiritual Knowledge and the divine Ray.

[36] The Great Seal is the Shakespeare's lost Perdita, who is found at the end; "Our Perdita is found" (**The Winter's Tale** V.III).

[37] Miles Hendon resembles the Knights of the Round Table. Mark Twain's interest for the Arthurian legends is well known. Miles' elder brother is called Arthur and Edith "was betrothed to Arthur from the cradle" (74). Miles' love for Edith is Lancelot's love for King Arthur's wife, Queen Guinevere. In fact, Miles and Edward, they both are substitutes of Lancelot. Lancelot, when he arrives at King Arthur's court, is just a boy, a "youth" like Edward, and he is called "the King's son," which entitles him to be a "little prince." King Arthur makes Lancelot a knight on the feast of Saint John (the summer solstice); we see something similar when Edward makes Miles a knight (77). Saint John has a major importance in Chivalry and Freemasonry. "My lord Saint John was the most praiseworthy and meritorious man ever conceived of a woman by fleshly union," says Lancelot's mentor, the Lady of the Lake (See **Lancelot of the Lake**, Oxford Univ. Press, 1989, p. 58); by coincidence, lord St. John is the one who, following King Edward's orders, brings the Great Seal from its hiding place. Also most interesting is the "lost identity" of Lancelot. No one knows Lancelot's name and origin, even Lancelot doesn't know his name, and his initiation has as goal exactly the uncovering of his "lost identity" (**Lancelot** 71). Lancelot is a "nobody" and so are Miles and Edward. No one recognizes little prince's identity and Hugh doesn't admit that Miles is his brother (153). Only at the end, they recover their "personalities," the "lost identity" playing the role of the "Lost Word" or of the Holy Grail.

The Twins

An interesting character is the "whipping boy" that helps Tom behave like a prince, teaching him the rules (89-91). He is an historical character, used by King Henry VIII for his son (Hendrickson 716). The term became afterwards identical with "scapegoat," which derives from the *Bible*: a goat is charged with all the sins of the sons of Israel (**Leviticus** 16:20-22). For the Western world, the most illustrious "scapegoat" is Jesus Christ who came down to redeem the sinful humankind, and who is the "whipping boy" too, because before to be crucified He was whipped for our sins.[38]

This idea, combined with the twins' theme, is used by Daphne du Maurier, the author of the once famous *Rebecca*, in the novel *The Scapegoat*, written about 70 years after Twain had written *The Prince and the Pauper*.[39]

We see a similar beginning of the plot. Two complete strangers, one a poor teacher, an Englishman, the other one a noble, a French count, meet and change clothes and places. John has no family, a reflection of the divine orphan; he is very unhappy with his mundane life, a lonely person, dreaming in another world and disgusted by his terrestrial failure. John comes to France and wants to go to a monastery, "Abbaye de la Grande-Trappe" (the "spiritual center"), "to find the love of God" (11). He is looking for a spiritual goal, for a "returning home," wondering about the "inner man." Jean is the master of the castle, which represents our dying world. He is evil, though human also, because at the end of time, humankind has evil tendencies. "The motive force in human nature is greed," says Jean (17), and we know that for Dante greed is a most terrible sin of humanity and marks the end of the world, the reign of devils and infernal forces. Jean manipulates his family (which symbolizes the decayed humankind) and each member is in distress. The well of the castle is dry and useless (167) – a striking "sign of times" illustrating the "abduction of waters" at the end of the cycle and hu-

---

[38] It is interesting that Iamblichus suggests that the stork is such a "scapegoat," analogous to the Christian symbolism of the pelican (Iamblichus 11). During the Quest of the Holy Grail, Bors has a vision of a great bird that stabbs its breast and revives its dead young with the dropping blood (**The Quest** 181).

[39] See Daphne du Maurier, **The Scapegoat**, Simon & Schuster, 1970.

mankind's ignorance.[40] Jean meets John by chance and they stare at each other and look into the mirror, being, like Tom and Edward, amazed by the resemblance. They are so alike, that "it was as though one man stood there" (9).

John is the "scapegoat" (49, 290). He is a substitute of Christ, who was the "scapegoat" of mankind; yet John pretends to be a fool not a saviour (313), which only stresses his divine-like mission. The whole story develops in seven biblical days (309), during which John tries to save Jean's family and succeeds at the end in making them hope for a future. John plays the jester, and tries to be detached; for him Jean's relatives are puppets, and everything is just a play, a sport (66). He plays with the human puppets to end the world and starts a new one. The well will have water again (293), and "the sun rose" (287).

At the same time, Jean, replacing John in England, cuts all his mundane ties (he quits the teaching job and sells the furniture and ends the rental of the apartment in London). Now John has "no future" (317); in fact, he becomes free, he gets his Liberation. A new cycle begins (328), with Jean coming back as a new regent and John retiring to the monastery.

John and Jean are the twins. Jean's name is the French translation of John and it is obvious that we have in front of us the symbol of the two Saint John, a very precious emblem of the Western tradition. St. John the Apostle, the most beloved disciple of Jesus, corresponds to winter solstice and to the "gate of gods," being a direct substitute of Christ who is born at winter solstice. St. John the Baptist, who is born six months earlier than Jesus, corresponds to summer solstice and to the "gate of ancestors." John reflects the first one, Jean the second one. But Daphne du Maurier's novel is not transmitting a well-defined symbolism and sometimes John and Jean appear mixed together.[41]

---

[40] "People like this (i.e., sinners) are dried-up wells" (**2 Peter** 2:17).
[41] Even when the twins seem to be clearly differentiated, decoding the meaning is not easy. A famous example is the twin children of Odin and Frigga, Balder and Hodur. The Norse twins are, like Shakespeare's Helena and Hermia, opposite in appearance and character. Balder is solar, shining and beautiful, with golden locks;

The Twins

The "country of dreams" is present too: "So often, dreaming, I was the shadow, watching myself take part in the action of the dream. Now it was happening.... Everything I saw had the quality of a dream," John confesses (13, 28). A singular character is a child, a little girl (Latin *pupilla*), Marie-Noel, whose name directs us to the winter solstice and the Virgin. She is a mystic, a God worshipper, and has dreams and visions (43), being comparable with Ariel (78). Marie-Noel gives us an important clue regarding the recognition of the sacred kernel, especially when we deal with mundane literature. "Sometimes," says the child (299), "the devil tempts us in disguise.... The point is to discover which is which, who gives us the things we want, the God or the devil. It must be one or the other, but how do you tell?"

The answer is what the traditional doctrines call the "power of discrimination."

Hodur is sombre, taciturn, and blind (Guerber 197). Obviously enough, Hodur represents the dragon without feet and eyes; he is an emblem of Meister Eckhart's Godhead (the Principle *ab intra*) and Balder is the Sun with "one thousand feet." Hodur is only apparently the evil brother or the mortal soul. In fact, Balder is the mortal soul (despite his invulnerability), and only when Hodur kills him with the mistletoe, he becomes immortal.

Chapter Ten

THE EYE OF THE HEART

ÂTMÂ, THE UNIVERSAL SPIRIT, which is not different from Brahma, is concealed from our eyes by three main veils that – so the Hindu tradition states – represent its "limitative conditions" and correspond to the threefold-partition of the universal manifestation (the "Three Worlds") and, accordingly, to the tripartite constitution of the total being (*Corpus-Anima-Spiritus*). The "waking" and the "dream" states (**Mândûkya Up.** I, 3-4), components of the changeable and perishable individuality, embody the external grosser veils. Closer to *Âtmâ* is a diaphanous veil, the "deep sleep" state, a state without dreams and full of bliss (*ananda*), but beyond these three states there is the supreme and unconditioned one, "The Fourth," where *Âtmâ* dwells in itself (**Mândûkya Up.** I.5-7). These last two are essential for a complete initiation and spiritual realization. The "deep sleep" state, corresponding to Dante's *Paradiso*, leads to the Gate of Liberation, yet it is still a limitative state and the truly effective and total liberation through the Sun-door aims for *Turîya*, "The Fourth" state.[1] Consequently, the grosser states are inadequate for a full initiation and in the best case they could provide support for a realization of the *Lesser Mysteries*.

In the domain of *Lesser Mysteries*, the danger is tremendous. The "waking" and "dream" states constitute the realm where the satanic

---

[1] "The Fourth" state corresponds to Meister Eckhart's Godhead, the divine abyss, where God appears without names and attributes (Eckhart, **Sermons**, I, 56).

The Eye of the Heart

forces have access and, the closer the end of time is, the stronger they act. The communication with the superior states breaks and the path towards *Turîya* (or at least towards the "deep sleep" state) is lost, which facilitates the chaos and confusion in the individual order. And the corporeal sheath, the grossest, is not the most vulnerable, even if the lower appetites and desires are its emanations; but the psychical sheath, with all those sentiments and emotions, and especially the mind which represents the favourite place for mixed influences. The mind is the fanatical sustainer of duality that permits the Devil to feel legitimated. "As in dream the mind acts through Mâyâ presenting the appearance of duality, so also in the waking state the mind acts, through Mâyâ (the art of illusion), presenting the appearance of duality" and only in the "deep sleep" state the mind ceases to act and "becomes identical with fearless Brahma" (**Mândûkya Up.** III.29-35). An untamed mind maintains the illusion of reality; that is what happens in the "waking" and "dream" states. The world perceived in dream is illusory, but also the objects seen in the waking state are illusory. "The nature of objects is the same in the waking state and dream" (**Mândûkya Up.** II.4). In Daoism, the famous Zhuang Zi tells about his dream in which he was a butterfly, and he puts the essential question: "Who actually am I? A butterfly dreaming to be Zuang Zi, or Zuang Zi dreaming to be a butterfly?" The answer of Daoism is similar to that of the Hindu doctrine: both are illusions of the One (of his "art," Mâyâ), and life is just a dream; the Principle alone has absolute reality (Wieger 225-7).[2]

It is desirable then to abandon the illusion and look upwards to the everlasting and non-dual Principle. Shakespeare's *A Midsummer Night's Dream* repeatedly illustrates the above fundamental doctrine.

---

[2] Life as an "illusion" has to be understood as a relative reality, a reality depending on a principle that gives and guarantees it. The "waking" and "dream" states have a relative reality, which is illusory by itself. The "creatures" are pure nothingness, having no reality by themselves. This nothingness has no common measure with the Nothingness (the Godhead as pure Reality). Giving up God (as Creator of nothingness) the initiate obtains God (as Nothingness) (Eckhart, **Sermons**, I, p. 122).

The Everlasting Sacred Kernel

Illusion, "country of dreams," chaos and confusion, sports, characterize this special night; yet at the end order is restored and a new luminous cycle is ready to begin, proving the ties with the Principle. Dante travels through Hell (where there is no hope), yet at the end he rises to Heaven, reaching the Celestial Paradise. "No hope" is only for those lost into the labyrinthine "outer darkness," those who look downwards and not upwards, those who wander without a guide or having a deceiving one. With the evolvement of the cycle, more and more often the interest is directed towards Hell, ghosts, dreams and "chthonic gods"; the tendency (*guna*) *tamas* (error, inertia, darkness and ignorance) dominates, and these who follow *tamas* go downwards, *Bhagavad-Gîtâ* says (XIV.18). For the *tamasic* individuals, the monster's jaws are the Jaws of Death and not the Gate of Liberation, and Existence is a chaos containing nightmares, spirits, fear and death.[3]

This kind of limitation due to the ignorance of the decaying world happens equally for extensive and secondary cycles. We noted it with the evolution in time of Western literature. Alexandre Dumas, Jules Verne, Bram Stoker, Edgar Poe, even if they are forced to provide dwelling for the sacred kernel in their works, all are more concerned with looking downwards. For Melville, the quest of the white whale is a fearful enterprise, Moby Dick illustrating the Jaws of Death.[4] For Verne, the journey through Hell leads to illusion and destruction.

---

[3] A Romanian legend, quoted by Coomaraswamy, after Geticus (**La Doctrine**, p. 115), says that from the middle of the sea rose a worm, which became a butterfly. The butterfly was God and the remains of the worm became the Devil. The butterfly corresponds to *sattva*, the ascending *guna*: "those who follow sattva go upwards," *Bhagavad-Gîtâ* states (XIV.18). The rest of the worm corresponds to *tamas* and to our lower appetites and desires. "The knowledge of men of heart bears them up, the knowledge of men of body weighs them down" (Rumi 52), where "heart" is *Spiritus*.
[4] This representation prevailed already during the Renaissance, after the decline of the traditional society in Europe. A German incunabulum printed in 1473 shows the mouth of Hell as the jaws of a sea monster. Breughel the Elder engraves in 1558 a picture showing a huge whale's throat as the entrance to Hell (See Grillot de Givry, **Witchcraft, Magic & Alchemy**, Dover Publ., 1971, pp. 30-1).

The Eye of the Heart

In Shakespeare's *The Winter's Tale*, Hermione, whose illusory "image" is a statue – a perfect copy of herself, symbolizes *Madonna Intelligenza* and *Shekinah* (the "divine presence" of *Kabbalah*), the immortal Knowledge and Tradition descending to initiate a new cycle and establish a new spiritual center. Hermione is absolutely real, infinitely more real than the world. When Paulina, the Initiatress, commands her to descend, she says: "Music, awake her: strike!" (V.III). The music has divine powers providing resurrection and life. For Verne, on the contrary, music causes death and is, like Stilla's image, just an illusion, a devil's trick. In the same way, Dumas and Stoker, instead of suggesting a luminous way upwards, maintain their stories at the level of graveyards, vampires and death.[5] Yet, in the modern times, especially these authors, with interest in extraordinary tales, afford the opportunity to the sacred kernel to find refuge in their work. Despite their attraction to the *tamasic* domain, a spiritual symbolism is very likely to hide under the fictional surface, even though oppressed by parody, abuse and inferior attacks.[6] Beside the rare authors who still consciously know some genuine traditional data, the majority are more or less innocent transmitters and it is the reader's responsibility to be capable of unveiling or restoring a sacred meaning where this is the case. Not sentimentalism and profane analysis, but the power of discrimination in accordance with the sacred writings of divine inspiration should be the infallible guide – say the seers. The power of discrimination (symbolized by *Hamsa* in the Hindu tradition and by *Qor'ân* in Islam) guarantees the right choice between heavenly (su-

---

[5] It seems that E. T. A. Hoffmann played a very suspect role in all of this. His work influenced not only Dumas, Verne and Poe, but also Freud and Carl Jung.

[6] It is a special sort of a game. The Devil's parody of the spiritual domain and sacred rituals, its monkey-like aping of symbols, constitute an attempt to confuse and delude, in a vain hope of eliminating the celestial influences. The Devil is tricky, a master of deception, and altering the divine symbols and mystifying their meaning, it tries to take control over the sacred kernel. On the other hand, the sacred kernel takes advantage of this parody to remain alive and accessible to a true quest. The inferior influences have no access to the spiritual and celestial domain, only to the psychical one, therefore the sacred kernel, even when covered with dirt or devilish illusions, will preserve its divine significance.

pernal) and terrestrial (infernal) symbols, between the immortal and mortal twin, between the wheat and the darnel (**Matthew** 13:24-30), which could cohabit together, as happens in Christ's parable. The same cohabitation appears in the literary works, which always imposes a selective approach.

Edgar Allan Poe's *Pym* is mostly concerned with evil and infernal trials; even at the end, we are not sure if Poe was looking upwards when he made the shrouded human figure appear, or if he was subtly influenced by spiritualism or other occultist movements. Poe considers that the world with good and bad, and all the contradictions, is initially created from One, the pure Spirit, and the supreme Being. As in the Hindu tradition, to manifest itself, the supreme Spirit has to express the duality, which is the cause of evil, and the world exists supported by action and reaction, attraction and repulsion.[7] The elements of the world created by the action of One have inside them as reaction the tendency to return to the origin, to unity. Creation is multiplication, the dismemberment of Osiris; the final goal is the recreation of unity, putting back Osiris, and that can happen only by exaggerating the evil part that will produce the destruction of it. In a way, that is the reason of the carnivals, which permit free action of the evil and encourage the manifestations of evil in order to consume it. It seems that Pym is doing the same thing: he wants to exhaust the evil, and his dreams about infernal events, his tenebrous desires ("for they amounted to desires") are part of his salvation; but Poe's vision of redemption and spiritual trials, even if, apparently, corresponds to some traditional data, is a very dark and deceiving vision. Poe is so attracted towards the infernal experiences that he forgets St. Paul's sayings: "You might as well say that since my untruthfulness makes God demonstrate his truthfulness and thus gives Him glory, I should not be judged to be a sinner at all. That would be the same as saying: Do evil as a means

---

[7] About a comparison to the Hindu tradition see Arnolds Grava, **L'aspect métaphysique du mal dans l'oeuvre littéraire de Charles Baudlaire et d'Edgar Allan Poe**, Slatkine Reprints, 1976, pp. 81-2 (Poe's *Eureka* is discussed, yet Grava confounds manifestation with non-manifestation).

to good. Some slanderers have accused us of teaching this, but they are justly condemned" (**Romans** 3:7-8).[8]

In *Ms. Found in a Bottle* Poe describes the pole, the center, as a fearful abyss, a whirlpool in which, amid a bellowing and thundering of ocean and tempest, the ship, whirling in concentric circles, is falling down. Mark Twain wrote in 1896 a similar story, unfinished, called *The Enchanted Sea-Wilderness*, in which he depicts an infernal abyss, close to the South Pole, and named the "Devil's Race Track."[9] The sea voyage starts at the winter solstice and it is directed southward; eventually, the brig reaches the "bewitched domain" of circular shape, being "in the whirl and suck of the Devil's Race-Track." The "Great Dark" governs there, but in the center there is "a trap" called the "Everlasting Sunday" where ghost-ships keep rotating and a forever bright sky replaces the darkness. Like in Poe's *Pym*, black and white alternates, marking the center, but in Twain's case it is more obvious the infernal character of the abyss; even the "Everlasting Sunday," which normally should symbolize the eternity and peace of the spiritual and paradisiacal center, is a "ghostland."[10]

Another unfinished story, so-called *The Great Dark*,[11] presents an illusory world seen through a microscope, which reminds of Verne's

---

[8] St. Paul's sayings may be compared to the idea found in different traditions about the advantage of the "Iron Age" (Georgel 218 ff.). However, all the spiritual teachings are peremptory in stating that liberation doesn't mean enhancing our evil side; on the contrary, we have to fight the devils within us, which provoke the evil to enhance itself towards its own destruction.

[9] **The Devil's Race-Track: Mark Twain's Great Dark Writings**, Univ. of California Press, 1980, p. 29.

[10] In August 1896, Mark Twain's favorite daughter, Susy, dies. This misfortune and others made Twain turn to spiritualism and develop his "dark" writings. He is not an isolate case; tragic deaths in the family made others to find consolation in spiritualism (Guénon, **L'erreur**, p. 372). Hasdeu, a brilliant scholar we referred to, became a spiritualist after his beloved young daughter died. But for Twain, the "ghostland" is interwoven with the "country of dreams" and he studied William James' theory about dreams (note that James at the end of his life became involved with spiritualism). See John S. Tuckey, **Mark Twain and Little Satan**, Purdue Univ. Studies, 1963, p. 27 and Guénon, **L'erreur**, p. 89.

[11] See Bernard DeVoto's commentary in **Mark Twain, Letters from the Earth**, Crest Book, 1964, pp. 231 ff.

telescope that opened the window to illusion and evil. In this story, Mark Twain introduces a "master puppeteer" named the "Superintendent of Dreams," who in *The Mysterious Stranger* becomes the Little Satan.[12] *The Great Dark* uses, like *The Enchanted Sea-Wilderness*, *Pym*'s skeleton: a ship aiming at the South Pole, enters a zone of total darkness (the Great Dark) and is sailing toward a Great White Glare, a zone of "disastrous bright light" (Twain, **Letters**, p. 227). As Melville's fearful white, Twain's light is not the spiritual illumination but a terrible, demonic light.[13] This story seems to be not about "ghostland" but about the "country of dreams," suggesting that life is an illusion, and showing the confusion between "waking" and "dream" states.[14] Twain appears in agreement with the Hindu tradition and Zhuang Zi, yet for him there is no other reality. This limitation to the individual order, without any link to the supernal levels

---

[12] "Little Satan" is a suitable expression used by Tuckey.

[13] That is not surprising, thinking of some occultist movements, in Twain's time, which praised Lucifer as "light-carrier" and "Creative Intelligence" (Guénon, **L'erreur**, p. 303). Unfortunately, this Lucifer isn't different from Satan, which makes his "light" a satanic light.

[14] Henry, the main character of the story, considers the miniature sea voyage only a dream, not real life, but his wife, Alice, regards their previous life as a dream and this one, on the ship, as real (Twain, **Letters**, pp. 207-8). Normally, the "dream" state, as part of the psychical domain, is open to influences coming from "above" and "below." The former are, as Titus Burckhardt says, "the dreams coming from the Angel"; they carry a genuine spiritual symbolism and sometimes they have a providential meaning (see Joseph's dream about Christ's conception, **Matthew** 1:20). The latter are "dreams of satanic impulsion, containing palpable caricatures of sacred forms" and opposing the "dreams of divine or angelic inspiration." The satanic dreams bring a sensation of "obsession and vertigo; it is the attraction of an abyss" (Burckhardt, **Mirror**, p. 57). In some ancient *Mysteries*, this abyss was described as mire, symbolizing Hell, but it is a huge difference between the initiate "descending to Hell" and then ascending to Paradise, and the profane "falling into the mire." Descending to Hell, the neophyte transforms and integrates his inferior levels; falling into the mire, the profane is caught by the mire without hope of salvation (Guénon, **Le règne**, p. 310). This very abyss is described by Poe and Twain in some works as a whirlpool, a Hell without salvation, indicating the "fall into the mire." Still, we have to keep in mind that in *Pym*, God's support is invoked continuously, which suggests an upcoming deliverance. Also, in Twain's "dark" stories the "country of dreams" is "open" downwards and "sealed" upwards, yet in *The Prince and the Pauper* Tom's dream world is "open" upwards and his dreams actually initiate the whole spiritual process.

The Eye of the Heart

of more consistent reality, facilitates the *tamasic* actions, which try to replace the traditional symbolism of the sacred kernel with counterfeits and deceiving meanings.[15] Therefore, Twain's "country of dreams" is also a "ghostland," wherein during the process of confining everything to the psycho-physical domain the spiritual order (the "deep sleep" state as super-individual, celestial world) is being replaced with "spiritualism" or other hoaxes, which can be crowded into the individual plane.[16] For that reason the "Superintendent of Dreams" is described as a spirit, a ghost (Twain, **Letters**, p. 195).

A detail of this strange story brings further clarification: the "Superintendent of Dreams" plays with Turner, emptying unnoticed a couple of times his coffee cup (Twain, **Letters**, pp. 195-8). He is not only a transparent ghost, but also a jester. He is a "master puppeteer," creator of a dream world in which he plays tricks. Not once Shakespeare suggested that life is just a play, rephrasing the traditional point of view that Brahma created the world by way of sport. In *A Midsummer Night's Dream*, the jester has an important role. He represents the sum of celestial (supernal) and terrestrial (infernal) influences, he is the expression of *yin-yang* or better, of the chessboard; he is the illustration of God's creative work as a playful sport or a game, the creatures being God's toys or puppets.[17] It is interesting that Shakespeare, as if he wanted to stress the ambiguity of

---

[15] As we said before, there is no perfect deception; there is always a hint to reveal the truth. For example, in Twain's unfinished story, Turner, the mate, thinks, "that the world has come to an end," because there is no sun or moon or stars (Twain, **Letters**, p. 200). This remark is enough to warn us. At the end of a cycle, the link with the Principle is extremely damaged and everything is limited to the individual order, which implicitly explains Twain's attitude.
[16] Another "hoax" could be the theory of subconscious. G. K. Watkins, comparing Poe's *Pym* to Twain's *The Great Dark* (**God and Circumstances**, Peter Lang Publishing, 1989), makes the common error to confound the subconscious with spirituality, that is, to confound the "below" with the "above." Spirituality belongs to the "super-conscious" and to the "super-rational" (see Shri Aurobindo, **Le guide du Yoga**, Albin Michel, 1970, pp. 115-6, Guénon, **Le règne**, pp. 303-313, and Burckhardt, **Mirror**, pp. 45-67).
[17] About the world as a play (in the Hindu tradition *Lîlâ*) see Coom., **Metaphysics**, pp. 148 ff. About the world as a chess-board see Burckhardt, **Mirror**, pp. 142 ff.

the jester, calls him now Puck, now Robin Goodfellow.[18] Puck is usually represented as a child, a boy, which is very significant. Generally, all the magic entities and forces of the psychical world are described in different traditions as dwarfs or giants or strange creatures.[19] The goblins, elves and fairies are "little people," and in Shakespeare's play, the fairies in Titania's service are insignificant, of a mustard seed size. But Puck is not only a "little" one, he is a child, which suggests, as we saw in the case of the fairy tales, a sacred meaning.[20]

The children, with their innocence, are the best representation of an *avatâra* or of an "elected" one[21]; also they illustrate, with their involvement in playful activities and games played just for the sake of them, God as Master Puppeteer. Puck's tricks and knavery, deliberate or not, reiterate the playful behaviour of a child. Robin

---

[18] Puck sings: "Up and down, up and down,/ I will lead them up and down;/ I am fear'd in field and town:/ Goblin, lead them up and down" (III.II.396-399), which illustrates the opposite tendencies governing the world. In the medieval legends, Robin Goodfellow, called also Hobgoblin, is a merry jester who "was to harm none but knaves and queans and was to love those that honest be, and help them in necessity." Puck, on the other hand, seemed to be a demon, an evil spirit (See Thomas Keightley, **The World Guide to Gnomes, Fairies, Elves and other Little People**, Avenel Books, 1978, pp. 287, 314-8). Usually, the "little people" (fairies, elves) represent subtle forces of the psychical domain where influences from "above" or "below" could also intervene. But Shakespeare's Puck is not an evil spirit. When Puck describes the damned spirits and the ghosts, spirits of the dark and afraid of light, urging Oberon to hurry up since soon the dawn will come, Oberon replies: "we are spirits of another sort/ I with the Morning's love have oft made sport" (III.II.378-389), which makes Puck a messenger of a supernal power. Puck is Oberon's jester (II.I.44); he is Robin Goodfellow, a shrewd and knavish sprite (II.I.33-39), and also Hobgoblin who brings good luck (II.I.40-1), yet he is used by a celestial influence and eventually, his jests and tricks are forced to obey a higher law.
[19] The "little people" are the "powers of the soul," good or evil, the "elementals" protecting the Psyche (as *jîvâtmâ*, the "living soul," which is the projection of the Self into individual life) (Coom., **Metaphysics**, p. 118).
[20] In the same way, the mustard seed, "the least of all seeds" (**Matthew** 13:31-2), symbolizes the everlasting, spiritual seed, which appears the smallest into the corporeal order and, in fact, is the greatest. Yet the "little people" are only indirectly related to this symbolism.
[21] "Therefore let a knower of Brahma remain in a childlike state (*bâlya*)" (**Brhadâranyaka Up.** III.V.1, and **Brahma Sûtras** III.IV.47, 50).

The Eye of the Heart

Goodfellow at the age of six, says the legend, was already a mischievous jester (Keightley 287). There are other famous examples, like Hermes who, barely born, stole Apollo's herds. But Puck's model is Cupid or Eros, whose representation oscillates between that of a young man and of a knavish child.[22]

Twain's "Superintendent of Dreams" is a kind of Puck, but he plays an ambitious role, which ruins the symbolism. He is not under a higher command, because there is no higher level. He creates a microscopic world, the "little people" constituting here the corporeal order, even if it is a "dream world." The character is more obvious in *The Mysterious Stranger* where he is Satan but called Traum (German "dream"); he is a boy, who creates a "small" world with small people and animals made of clay, indicating that Twain thought of him as Creator, yet even if he is presented as an angel and Lucifer's nephew, there can be no mistake: he is the Devil.[23]

---

[22] Cupid is present in Shakespeare's play, and he is as knavish as Puck: "Cupid is a knavish lad/ Thus to make poor females mad" (III.II.440-1). The magic flower used by Puck, "before milk-white, now purple," got its power from Cupid's arrow (II.I.155-167). Curiously, Shakespeare stresses that Oberon saw the flight of Cupid's arrow at the same time with hearing the celestial song of a mermaid on a dolphin's back (II.I.150-154). The dolphin bears an important spiritual meaning related to Apollo. Note that Cupid's mother, Venus, is a sea-maid. Cupid-Eros and Venus present a vast symbolism, cosmological and spiritual, closely linked to Love as Divine Madness, Creative Impulse and cosmic playful force, and used by Shakespeare in his plays. A comparison could be make between Cupid's playful role in Jason's initiation and Puck's similar function. Note that Medea is Hecate's disciple, and when Cupid shoots an arrow into her heart, she falls in love with Jason, the first man she saw; Titania falling in love with Bottom is the mockery copy. See Apollonius of Rhodes, **The Voyage of Argo,** Penguin Books, 1971, pp. 116-7, 123.

[23] Mark Twain names the village where Satan appears "Eseldorf," which means in German "the Ass' village." The village represents for Twain the whole mankind and the name suggests the degradation of the world and the evil and stupidity of the human race as Little Satan states it. But "Eseldorf" is a sign that betrays Satan: where else could the Devil land, if not in Bottom's village? The village is "in the middle of that sleep," which indicates the "country of dreams" (See Mark Twain, **The Mysterious Stranger,** Signet Classics, 1962, p. 161). Twain describes also a castle there, which is a copy of Dracula's castle; the oldest serving-man in the castle tells the children about ghosts, vampires, and other horrors he had seen in that region (*Ibid.,* p. 165). Little Satan is described creating a miniature world and destroying it after, without remorse, like a playful child (*Ibid.,* pp. 168-9, 173); but he is

The Everlasting Sacred Kernel

Cupid's tricks illustrate the world as a play, but Eros, as in Apuleius' story, or in *Orphism*, or in Plato's *Symposium*, symbolizes at the highest level the Principle itself; and Love is a spiritual way, as stated in the Hindu tradition or Sufism or the legends of the Holy Grail. Puck's knavery, enhancing the chaos, helps to exhaust the lowest elements of the dying cycle so as to replace it with order and a new golden age. Little Satan doesn't have such power. Even if Twain wants him to be an angel, he is limited to the individual order and doesn't have access to spiritual levels.

Little Satan has, from our point of view, another kind of merit. He can be used for comparison as a negative example, and there is in Western literature an excellent character to be compared to Little Satan: a boy coming from another world, a minuscule planet. He seems similar to Twain's Satan, being a mysterious stranger capable of producing wonders; he is a miraculous child, like Puck, belonging to the "little people"; he came down to earth flying from another planet, as Cupid came down "flying between the cold moon and the earth" (Shakespeare, **Dream**, II.I.156); he is a boy bearing the same title as Twain's Edward: "the little prince."

Antoine de Saint-Exupéry published *Le Petit Prince* (*The Little Prince*) in 1943 at New York. The story, having the flavour of a fairy tale, is more suitable than others to shelter a sacred kernel. The Little Prince, compared to Little Satan, is an angel (in a traditional sense), which opens to us the gates of Heaven and puts the individual order in its right place. Contrary to Twain's Satan, Saint-Exupéry's Prince expresses the reality of the divine world and his final laugh illustrates the felicity of spiritual realization.[24]

---

a spirit (*Ibid.*, p. 175). At the end of the story, Little Satan makes the terrible statement that no other world exists but this one (that means no supernal levels and no God), and that life is just a dream, a vision; in fact, nothing exists but a *thought* (*Ibid.*, p. 252). As we mentioned before, the mind is a favourite field of action for Devil, so Little Satan's affirmations that "there is no God, no universe, no human race, no heaven, no hell," and "it is all a dream" and "nothing exists but you, and you are but a *thought*" (*Ibid.*, p. 253), seem quite devilish.

[24] In his unfinished last work (*Citadelle*), Saint-Exupéry regards the human society as "a pyramid that doesn't make sense if it is not ending in God." As in the Islamic tradition, for Saint-Exupéry, God is beyond our human touch; climbing the moun-

The Eye of the Heart

Saint-Exupéry confesses that he would have liked to begin this story in the fashion of the fairy tales with "Once upon a time there was a little prince."[25] The story is a fairy tale, because it bears a sacred meaning and suggests, wittingly or not, an initiation as a spiritual journey, which makes it "children's literature." The hero is a child, but moreover, the tale clearly specifies the partition between the "children's world" representing the sacred and the essential wisdom, and the "grown-ups' world" representing the profane, the ignorance, and the reign of quantity.[26]

The Little Prince is similar to an *avatâra* coming down into our dying world to bring light and salvation.[27] The Sahara Desert, where

---

tain (of Purgatory), he didn't discover God but his symbol, a black rock (the Black Stone of Kaaba). However, we should not forget that Saint-Exupéry is a profane author, and we have to be careful not to confuse his tale with a sacred writing. In comparison, a more recent author, Paulo Coelho, even though he completed the pilgrimage to Compostela, was and remained a dubious character, with a work influenced by occultism and adverse forces, where the parody of initiation is well displayed.

[25] "To those who understand life (that means those who understand the reality beyond the illusion, the essence beyond the surface), that (the story told as a fairy tale) would have given a much greater air of truth to my story" (Antoine de Saint-Exupéry, **The Little Prince**, Harcourt, Brace & World, 1971, p. 17).

[26] "Grown-ups never understand anything by themselves" (4); "grown-ups love figures" (that is they love the quantities, the skin not the kernel) (16-17). "Only the children know what they are looking for" (89). "Men," says the little prince, "set out on their way in express trains, but they do not know what they are looking for. Then they rush about, and get excited, and turn round and round" (94). This "round and round" represents in the Hindu tradition the whirlpool of deaths and rebirths of the ignorant and profane people. "Living in the midst of ignorance and considering themselves intelligent and enlightened, the senseless people go round and round, following crooked courses, just like the blind led by the blind" (**Katha Up.** I.II.5 and **Mundaka Up.** I.II.8); the ignorant travels sometimes in one direction, sometimes in the other (Titus Burckhardt, **Letters of a Sufi Master**, Perennial Books, 1987, p. 29).

[27] He has a solar nature. The fox tells the Little Prince: "But if you tame me, it will be as if the sun came to shine on my life.... You have hair that is the color of gold" (83). Pryderi, the lost and found miraculous son of Pwyll prince of Dyfed, has also golden hair (**Mabinogion** 17). "Now, that golden Person who is seen within the sun has a golden beard and golden hair" (**Chândogya Up.** I.6.6); "that golden Person who is within the sun is even He (*Âtmâ* identical with Brahma) who dwells within the lotus of the heart" (**Maitri Up.** VI.1).

The Everlasting Sacred Kernel

the author had fallen with his airplane (6), represents the wasteland of the fairy tales, the savage and dark woods of Dante, the world at the end of time. The author, like Dante, is lost there and his fall illustrates the fall of the human cycle. On the contrary, the Little Prince is not falling; he is descending as saviour in the same place.[28] What characterizes the agonizing world is the thirst, understood as lack of spirituality; in many traditions, the divine activity and the celestial influences come down as rain or dew or tears to rejuvenate and sustain the Cosmos (Guénon, **Symboles**, p. 361). The author, placed in the middle of the desert, without any water left (91), reflects the situation at the end of time, and his thirst is the neophyte's longing for the beverage of immortality. "In this cycle of existence I am like a frog in a waterless well," complains the king thirsting for Liberation (**Maitri Up.** I.4). The Little Prince as saviour will miraculously provide the *Fons Vitae* with special water. The strange well that the Little Prince made miraculously appear in the middle of the desert (94) is the Fountain of Life, but also of Youth and Knowledge (Coom., **Trad. Art**, p. 405), which symbolizes at the same time the spiritual center as origins of the new world and as final goal of the initiation. The water (abducted by the Dragon) is now again available and a new cycle may start.[29] The Little Prince's mission is accomplished.

The water, drunk by the author (neophyte), operates his spiritual transformation. This water, says the Little Prince, "is good for the heart" (92), where "heart" means, as in the Hindu or Islamic tradition, not the soul but the center of the being where *Spiritus* dwells.[30]

---

[28] The Little Prince is talking about "my descent to the earth" (98) and he says to the author, "So you, too, come from the sky" (11), but that one's coming is a fall.

[29] "Beside the well there was the ruin of an old stone wall" (99). The old wall represents the old cycle. The same old wall and the fountain, with the same symbolical meaning, appear in the Romanian legend of the great mason Master Manole.

[30] In Sufism, the soul (*an-nafs*) as *ego*, is opposed to the heart (*al-qalb*) as Self. The Sufi "kills his soul and brings life to his heart" (Burckhardt, **Letters**, pp. 2, 5). "This water," says Saint-Exupéry, "was indeed a different thing from ordinary nourishment. It was as sweet as some special festival treat. It was good for the heart, like a present." And when they pulled the bucket, the well was singing (96). Note that Arabic *ayn* means at the same time "eye" and "spring" (Lings, **Sufism**, p. 50); *ayn al-*

The Eye of the Heart

The desert hides the well, says again the Little Prince, which is like a buried treasure (93), and a quest, a spiritual journey is needed to find that treasure; the author, carrying the Little Prince asleep in his arms as "a very fragile treasure," will discover the well at daybreak. The Little Prince is himself a "treasure," the same treasure as the hidden well, both symbolizing the absolute Knowledge and the everlasting Youth. Walking through the desert during the night, with the Little Prince as divine guide, the author fulfills an initiation finalized at daybreak, when the spiritual Sun rises at east.[31]

An *avatâra*, as we saw, is not a *Deus ex machina* but a child born miraculously who undertakes an initiation establishing a sacred pattern to be followed by those capable to look upwards. The *avatâra* commits self-sacrifice, coming down to save the Cosmos and the Man, and to renew the Year, yet it is not an instantaneous miracle. It needs a complete sacrifice, which implies initiatory trials, a ritual death and a resurrection, to give example and indicate that salvation demands also a personal effort, and not an easy one.

The Little Prince performs, therefore, an initiation as a spiritual journey. His small planet is the "mustard seed," the *minimum* of Nicholas of Cusa as Center, where grows the spiritual Rose, which is one with Dante's and Jean de Meung's rose, the rose of the Rosy-Cross.[32] The Rose is the hidden Self, which has to be unveiled and recognized, and Little Prince like a simple neophyte leaves his rose because he doesn't understand its significance, and he doesn't realize that the Heavenly Kingdom is within us. He starts a spiritual voyage far away, apparently leaving the rose behind, but in fact his

---

khuld means "the eye of immortality" but also "the fountain of immortality" (Guénon, **Symboles**, p. 432). The desert without fountain and water describes then the "heartlessness" and the "blindness" of the world at the end of time.

[31] The spiritual Sun is also the Eye of God. Finding the well (the treasure) means finding the Center and the Eye, which is the Sun.

[32] The Little Prince's planet has the size of a house (14), suggesting the Cosmos as "World Egg"; the smallest is the lamplighter's planet: "there was just enough room on it for a street lamp and a lamplighter" (57), which is an even better symbol for the non-dimensional Center.

The Everlasting Sacred Kernel

aim is the same rose, and only the initiation will open the heart allowing him to see that all the time the rose was there.

The Little Prince's journey to Earth should be a descent to Hell and an ascent to Purgatory and to the Earthly Paradise (symbolized by the well). Saint-Exupéry depicts a journey through seven planetary levels, apparently similar to Dante's voyage and to Islamic tradition, yet there is no clear initiatory symbolism.[33] We could say, forcing the interpretation, that the Little Prince's path is a journey to spiritual humility, from master to servant. In the Romanian fairy tale, *Harap Alb* has to accept becoming the servant and the servant takes his place. The little prince Edward changes positions with Tom and becomes a beggar. Grimm's Cinderella is a servant before becoming a queen. The whole Islamic tradition is built on this principle.[34] The Little Prince's voyage happens from a king who knows

---

[33] This part of the voyage starts and ends symmetrically, with a story about the power of discrimination. On the Little Prince's planet grow good and bad plants (20), in accordance with Christ's parable of the darnel. The bad plants (the baobabs) try to split the planet into pieces (22), producing the multiplicity (the profane). The good plant, the rose, which was "born at the same moment as the sun" (33), stands for One-and-only (the sacred). The grown-ups (the profane people) don't know to discriminate between good and bad plants. They are confused and forlorn. They are "bad plants" like the baobabs ("they fancy themselves as important as the baobabs," 68), lost into illusory multiplicity. On earth, little prince meets a railway switchman who sends the trains "now to the right, now to the left." The travelers (the grown-ups) represent the wandering profanes, never satisfied, always restless, "pursuing nothing at all"; they sleep in the trains, their Self is not "awake" (88-9). The seven planetary levels constitute a mixed, and somehow confused, model of the infernal-celestial circles; there is no clear illustration of the two-faced character of any symbolism and the ambivalence divine-human of any perspective. Though a descent to Hell, the levels correspond not only to different "sins," but also to "virtues." For example, the unique rose on the Little Prince's planet symbolizes the Self (the immortal "soul") and the Knowledge, yet at the same time she is ephemeral (65) and full of vanity (33). The same ambivalence is true for the king, the lamplighter, or the geographer. However, the conceited man, the tippler, and the avaricious businessman, placed between the king and the lamplighter, represent plainly the sins and Hell.

[34] *El-Islâm* means submission to God (to his Divine Will) and *muslim* is the one who respects this submission. See Frithjof Schuon, **L'Oeil du Coer**, Dervy-Livres, 1974, pp. 91-3. "Seek the treasure with humility" (Rumi 303), where the "treasure" is Allâh.

The Eye of the Heart

only to command, to a "muslim" who knows only to obey orders. Between those two is placed the Hell represented by "grown-ups" lost into the realm of quantity.[35]

Reaching the Earthly Paradise, the Little Prince learns and understands the essence of his initiation: the illusion of multiplicity and the reality of One without a second. His rose in unique, in fact it is the Rose, the only One.[36] Now, the Little Prince is ready for the great voyage of the *Greater Mysteries*, the celestial journey to the Heavenly Paradise, where the Rose reigns. He suffers, similar to Christ, ritual death (105) and rebirth (106) through the dragon's jaws

---

[35] The king illustrates one of Dante's most hated sins, *superbia* (pride). The lamplighter represents the sloth but Saint-Exupéry points out the ambivalence, stating that the lamplighter is also faithful (61). Similarly, the king illustrates the Daoist concept of kingship: he gives only orders that are in accordance with the natural laws and tendencies ("One must require from each one the duty which each one can perform") (45). The lamplighter obeys totally the orders he received and his job could symbolize the vortex of the cycles and also of one cycle ("from year to year the planet has turned more rapidly"; the traditional theory of cosmic cycles states that a cycle evolves faster and faster to its end). As a lamplighter, and showing a complete submission and faithfulness, he also suggests the spiritual "illumination." In the Islamic tradition, Allâh is the Lamp (**Qor'ân** XXIV.35), and the Sufi is the perfect vassal. The businessman, obsessed with counting and figures (29), symbolizes the bottom of Hell, where the pure quantity reigns (See Guénon, **Le règne**, p. 21). The last planet, before Earth, is inhabited by a geographer who writes in a big register of "eternal things" and who stirs in the Little Prince the first desire to return to his unique rose (66), suggesting (together with the lamplighter) the ascension to the Earthly Paradise (the ambivalence is still present because the "eternal things" that concern the geographer are the corporeal elements of the ephemeral reality, and the flower, having an "ephemeral" character indicated by the geographer, is the kernel of absolute Reality).

[36] "Go and look again at the roses (the roses which the Little Prince met on Earth in a garden, representing the profane multiplicity). You will understand now," says the fox, "that yours is unique in all the world" (86). This unique rose is identical with the unique lamp and dwells in the Little Prince's heart: it is a rose "that shines through his whole being like the flame of a lamp" (93-4). In the Hindu tradition, this lamp is *Âtmâ*, the Universal Spirit (Self): "There (in the Heart or Center) the sun does not shine, neither do the moon and the stars. He (*Âtmâ*) shining, all these shine" (**Katha Up.** III.II.15). The same lamp is the Lamb in Christian tradition: "and the city (Center) did not need the sun or the moon for light, since it was lit by the radiant glory of God and the Lamb was a lighted torch for it" (**Revel.** 21:23).

(the dragon being here a poisonous snake), followed by the celestial (*sattvic*) ascension, which crowns his Liberation.[37]

Saint-Exupéry's *The Little Prince* is a good imitation of an initiatory tale. It is an enchanting children's story barely veiling the sacred kernel. Even if the influence of Sufism is perceptible, it is a universal tale of all traditions and of all times. But most of all, it strongly indicates the *absconditorum clavis*, "the key of the hidden things," the key that opens the gate to the everlasting sacred kernel.

There are other traditional elements, like the idea of silence, that suggest a sacred kernel. "Words are the source of misunderstandings," says the fox (as spiritual master) (84); "And now," the fox adds, "here is my secret, a very simple secret: It is only with the heart that one can see rightly; what is essential is invisible to the eye," and the Little Prince will repeat it, using a traditional way of learning: "What is essential is invisible to the eye" (87).[38]

Only the Eye of the Heart has access to the invisible domain. "But you are not able to see Me with your (corporeal) eyes. I give you a divine eye" (**Bhagavad-Gîtâ** XI.8). The "divine eye" is not different from God's Eye, because, as stated in different traditions, only God knows God, and only God sees God, which is an illustration of the Supreme Identity, taught in Sufism, or of the Hindu *Tat tvam asi* ("That you are") and *Aham Brahmâsmi* ("I am Brahma"). God's Eye is "The All-Seeing Eye" of Christian tradition and Masonry (the eye inside a triangle), but this Eye is the spiritual Sun, and actually God *is* the Eye (Guénon, **Symboles**, p. 430, Coom., **Trad.**

---

[37] "That which is like poison at first, at the end, like nectar that pleasure is declared to be sattvic, born of purity of one's own mind" (**Bhagavad-Gîtâ** XVIII.37).
[38] The Hermetic tradition tells also about a silent vision of God, seen with the "intellectual eyes." "In this life," Hermes Trismegistus says, "we are still too weak to see that sight (the vision of God); we have not strength to open our intellectual eyes, and to behold the beauty of the Good, that incorruptible beauty which no tongue can tell. Then only will you see it, when you cannot speak of it; for the knowledge of it is deep silence, and suppression of all the senses" (**Hermetica**, Shambhala, 1993, tr. by Walter Scott, p. 191).

The Eye of the Heart

Art, pp. 372-5).[39] Seeing with the Eye of the Heart means God seeing God with God (as Eye).[40]

The Eye of the Heart is a universal symbol. In the Hindu tradition it is called also the "eye of knowledge" (*jnana caksus*) (**Bhagavad-Gîtâ** XV.10), representing the "intellectual intuition," the only instrument that has direct and immediate (not mediate) access to absolute Knowledge and the celestial levels.[41] "It is not possible to see the Principle with the corporeal eyes. Those who know him with the heart, as dwelling within the heart, become immortals" (**Svetâsvatara Up.** IV.20). About the Eye of the Heart Plato teaches: "the soul sees by itself the intelligible and invisible things" (compared with the eyes seeing the sensitive and visible objects) (**Phaedo** 83c), and St. Paul, who says, "may he enlighten your eyes of heart (*oculos cordis*)" (**Ephes.** 1:18), and also Philo ("for what the intellect is in the soul, that the eye is in the body," Philo 8). In Oglala Sioux tradition, during a rite of purification, the leader of the rite says: "For it is the wish of *Wakan-Tanka* that the Light enters into the darkness, that we may see not only with our two eyes, but with the one eye which is of the heart (*Chante Ishta*), and with which we see and know all that is true and good" (Brown 42).

However, the metaphysics of the Eye of the Heart is best developed in Sufism. *Ayn el-Qalb*, the Eye of the Heart, sees the Face of God, which is its eternal vision and is called "absolute Invisible" (*El-Ghayb el-mutlaq*) or "the Invisible of the invisibles" (*Ghayb el-ghuyûb*).[42] Seeing the Invisible with the Eye of the Heart is Saint-

---

[39] "The One within the Sun and the Eye is Brahma" (**Brahma Sûtras** I.I.20).
[40] As Ibn 'Arabî affirms, "someone else than Himself can not see Him; therefore, with His essential Eye I see Him" (Ibn 'Arabî, **L'Arbre**, p. 157). It is the same with saying that "if you do not make yourself equal to God, you cannot apprehend God; for like is known by like. Leap clear of all that is corporeal, and make yourself grow to a like expanse with that greatness which is beyond all measure; rise above all time, and become eternal; then you will apprehend God" (**Hermetica** 221).
[41] The "eye of knowledge" corresponds to Nicholas of Cusa's "the eyes of my mind and understanding" (Cusa 23) and to the "intellectual eyes" of Hermeticism (the heart being the traditional seat of the Intellect).
[42] About *Ayn el-Qalb* see Schuon 13-19. The heart is the residence of the Intellect (*Spiritus*), but for the majority (the ignorant) the Eye of the Heart is blind: "It is not

The Everlasting Sacred Kernel

Exupéry's perspective too. "What is most important is invisible" (93). "But the eyes are blind. One must look with the heart" (97). "The thing that is important is the thing that is not seen" (103). And the well with water that is "good for the heart" is, like in Sufism, the Fountain and also the Eye in the middle of the World.

Yet there is in *The Little Prince* another symbol, very graphic, which illustrates this invisibility. Almost at the beginning of the story, when the author meets the Little Prince for the first time, that one asks the author to draw him a sheep. After three unsuccessful tries, the fourth one pleases the Little Prince. The first three are drawings showing explicitly the small sheep and they are rejected one by one: the first one because it is a sick-looking sheep, the second because it is not a sheep but a ram, and the third one because the sheep looks too old (8-9). This vividly reminds us of Buddha's Four Signs (or Encounters), the first three of which being an old man, a sick man and a dead man. The Fourth Sign is a seer, an "elected" one, corresponding to "The Fourth" state of Hinduism and to Saint-Exupéry's fourth drawing. The fourth sheep is invisible, unlike the first three sheep that are very visible. The fourth drawing shows just a box (10), but the Little Prince knows that inside hides a sheep, because the Little Prince sees the Invisible with the Eye of the Heart.

The sheep is the Hidden Treasure, its symbolism being related to that of the ram and the lamb, and representing the spirituality.[43] Its fleece is the Sufi's wool, which suggests that the invisible sheep is an emblem of the Sufi. Moreover, the box with the sheep inside represents the fruit of immortality, the box being the skin and the sheep the sacred kernel.[44]

---

the eyes that are blind but the hearts," **Qor'ân** XXII.46 (Lings, **Sufism**, p. 48). In the Hindu tradition, Brahma is also the Invisible: "That which possesses the attributes of invisibility and so on is Brahma" (**Brahma Sûtras** I.II.21).

[43] The same meaning bears, we saw, the Romanian little sheep, Miorita. In the Islamic tradition, the "hidden treasure" is a symbol of Allâh: "I was a Hidden Treasure and I wished to be known, and so I created the world" (Lings, **Sufism**, p. 15).

[44] Jason's Golden Fleece is too the fruit of immortality, hanging on a huge oak and guarded by a dragon with unsleeping eyes (Apollonius 150). The skin (*el-qishr*) and

The Eye of the Heart

---

the kernel (*el-lubb*) of the fruit were used by the greatest *shaykh* Muhyiddin Ibn 'Arabî to express the relation between exotericism (visible) and esotericism (invisible); the same symbolism appears in Hebraic *Kabbalah* (**Zohar** I.19b).

TEN YEARS LATER – AVOWAL

IN *THE EVERLASTING SACRED KERNEL*, our goal was to follow the Hindu method called *Arundhati-darshananyâya*, a method based on the obvious fact that not all individuals are capable of understanding the same truth.[1] To reach the Principle – Brahma –, the Hindu teachings say, is such a difficult task for the majority of honest seekers that the master advises the student to meditate first on a physical object, let's say the physical sun (or the star *Arundhati*, which is usually given as example); after a while, the student will understand that the physical sun is not his real target and will move to a higher object and so on, until the spiritual Sun, the supernal Sun is reached.

This method is used in different traditions, from Yoga-mârga to Hesychasm. The neophytes simulate a state of peace and bliss, which will really become their transformed and permanent nature only after a spiritual realization. Such a *modus operandi* offers also the possibility – at least, theoretically – of integrating the series of disharmonies (the lower or external stages) into a final perfect harmony. René Guénon, writing about contrarieties and contrasts that function at the corporeal and subtle (psychical) levels, but disappear at a higher level, explained: "Who says contrast or opposition, says, by this, disharmony or unbalance, that is, something that can exist only from a very particular and limited perspective; as a whole, the

---

[1] In the Hindu tradition, this is related to *adhikâribheda*.

Avowal

equilibrium is composed of the sum of all the unbalanced parts, and each partial disorder concurs, willy-nilly, to a perfect order."[2] For Guénon, this truth is so important that he uses it to explain the rank of the profane and antitraditional elements in our modern world. He states that any antitraditional, profane and even counter-initiatory actions or forces cannot surpass the individual domain (the "psycho-physical" world) and it is an illusion to think that they can oppose the spiritual order itself. Without their awareness and despite their will, these entities are subjugated to *Spiritus*, the same way everything is, even if unwitting or involuntarily, subjugated to the Divine Will. And they are used, against their will, to the realization of the "divine plan in the human domain." And Guénon added:

> If we consider the matter from an overall perspective, and not only in respect of these beings [representing the counter-initiation], we may say that, similar to all the others, they are necessary in their places, as elements of the assembly, and as "providential" instruments – speaking in a theological language – of the advance of this world through its cycle of manifestation, because in this way each partial disorder, even when it appears as *the disorder*, concurs necessarily to total order. (Guénon, **Le règne**, p. 355)

The traditional vestiges, that is, the debris that survived the disappearance of different genuine traditions and traditional civilizations, could become part of these disharmonies, after the spirit withdrew and inferior forces took control of them. It was very common during recent centuries to collect all kinds of vestiges belonging to various traditions and build a so-called "doctrine," which is purely and simply a fake (Guénon, **Le règne**, p. 328), without any spiritual power and often open to counter-initiatory influences. The interference of a human or individual element, that is, reorganizing, changing, abusing and altering the traditional vestiges, constitutes a

---
[2] René Guénon, **Études sur l'hindouisme**, Éd. Trad., 1979, p. 15.

significant danger. The traditional doctrines that are alive suffer the same abuse and alteration, yet their representatives can still react and protect them against "maleficent" actions; by contrast, the traditional vestiges are without protection and consequently more exposed to the dangers of counter-initiatory influence. It is no surprise that Muhyiddin Ibn ʿArabî wrote:

> It is better if the companions of our Way keep silent on the subject of the operative sciences of the spiritual order. Moreover: it is forbidden to expose them in a manner that makes them comprehensible at the same time to the initiatory elite and to the common people, because the corrupters could use them in their malefic works.[3]

This kind of subversion and abuse is, today, almost impossible to stop. The least we can do is to try to suggest the real meanings of the symbols that are still alive. About the importance of the symbols, René Guénon wrote:

> For the people who succeeded in penetrating its profound significance, the symbol can transmit inestimably more [sacred knowledge] than any direct discursive teaching; thus, it is the only way to transmit – insofar as is possible – the inexpressible that constitutes the proper domain of initiation ... We must not forget that, if the symbolic initiation, which is merely the base and the support of the effective initiation, is inevitably the only one that can be communicated on the outside, at least this symbolic initiation can be preserved and transmitted even by people who don't understand its meaning and importance; it is enough to keep and preserve the symbols intact, and they will always be able to awaken – in those who are capable – all the concepts they contain in a synthetic mode. (Guénon, **Aperç. sur l'Init.**, p. 205)

---

[3] Ibn Arabî, **Le Livre du Mîm, du Wâw et du Nûn**, trans. in French by Charles-André Gilis, Albouraq, 2002, p. 59.

Avowal

Modern literature can serve as a preparatory exercise to understand how fundamental symbols operate, but at the same time it shows how dangerous and pernicious are the effects of "originality," "individuality" and "inventiveness," by altering and diverting the essential meanings of symbols. A special case is that of so-called "folklore." Folklore, like mythology, is a reservoir, which preserves the vestiges of vanished traditional societies, of sacred rituals and initiatory rites. If modern mentality didn't touch it, that is, if nobody tried to alter its content and form, "folklore" could be a valuable support in the study of traditional symbolism (*supra*, pp. 40 ff.); otherwise, "fabricated" folklore is no better than profane and "original" literature.[4]

We must stress that literature has no initiatory power and does not constitute an initiatory tool of any kind. Moreover, the popularity of the authors, or the fact that they are some famous characters in the international literary domain, means nothing. If we talk about Balzac or Patrick Süskind, for example, their works are not initiatory because the authors are profane and there is no "super-human" element involved. If the literary works carry some traditional data or initiatory symbols, it does not mean much if the author does not have the necessary esoteric qualification; on the contrary, the author's intervention can bring a counter-initiatory viewpoint, as was the case of Umberto Eco or of Paulo Coelho.

In short, we may view modern literature from a quadruple perspective, with respect to the author: there are authors, albeit very few, who possess initiatory data and these are reflected in their works[5]; there are authors who, unconsciously, transmit in their works unaltered traditional vestiges; there are antitraditional authors

---

[4] We have shown, in another work, the difference between modern literature and genuine fairy tales, between pseudo-initiatory texts and the legitimate symbolism safeguarded in myths, ballads and fairy tales (See **Agarttha, the Invisible Center**, Rose-Cross Books, 2002).

[5] Of course, in the situation where the authors only think that they are endowed with an initiatory knowledge, fantasizing that they have the key of the secret treasure, without actually belonging to an initiatory organization or an authentic tradition, their work possesses little if any worth.

who willingly abuse the sacred symbols and fabricate others, writing maleficent literature; finally, there are authors who, often manipulated without their knowing it by counter-initiatory forces, issue noxious writings.

In our present work, we did not limit our preferences to one type of authors. When, ten years ago, we decided to go public for a while and publish this first book, *The Everlasting Sacred Kernel* was specifically designed to target Occidental mentality, by using well known written texts.[6] The intent was to stir interest for the traditional perspective, to show that we still can reverse our upside-down and profane state of mind, and to stress how essential it is to open the "eye of the heart" and choose between "the wheat and the darnel."

We used Western literature as a pretext. It was a risky endeavour, considering the subversive modern mind, which postulated that humankind hides an unconscious yearning for initiatory subjects and initiatory symbolism, and has a secret need for religiosity. Such an opinion degrades the spiritual domain, bringing it down to the psychological level of individuality. And not once was the attraction towards initiatory meanings and religious implications in literary works considered a confirmation of this unwitting longing for a spiritual completion.

It is dangerous to consider literary texts, especially the modern ones, as initiatory means. What is usually called "literature" belongs completely to the profane order. As we said, modern and profane literary works have no power to transmit an initiation or to be a support for spiritual realization. Even sacred writings do not automatically confer initiation on an individual. Reading a sacred text or a thousand sacred texts doesn't allow readers to initiate themselves.

In our present work, *The Everlasting Sacred Kernel*, we only used Western literature to introduce the essence of traditional thinking

---

[6] Coomaraswamy mentioned oral and written literature; of course, he used the word "literature" in its general sense, even if in Latin *littera* represents mainly "written letters, inscriptions." For modern man, as well, "literature" refers firstly to written works, and especially to fiction.

and to illustrate how the laws of sacred symbolism should be considered. We stressed the importance of looking upwards, in a *sattwic* manner, and not downwards as many are doing today. We assumed that, looking upwards, it is still possible to uncover a sacred kernel in literature, even if this had become desecrated. We underlined the major role of the power of discrimination to identify the traditional vestiges carried by profane literature, and in some cases we showed how these were abused and altered.

In fact, our work distinguished between two types of "literature": one initiatory and traditional, the other occult and antitraditional. In the first category we included the biblical story of Samson, Homer's epics, fairy tales, Dante's *Divine Comedy*, Shakespeare's plays, and two modern works, *The Three Musketeers* by Alexandre Dumas and *The Little Prince* by Saint-Exupéry; in the second category, which is extremely rich, we chose as exemplification other works by Dumas and also works by Jules Verne, Mark Twain and Edgar Allan Poe.

The fact that we included *The Three Musketeers* and *The Little Prince* in the first class was done for "didactic" reason: to illustrate how we should read the dormant symbols and how we should purify our profane mentality. Yet, we never suggested that such works, belonging to profane literature, could be called "initiatory," or that they can confer an initiation, or even that their authors were some sort of initiates. Contrary to Homer, Dante and Shakespeare, who represented genuine initiatory currents (not to say more), authors like Alexandre Dumas or Antoine de Saint-Exupéry did not have any spiritual qualification and their books have nothing sacred about them. What happened was that literature inherited some esoteric vestiges and transmitted them further, yet they were all too often altered, misunderstood, or counterfeited.

In Alexandre Dumas' case, for example, *The Three Musketeers* is an exception. Dumas (and, of course, his readers) knew nothing about

The Everlasting Sacred Kernel

any initiatory symbolism and rather enjoyed "dark" subjects.[7] We described Dumas' interest in vampirism, ghosts and infernal characters; even in *The Three Musketeers*, there are two demonic characters: Rochefort and Milady,[8] both without real names (here it is not about a supernal anonymity, but an infernal one); nonetheless, we could consider that they represent the dragon, and their roles and fate are in accord with a traditional scenario, which makes *The Three Musketeers* not a "dark" story or parody, but a sort of fairy tale, hiding traditional data.

On the contrary, the modern Spanish novel, *El Club Dumas*, by Arturo Pérez-Reverte, is nothing else but a parody, an occultist and infernal tale, using Rochefort to stress the demonic characteristic of the story[9]; it combines fiction with non-fiction, where the non-fiction includes Alexandre Dumas' work and his sources.[10] If, in

---

[7] However, the modern society's attraction for the infrahuman domain was not a phenomenon limited to the 19th century, and it developed continuously in the 20th and 21st centuries.

[8] Milady appears to be a ghost from hell. Rochefort is "the cursed man, my evil genius," as d'Artagnan says, "the devil," as Athos says. Rochefort and Milady are "two kinds of demons," and Rochefort will salute Milady saying "My compliments to Satan!" (*supra*, p. 118).

[9] The movie, *The Ninth Gate* (1999), based upon the novel *The Club Dumas*, pushed the infernal and parodistic characteristics to the extreme. Similarly, the recent movie *The Three Musketeers* (2011) is nothing else than another degradation, where the "Star Wars & ninja" style is visible, illustrating how successful the infernal forces are today.

[10] No doubt, the main source for Dumas' *The Three Musketeers* was *Mémoires de Mr. D'Artagnan*, written by Gatien de Courtilz de Sandras in 1700 (the edition available to us was published in 1966 at Jean de Bonnot, Paris). We find here the main characters, some episodes, including the one about Milady and her chambermaid (Bonnot edition, pp. 203, 239). The same Gatien de Courtilz wrote in 1687 *Mémoires de Mr. M.L.C.D.R.* (*Mémoires de Monsieur Le Comte de Rochefort*) (the edition available to us was published in 1710, at Henry van Bulderen), and this book is the source for the name of Dumas' Rochefort, but there were other elements that inspired Dumas and Maquet: Rochefort's journey to Brussels (**Mémoires de Mr. M.L.C.D.R.**, pp. 53 ff. and Alexandre Dumas, *The Three Musketeers*, Peter Fenelon Collier Publisher, 1893, p. 19); the involvement of Rochefort's father with a branded (marked with a fleur-de-lis) woman (**Mémoires M.L.C.D.R.**, p. 5) inspired the episode about Athos and his wife; and Dumas used even a verbal expression found in Rochefort's *Mémoires*, where Rochefort admitted to be one of Richelieu's "creatures" (p. 93), and that is how Milady is described ("she was some creature of the cardinal's," **The**

Avowal

some cases, finding the sources is a *sine qua non* (or seems to be), then these sources must be verified and not taken from second hand references, as it happens with many occultist and New Age works, and even with some works about traditional subjects.[11]

Let us say one more word about *Les Trois Mousquetaires*. After Dumas' death, many epigones invaded the book market with sequels exploiting the success of the *Musketeers*. The first assault was carried immediately after Dumas' disappearance, with Albert Maurin publishing, in 1874, *Les Véritables Mémoires de D'Artagnan le Mousquetaire*. This work, compared to Dumas' *Les Trois Mousquetaires*, discloses another "classification": there are texts that shelter a sacred kernel, and *The Three Musketeers* is one of them; then, there is neutral "literature," like Maurin's book, which hides no symbolism, no traditional elements, but it is built on fiction and some historical facts.[12] Finally, there are texts plainly directed against any traditional elements that could still subsist in our modern world, and we should say a few words about this last category.

Three Musketeers, chapter XXXI, p. 186). The episode of the twelve diamond studs has an important place in Dumas' novel. There is more than one source for it: *Mémoires du Duc de la Rochefoucauld* and Antoine-Marie Roederer, *Intrigues politiques et galantes de la Cour de France* (Librairie de Charles Gosselin, 1832, *Les aiguillettes d'Anne d'Autriche*, pp. 195 ff.). However, the printing history of La Rochefoucauld's *Mémoires* is a tumultuous one, and therefore, the mentioned episode is not to be found in the early editions (the edition available to us was published in 1664, at "Pierre van Dyck," as *Mémoires de M.D.L.R.*), but much later (see, for example, *Mémoires du Duc de la Rochefoucauld*, première partie, Renouard, 1817, pp. 8-9).

[11] Arturo Pérez-Reverte, in his *El Club Dumas*, refers to all the three *Mémoires* and to Roederer's work we cited in the previous note (**The Club Dumas**, Vintage Books, 1998, pp. 14-15, 96, 196), but he adds *Mémoires of De La Porte* (p. 196) as a source for "Constance [Bonacieux]'s kidnapping." Constance Bonacieux, as D'Artagnan's mistress, appears (without a name, just as "la cabaretière") in the *Mémoires de Mr. D'Artagnan*, p. 121. Nonetheless, for "Constance's kidnapping," it is true that the *Mémoires de M. de la Porte* (the edition available to us was published in 1756, in Geneva) was the source, but in the *Mémoires* La Porte describes his own kidnapping (p. 121) and not Constance's (a character invented by Dumas, who said she was La Porte's goddaughter).

[12] If someone had the patience to read *Les Véritables Mémoires de D'Artagnan le Mousquetaire*, this someone would see what a fundamental difference is between this book and Dumas' *Les Trois Mousquetaires*, a difference almost identical with the one between the profane and sacred viewpoints.

The Everlasting Sacred Kernel

The counter-initiatory forces have no access to the "power of discrimination." On the contrary, they use indiscriminately all the tools they can get and, because they need to create confusion, these tools can appear as being opposed to one another. Some of these tools are writers like Edgar Allan Poe (1809-1849), Mark Twain (1835-1910), Gustav Meyrink (1868-1932) and Alfred Kubin (1877-1959). We already mentioned Poe and Twain in the main text; however, it is instructive to augment the exposé by concisely examining the last two authors.

Alfred Kubin, a friend of Meyrink and so foolishly labelled "prophet of Agarttha,"[13] is a sad and troubled character. In his *My Life*,[14] Kubin describes a life that is interesting only because illustrates pseudo-tradition, pseudo-initiation and counter-initiatory influences at work. His main work, *The Other Side*,[15] is a dark parody, where the "center" is called the "Dream Empire," and we see the same idea like in Mark Twain's case. The "Dream Empire," located in Asia, is isolated by an impenetrable wall, a parody of Cusanus' paradisiacal wall; it is a shelter, Kubin says, for all who are against the modern world and everything is organized with respect to a higher spiritual life.[16] The author is invited to travel to this "Dream Land," a "secret" place, having as center a city called Pearl.[17] Yet, what seems to be just a parody of Agarttha, of a spiritual center, is, in fact, an anti-center.[18]

---

[13] Louis de Maistre, **L'Énigme René Guénon et les "Supérieurs Inconnus," Contribution à l'étude de l'histoire mondiale "souterraine,"**, 2004, Archè – Milan, p. 133.
[14] Alfred Kubin, **Ma vie**, Allia, 2000.
[15] Alfred Kubin, **L'Autre côté**, Jose Corti, 2007.
[16] *Ibid.*, p. 12.
[17] *Ibid.*, pp. 21, 27.
[18] *The Other Side* is really boring. But North-American schools would love to have it for their students, since the only interesting works for the School Boards are those connected with mental illness and psychical disorders (hence their favourite painter is Van Gogh). They are not alone, of course. We should mention here a curious fact: the most famous ancient sculptures exposed in the Louvre Museum are *Venus de Milo* and *Victory of Samothrace*. Why, when there are many others similar beautiful ancient Greek sculptures, these two became the most celebrated? The only reason is that these two specific pieces have something special: *Venus de Milo* has no arms and

Avowal

The other author is Gustav Meyrink, who makes good company with Kubin, Verne, Poe and Twain. Likewise, he uses some symbols, but it is obvious that his work is a "parody" of the genuine initiatory stories and creates a terrible confusion. Like Kubin, and akin to Jules Verne in his works *The Carpathian Castle* and *Mathias Sandorf*, Gustav Meyrink uses (in fact, abuses) the symbolism of the center. The centers presented by Kubin, Verne and Meyrink are pseudo-centers or even anti-centers, "occultist" centers, a caricature and a mockery, suspect centers influenced by counter-initiatory forces, and we have to use our power of discrimination to understand Guénon's sayings that the "'counter-initiation' derived from the unique source to which every initiation is attached."

In a letter to Julius Evola (from 1949), René Guénon wrote: "There are cases in which the influence of counter-initiation is clearly visible. Among these cases we must include those in which the traditional elements are presented in an intentionally 'parodistic' form; this is, in particular, the case of Meyrink, which, of course, does not mean that he was clearly aware of the influence which was exercised upon him. Therefore, I am surprised to learn that you seem to respect Meyrink."[19]

When Meyrink's last book, *Der Engel vom westlichen Fenster* (*The Angel of the West Window*), was translated in French, it was published with a *Foreword* by Julius Evola, and this *Preface* shows how such books can create confusion, even in the case of people like Evola, who knew Guénon's teachings. However, Evola himself made his contribution to the general confusion, with his erroneous ideas about initiation, Masonry and spiritual authority. Even though Evola tried to highlight some of Meyrink's errors, the *Preface* remains dubious, especially at the end when Evola compares Agarttha from Guénon's *Le Roi du Monde* to Meyrink's Elsbethstein.[20] Mey-

---

Victory of Samothrace has no head, and these kinds of mutilations are compatible with the mutilated state of the modern mind.

[19] Julius Evola, **René Guénon, A Teacher for Modern Times**, Sure Fire Press, 1994, p. 33.

[20] "[Meyrink] talks about a supreme center of the world (Elsbethstein, an analogue idea to that of Agarttha)" (Gustave Meyrink, **L'Ange à la fenêtre d'Occident**, La

rink's center is, at best, a pseudo-Agarttha; nonetheless, it is instructive to see how Meyrink abuses the traditional symbols. For example, in Evola's opinion (expressed in his *Foreword*[21]) the novel transmits a real teaching when, at the end, the Angel is denounced as just an echo, an illusion,[22] a spiritist error. What Evola could not see is that the title, which represents the quintessence of the work, is *The Angel of the West Window*, emphasizing the importance of this "Angel," and if Meyrink at the end negates it, he only divulges his own confusions. Not to say that the idea of using the term "angel" for this ghost is not only inadequate, but directly diabolical, and even if it seems that Meyrink eventually rejects the "Angel," his book extensively presents spiritist sessions.[23]

The Angel of the West Window continued the confusion created by Verne, Poe, and Twain, and influenced modern antitraditional authors. Meyrink introduces a character called Lipotine or Nitchevo,[24] a name similar to Verne's Nemo (in Russian, *nitchevo* means "nothing"). As in Twain's case, the (malefic) dream plays an important role[25]; but also the abyss, the Templars[26] and Baphomet, which becomes a substitute for the Principle, the head turned backward,

---

Colombe, 1962, p. 17). We should add that, inexplicably, Julius Evola considered Gustave Meyrink as expressing in his work some "magico-initiatory teachings" (Julius Evola, **Masques et visages du spiritualisme contemporain**, Les Éditions de l'homme, 1972, p. 271).

[21] See also **Masques et visages**, p. 288.

[22] That is what Meyrink says at the end of his book (Gustav Meyrink, **L'ange de la fenêtre d'Occident**, Le Rocher, 1986, pp. 292, 312-313). We see here the same pattern that Twain used in *The Great Dark*, where the conclusion was that everything is illusion, but, in comparison with the sacred writings, there is nothing beyond this illusion. The Angel could be compared to Twain's "Superintendent of Dreams."

[23] **L'ange de la fenêtre d'Occident**, p. 138. Marcel Clavelle (Jean Reyor) published in 1932, in *Le Voile d'Isis*, un article about Meyrink, and it is depressing to read that this collaborator of Guénon could say that Meyrink's *Green Face* offers practical guidance with respect to the initiatory process (Jean Reyor, **Études et recherches traditionnelles**, Éditions Traditionnelles, 1991, p. 179); however, Clavelle and Evola were not the only dupes, since Vasile Lovinescu appreciated Meyrink too.

[24] *Ibid.*, p. 9.

[25] *Ibid.*, p. 11.

[26] "The Knights Templar of the New Grail," see *ibid.*, p. 254.

Avowal

the blood, Tula,[27] St. Patrick and St. Dunstan,[28] are elements participating to the general confusion. Meyrink makes of Bartlett Green a mock imitation of Christ.[29] Even though Evola tried to defend Meyrink, the latter uses the erroneous theory of reincarnation[30] and employs expressions such as "the satanic astral body,"[31] "Golden Rose,"[32] "vampirism,"[33] "the Lodge of the West Window,"[34] and "the realization of Baphomet."[35] We find in this work the same pattern used today in books like *The Da Vinci Code*, *Mysteries and Secrets of the Masons* and many others, where Alchemy, the Rose-Cross, Masonry, Templars, etc. are mingled in an atrocious way. But *The Angel of the West Window* is not only a sinister mixture; it is a "parody"[36]; and furthermore, it transmits an upside down symbolism, which represents actual "Satanism." Alchemy is combined with Chemistry,[37] the Pentagram is abused,[38] the angels are ghosts, and the spiritual forces are magnetic forces.[39] At the end, it is said: "Brother, you have crossed the threshold of initiation with your face turned backwards."[40] In fact, in a genuine spiritual realization, the neophyte must not look back, and all the initiatory stories are adamant in warning about it.

---

[27] And also Thule of Greenland, *ibid.*, pp. 84-5.
[28] It is known that both, St. Patrick and St. Dunstan, were connected by some authors to Glastonbury. "St. Patrick's well," often used by Meyrink, is, in this case, similar to the abyss of Poe and Twain, or to Dumas' "le trou de l'enfer." *Ibid.*, pp. 21, 30-31, 133.
[29] *Ibid.*, pp. 60-61, 63 (Green is resurrected), 65 (he comes back to visit the main character of the book, but he is a ghost).
[30] *Ibid.*, p. 70.
[31] *Ibid.*, p. 102.
[32] *Ibid.*, p. 114. Guénon revealed the imposture of an organization like *Rose-Croix d'Or* (**Aperçus sur l'initiation**, p. 246). Also, the symbol of the Rose-Cross is suggested by Meyrink at page 282.
[33] *Ibid.*, p. 233.
[34] *Ibid.*, p. 257.
[35] *Ibid.*, p. 158.
[36] It presents a parody of initiation (see *ibid.*, p. 175).
[37] *Ibid.*, pp. 147, 150.
[38] *Ibid.*, p. 140.
[39] *Ibid.*, p. 173.
[40] *Ibid.*, p. 315.

The Everlasting Sacred Kernel

Meyrink engages in a considerable effort narrating about the Angel to conclude in the end that the Angel is an illusion. The same effort is made in all the modern occultist books about the "Secret," which in the end appears to be something very disappointing, a *nitchevo*.[41]

With these two last authors we are far away from the works we presented in the first chapters. Nonetheless, they prove that, in our modern times, the doctrine of the Eye of the Heart is, more than ever, profoundly indispensable. There are other domains of our contemporary world where the sacred kernel is also present and ready to be seen. To see it, we have to open the Eye of the Heart and use the power of discrimination. Living in the world, we cannot expect to see only good or only evil. The good and the bad plants grow together as on the Little Prince's planet. But we can identify and remove the weeds and unveil the sacred kernel.[42]

> Tell the wary and discerning believer
> To distinguish the king from the beggar.
> If there were no bad goods in the world,
> Every fool might be a skilful merchant;
> For then the hard art of judging goods would be easy.
> If there were no faults, one man could judge as well as another.

---

[41] This is not new. When Baron Hund promised to reveal his great secret, everybody was thinking of something magic and miraculous, yet his secret was that every Mason is a Knight Templar. René Guénon was very explicit about what an initiatory secret really is. Today, many execrable books about Masonry abuse the word "secret" in their titles, but it is only a revival of the title of a book written at the end of the 18th Century.

[42] The *Qor'ân* is defined as *al-Furqân*, "the Instrument of Discrimination" (Lings, **Sufism**, p. 30). This is also the deep meaning of Solomon's heart; Solomon, the king of Peace and Wisdom, is an emblem of the Universal Man whose Heart is the Eye of discrimination. Solomon asks the Lord: "Give your servant a heart to understand how to discern between good and evil" (**1 Kings** 3:9). "The Lord gave Solomon immense wisdom and understanding, and a heart as vast as the sand on the seashore" (**1 Kings** 5:9).

Avowal

Again, if all were faulty, skill would be profitless.
If all wood were common, there would be no aloes.
He who accepts everything as true is a fool,
But he who says all is false is a knave. (Rumi 99)

www.ingramcontent.com/pod-product-compliance
Lightning Source LLC
Chambersburg PA
CBHW070735160426
43192CB00009B/1443